WEAK STRONGMAN

Weak Strongman

THE LIMITS OF POWER
IN PUTIN'S RUSSIA

TIMOTHY FRYE

With a new preface by the author

PRINCETON UNIVERSITY PRESS
PRINCETON & OXFORD

Published by Princeton University Press
41 William Street, Princeton, New Jersey 08540
99 Banbury Road, Oxford OX2 6JX

press.princeton.edu

All Rights Reserved

Library of Congress Control Number: 2022936587
First paperback printing, with a new preface by the author, 2022
Paper ISBN 9780691216997
Cloth ISBN 9780691212463
ISBN (e-book) 9780691246284

British Library Cataloging-in-Publication Data is available

Editorial: Bridget Flannery-McCoy and Alena Chekanov
Production Editorial: Nathan Carr
Jacket/Cover Design: Karl Spurzem
Production: Erin Suydam
Publicity: Kate Hensley and Kathryn Stevens
Copyeditor: Cindy Milstein

Jacket/Cover image: Shutterstock

This book has been composed in Arno

CONTENTS

AS I WRITE this new preface in March 2022, Russia has just launched the largest invasion in Europe since World War II. More than 200,000 Russian troops have entered Ukraine, but they have faced stiff resistance from the Ukrainian army and the local population. Russian forces have bombed residential areas in major cities, including the capital of Kyiv, launched more than 600 missiles into Ukraine, and even raised the specter of using nuclear and chemical weapons. More than three million refugees have fled Ukraine, and the scale of devastation and loss of life is staggering. With NATO members arming Ukrainian fighters via neighboring countries and Russia declaring these staging areas legitimate targets, observers fear the war may spread. The outcome is uncertain; some predict Ukraine's superior morale will lead to victory, but many expect the Russian army to eventually take control of major cities owing to its larger numbers and greater capacity, but to face attacks by insurgent groups as long as it occupies territory in Ukraine. The result could be a long and bloody war.

To date, the war has defied many predictions. Despite explicit warnings by US intelligence, few expected the Kremlin to launch an all-out invasion. Even those who might have known better were caught off-guard. One of Russia's top foreign policy analysts noted, "I was shocked because for a long time, I thought that a military operation was not feasible. It was not plausible."[1] Russian oligarchs failed to get their yachts to safe ports prior to the invasion, and the Russian stock market fell so far and fast that it remains closed as I write. The Ukrainian government too downplayed the threat of invasion, perhaps out of a desire to maintain public order. I had long been skeptical that Moscow, Kyiv, and the other countries involved in negotiations could reach a settlement and, in late January, predicted that an invasion was more likely than not, but I was still surprised by the timing of the operation.[2]

Surprises continued after the first bombs fell on Ukraine. Far from achieving a lightning strike on Kyiv as planned, the Russian military made slow progress at great cost. Rather than collapsing, the Ukrainian army resisted Russia's advance far better than expected. Ukraine's president, Volodymyr Zelensky, became a symbol of resistance. The political novice, who had played a president in a popular comedy series before taking office and had just a 23 percent approval rating at the start of the war, did not flee but stood his ground and rallied his country against long odds. NATO members and partners put aside their many differences and levied economic sanctions of unprecedented scope and scale against Russia.[3] Switzerland, long the paragon of neutrality, openly backed Ukraine and joined the sanctions regime. Germany conducted a stunning about-face by announcing plans to vastly increase defense spending and denying approval of the Kremlin's most favored economic project—an $11 billion pipeline to bring gas from Russia to Europe.

If the outcome of the war is uncertain, so is its impact on Russian politics. Some argue that the invasion of Ukraine will mark the beginning of the end of Putin's rule, as military defeats and economic collapse are especially dangerous in autocracies.[4] Others expect a long, dark night of international isolation and severe repression in Russia—a nuclear-armed Belarus on steroids. How this war ends is unclear, but its importance is not. Putin's decision to invade Ukraine will echo for years. Understanding the causes and consequences of this decision will take time and effort, but even at this early stage of the war, the argument put forward in *Weak Strongman* helps to shed some light on the topic.

In the pages that follow, I argue that politics in Putin's Russia often follow a logic common to autocratic regimes ruled by a single individual. At the heart of these "personalist" autocracies is a dilemma: to stay in power, autocrats must cope with the dual threats of an elite coup and mass revolt, but they can rarely reduce these threats simultaneously. Decreasing the risks of coups often makes a mass revolt more likely, and vice versa. This political logic compels autocrats like Putin to balance these competing threats using a variety of rather blunt tools, including personal popularity, economic growth, policy success, corruption, propaganda, and repression. It also leads to a host of pathologies, such as difficult policy trade-offs, distorted information, and weak institutions that made an invasion of Ukraine far more likely.[5]

The difficult policy trade-offs that confront all autocrats led Putin in recent years to rely on a narrow group of hawkish national security officials and to sideline other voices. In his first decade in office, an oil boom and sound economic management allowed Putin to resolve the dual threats by not only vastly increasing living standards for the mass public, but also by fantastically enriching his cronies. In his second decade in office, he used the wildly popular annexation of Crimea to keep both groups on board. But since around 2018, the balancing act of keeping key elites and the mass public satisfied has become more difficult because of flat economic growth, massive corruption, public fatigue with Putin's long term in office, less effective propaganda, a botched response to the pandemic, and the fading of the warm glow of the Crimea annexation. As other tools for governing Russia have become blunter, Putin has increasingly turned to his security apparatus—the successor to the KGB, known as the Federal Security Services (FSB), the military, and National Guard—to keep other elites and the mass public in line through a mixture of repression, intimidation, and censorship. The most vivid example of increased repression is the change in treatment of Alexei Navalny, who for ten years publicized the egregious corruption of Putin's inner circle to great fanfare, but was jailed on dubious charges in the summer of 2021.[6] The puzzle is not that Navalny was arrested and jailed—a common occurrence in autocratic regimes—but that he was allowed to operate for so long.

The rise of the security services is reflected in other ways as well. In January 2020, the Russian government hiked the pay of those forces responsible for internal security. To protect the agency from the prying eyes of journalists, human rights activists, and anti-corruption campaigners, the FSB vastly expanded the scope of activities that could label anyone reporting on the organization a "foreign agent" in 2021.[7] One Russian expert called this move "secrecy taken to a monstrous extreme."[8] Following perceived successes in Crimea and Syria, the

Kremlin showered praise and resources on the Russian army. Defense spending increased dramatically in the past decade, and Defense Minister Sergei Shoigu assumed a much more public profile. Public opinion surveys reveal that the army has become Russia's most trusted institution, thanks in part to fawning coverage in the state-controlled media.[9]

Putin's increasing reliance on a handful of security officials to make policy at home and abroad has sidelined voices that might have preached a more cautious approach. When making the decision to go to war Putin likely consulted only a half-dozen or so hard-liners in his war cabinet who were well-known for their anti-Western views. These are men like Nikolai Patrushev, who argues that the United States has developed chemical and biological weapons in labs on Russia's borders and uses NATO to weaken its own allies in Europe.[10] A week into the invasion of Ukraine, he noted, "The West does not only want to encircle Russia with a new iron curtain, but to dismember it completely."[11]

The militarization of Russian foreign and domestic policy benefits the national security hawks by increasing the value of their expertise to Putin and benefits Putin by making repression at home more reliable. Aggression in Ukraine both flows from and reinforces Putin's bargain with the men in uniform, as Putin becomes more dependent on those groups who benefit most from Russia's muscle flexing.

The invasion of Ukraine highlights a second problem of personalist autocracies: the difficulty of obtaining accurate information from elites and society. As political scientist Erica Frantz points out, over time personalist autocracies tend to rely on ever narrower groups of officials, because they prize loyalty over merit.[12] This is certainly the case in Russia, where turnover among members of the powerful National Security Council is far lower than in any other part of the bureaucracy. The average age of the twelve-member National Security Council is sixty-four, with heavyweights, such as the ministers of defense and internal security, and the heads of foreign intelligence, the FSB, and the National Security Council, skewing even older. These five members of Putin's war cabinet have held their current positions for an average of almost twelve years.

Moreover, personalist autocracies provide few incentives for lower-level bureaucrats to provide accurate information to superiors when that information will be inconvenient or undesirable. The weak institutions inherent to personalist autocracies typically reward loyalty over competence and provide few protections for those who speak out against current policy. Far better to pander to the bosses with soothing refrains than to challenge them with independent judgment.

These common features of personalist regimes like Putin's Russia may have contributed to the faulty premises on which Putin launched this war.[13] The Kremlin's initial strategy of a lightning strike on Kyiv with the expected defection of some Ukrainian elites, support from the Russian-speaking Ukrainian population, and noisy acquiescence from the West has not been borne out. While more research is needed, it seems likely that Putin's subordinates provided inaccurate information about the state of affairs on the ground in Ukraine, whether through fear of contradicting the boss or the simple information deficit that is common to autocratic regimes.

One telling detail supports this view. Just two weeks into the invasion, two high-level officials in the Fifth Service, the foreign intelligence branch of the FSB were reportedly placed under house arrest for financial abuses and providing inaccurate information about the war.[14] Operatives in this branch had long been active in spreading misinformation, recruiting sources, and gathering intelligence on political affairs in Ukraine for the Kremlin. A leading Russian expert on the FSB noted, "After two weeks of war, it now appears that Putin has finally realized that he was misled: afraid of angering the Russian leader, the Fifth Service simply told him what he wanted to hear."[15] A similar argument may account for the overly rosy assessment of the chances of Russia's military after its dismal performance at the start of the war.

The logic of personalist rule tends to bias the flow of information from the bureaucracy to the autocrat, but the problem is even larger. The crackdown on independent sources of information also hinders policymaking. In the past three years, the Russian state has all but eliminated Russia's small but feisty independent news organizations and civil society groups that regularly provided counterpoints to the state media. Extinguishing private sources of information likely made it more difficult for Putin—a man who does not use the Internet and e-mail—and

for his subordinates to gather accurate information about public sentiment and the quality of state institutions in Ukraine and Russia. The
informational problems common to personalist autocracies are on full
display in the decision to launch the war in Ukraine.

Finally, Putin's decision to invade Ukraine is consistent with the
broader logic of personalist rule: weak institutions may allow a ruler to
take power in his or her own hands, but they make policy mistakes more
likely. Because Russia is an unusually powerful player in global politics,
comparisons to the foreign policies of other autocracies should be made
with care, but cross-national research suggests that personalist autocracies like Putin's tend to be more likely to go to war than other types of
autocracies because their leaders face fewer institutional constraints.[16]
More limited evidence indicates that militaries in personalist autocracies fight less effectively than in other types of autocracies.[17] Personalist
autocrats may fight wars that are more difficult to win because they receive low-quality information about their chances of success and
because soldiers are less motivated to fight on behalf of a corrupt elite.

To be sure, the logic of Russia's personalist autocracy is not the only
factor that led to Russia's war on Ukraine. In *Weak Strongman*, I critique
approaches to Russian politics that emphasize Putin's personality and
occupational background, but these factors matter more in foreign policy than in any other realm and take on even greater weight during crises
when decisions need to be made quickly under great duress. In announcing the decision, Putin emphasized his personal role by noting,
"I have made the decision to begin a special military operation." Putin
may believe that he is righting an historical injustice by trying to unite
Ukraine and Russia, but his views that Ukraine is "not a real country"
and that Ukrainians and Russians are "one people" are not widely held
in Russia.[18] In regular surveys over the past decade, fewer than
20 percent of Russians supported the idea that Russia and Ukraine
should unify into a single country, and close to 80 percent preferred
friendly relations with a sovereign Ukraine.[19] A different leader might
have made a different choice. Yet even a different leader in a personalist
autocracy would have faced similarly difficult trade-offs, received

similarly biased information, and faced institutions too weak to counter his or her personal views.

Looking forward, the framework developed in *Weak Strongman* also suggests that Putin's balancing act will be much more difficult should the war continue on its current path. Putin launched the invasion with little buy-in from economic and foreign policy elites and without a clear narrative to sway the mass public. This preserved the element of surprise but also made it more difficult to build a case for why Russia needed to go to war. Putin's contentions that the invasion was undertaken to liberate Ukraine from "Neo-Nazis and drug addicts" in the Kyiv government may sway some in Russia, but it rings hollow to many others in the country and abroad.[20]

In addition, as sanctions and the withdrawal of foreign companies put great pressure on the Russian economy, Putin's ability to satisfy both elites and the masses will be tested. Already, we have seen the ruble crash, threats of a government default, and predictions of a steep drop of output in Russia in 2022. To date, many elites have remained silent, but some have called for a quick end to the fighting. Ukraine-born billionaire Mikhail Fridman, whose parents live in Lviv, "joined those whose fervent desire is for the bloodshed to end," and metals magnate Oleg Deripaska called for "peace as fast as possible."[21] The economic and foreign policy elites who have enjoyed the benefits of a globalized Russia did not sign up to become the symbols of an international pariah state.

While these elites may oppose the war and suffer by sticking with Putin, they may fear losing more should they express their opposition without other elites supporting them. Collective action by economic elites in personalist autocracies is made difficult by the lack of organizations like independent parties or business groups to coordinate their actions. One group not likely to be affected by the economic sanctions is Putin's inner circle of national security men. They have long been under sanctions and harbor few illusions that they will ever travel freely outside of Russia. We are likely to see tension among elite groups in Russia as Putin's war cabinet and economic elites have interests that largely conflict.

The fracturing of elite groups is likely to be mirrored in the mass public, further complicating Putin's balancing act. We are likely to see the cleaving of Russian society into those who favor a "fortress Russia" of economic isolation, anti-Westernism, and state control, and those who favor a "global Russia" of integration with the world economy, access to non-state information, and greater political openness. Older, less well-educated Russians, and those who depend on the state for their livelihood or their information are likely to rally around the leader in the short-run, but we have not seen anything like the surge in genuine support for Putin across all social groups that followed the annexation of Crimea. Many Russians seem to be taking a wait and see attitude as they struggle to piece together their views from state sources that obfuscate the causes of the war and downplay the scope of the destruction in Ukraine.

Some Russians will continue to support their government even in the face of damning evidence but others will not. In the past decade, younger, better-educated Russians who have benefited from openness to the world have been much less supportive of Putin. The Russian government's heavy-handed censorship, including bans on Facebook and Instagram, severe repression of even minor forms of protest, and anti-Western screeds will only harden their opposition. In addition, as noted in *Weak Strongman*, the mass public has long been skeptical of Russian military interventions abroad and keenly sensitive to casualties. Popular support for introducing troops in past conflicts in Georgia in 2008, in eastern Ukraine in 2014, and in Syria in 2015 has been rather weak. No wonder the Russian state has hidden the scale of the devastation in Ukraine, remained silent on the number of Russian fatalities, and clamped down so hard on alternative sources of information.

As I emphasize in *Weak Strongman*, it is much each easier to govern as a popular than an unpopular autocrat. The scale of the economic shock will likely cut into support for Vladimir Putin. Should Russian military efforts bog down and Russian casualties increase, his support will likely fall further. As more Russians become aware of the scope of the destruction in Ukraine, the scale of the international condemnation of Russia's actions, and the bravery of Ukrainian soldiers and ordinary citizens, many Russians will be forced to reassess their relationship with the current regime. For most Russians, Putin's greatest achievement was the stability and sense of normalcy that he brought to daily life, but having thrown in his lot in with the security services and launched a war with unpredictable consequences, he has put this all at risk.

The war has not only changed Russian politics but also how we study Russian politics. Should the war continue on its current path, academic research on Russia is likely to become simultaneously more difficult and even more important. Throughout *Weak Strongman*, I document the renaissance of the study of Russian politics over the past twenty years. Relative to other autocracies, Russia has provided far better opportunities for conducting surveys, richer administrative data, and greater scope for research. Russian and foreign scholars have taken advantage of these opportunities to produce impressive research on topics from vote fraud and repression to corruption and public opinion. Increasing repression against academics and journalists in Russia in recent years has hindered these efforts, but scholars continue to publish influential articles and books on Russian politics at rates not seen in decades.

The future of this renaissance is now very much in doubt. The Russian authorities are likely to pressure public opinion firms and state bureaucracies to falsify or hide their data, and the fear of showing disloyalty may reduce the willingness of survey respondents to provide honest answers on sensitive questions. Scholars will have to take extra care when interpreting survey results and data from the Russian state. The brilliant Russian journalists who produced searing exposés on abuses of power and provided invaluable political context are now largely silent as a result of a widespread crackdown and extreme censorship. The authorities have disbanded civic organizations like *Memorial'* that collected precious data on human rights violations both past and present. Russian society will likely become less legible to researchers, and we will have to find new ways to study it.

I fear for the future of my Russian colleagues who have proven so important to this renaissance. As I write, many Russian colleagues have fled the country. Some voluntarily, others under threat. In either case, it is unclear when and whether they will return. The presidents of almost all prominent universities in Russia sent a chilling message by issuing a collective statement in support of the war.[22] At the same time, many brave scholars have signed petitions opposing the war.[23] I continue to work with my Russian colleagues, but have taken leave from the Higher School of Economics in Moscow.

It may become more difficult to conduct research, but it is more important than ever to include academic voices in our national debate on Russia. Scholars cannot replace the rich reporting of journalists or the unique experience of policymakers, but they have much to bring to our national conversation about Russia. Social scientists with deep knowledge of the region are better positioned than most observers to sort through the biases in public opinion polls and distortions in administrative data, as these are common problems for scholars working in difficult research environments. They are well placed to put the Russian experience in perspective by drawing not only on the great research on Russia in recent years but also on the rich literature on autocratic rule in other countries. Finally, there is little doubt that our national conversation on Russia will become far more politicized and emotional in the coming years. For all its problems, the peer review process can help weed out the most partisan takes and reward analyses based on evidence rather than ideology.

I've been studying Russia for forty years through the excitement and disappointment of Gorbachev's reforms, the tumult and exhilaration of the 1990s, the optimism of Russia's economic boom in the early 2000s, and the long slide into repression that has marked the past decade. I have also conducted fieldwork in Ukraine, Georgia, Poland, and Bulgaria and made friends and colleagues along the way. My most ambitious effort in recent years is a project on legal reform in Ukraine funded by the US National Science Foundation. Each morning I now exchange texts with my closest Ukrainian colleague. We pretend that we are giving each other valuable information about the war, but we both know that these exchanges are a way for him to let me know that he is still alive. The horror inflicted on Ukraine will not be easily erased, and the lives of so many across the region will never be the same.

Many Russians have worked for a better Russia—a Russia less corrupt, more open to the world, with greater respect for individual rights; a Russia where people travel freely and speak their minds without fear of persecution; a Russia integrated into Europe, and at peace with its neighbors. For the moment, these hopes have been shattered. If Russian history is a guide, though, these setbacks are not the end of the story.

Over the past twenty-two years, Vladimir Putin had many paths to return Russia to prominence after the instability of the Yeltsin years. He could have built on Russia's rich cultural heritage to create a new brand for the country. He could have used Russia's well-educated populace to make it a center of international scholarship. He could have used Russia's natural resource wealth to rebuild the state. He could have used his personal popularity to combat corruption. Instead, he has returned Russia to global prominence using the costliest means possible: aggression abroad and repression at home. *Weak Strongman* tells this story.

New York City

March 17, 2022

ON THE NIGHT of February 21, 2014, Ukrainian president Viktor Yanukovych fled to Russia. His flight followed months of protest against his government for backing out of an agreement with the European Union—protests Yanukovych had tried to repress with ever-greater force. Fearing a loss of influence and the rise of a less friendly government in Ukraine, the Kremlin ordered Russian troops to seize the Ukrainian peninsula of Crimea and moved swiftly to annex the territory. Moscow then sent troops and matériel to local militia groups in eastern Ukraine hostile to the Kyiv government, fueling a six-year war that continues today.

As the fighting began, three scholars asked more than two thousand Americans to locate Ukraine on a map. Just one in six were able to do so.[1] This might just be an example of Americans' comically weak grasp of geography were it not for the second part of the study, which asked respondents whether Russia posed a threat to the United States, and whether the United States should intervene militarily in the conflict between Russia and Ukraine. The scholars found that the less people knew about Ukraine's location, the more they believed that Russia posed a threat to US interests and the more they favored military intervention. Whatever the pros or cons of US military involvement, these figures are disturbing. In democracies, we expect an informed public to guide policy makers and hold them accountable. This is not possible if the public holds opinions untethered from reality.

This book aims to improve our public conversation by drawing on a host of new research to reassess common narratives about Russian politics. Most observers view contemporary Russian politics as a reflection either of Vladimir Putin's worldview or Russia's unique history and culture. Yet these two narratives overlook a crucial body of scholarly research that understands Russia not as sui generis but instead as part of a group of modern nondemocracies. Tapping into this work allows a far richer—and more accurate—understanding of Russian politics today.

Recognizing Putin as an autocrat, and Russia as an autocracy like many others, may seem obvious—and yet doing so brings into sharp focus the inherent limits on his power that are common to autocratic rule, but are often overlooked in discussions about Russia. Throughout the chapters that follow, I look at three major types of constraints: the bluntness of Putin's tools for managing the country, difficult policy trade-offs that confront the Kremlin at home and abroad, and vast uncertainty generated by weak state institutions. For the last twenty years, Putin has been unrivaled at home, but achieving this primacy has come at the costs of a distorted economy, dysfunctional bureaucracy, and unsound policies—three keys to building state power. Rather than the omnipotent ruler depicted in popular narratives, Putin is like many autocrats. He is a strongman, but a weak one.

To make the case for this view of Russian politics, I draw on thirty years of scholarship and experience as a Russia watcher, including stints working as an "information warrior" for the US government in the Soviet Union, consulting for the Russian Securities and Exchange Commission in the 1990s, and coheading a research institute at the Higher School of Economics (HSE) in Moscow since 2011. These experiences— from being an accidental target of a honey trap by the KGB in the Soviet era to witnessing the fall of the Twin Towers from Moscow in 2001—helped me understand how Russia does and does not work.

More important, I rely on research by a new generation of scholars that is frequently at odds with conventional wisdom and has received little attention outside academia. In the coming pages, you will learn how my colleagues and I conduct surveys that detect whether Russians are lying about Putin's popularity; scrape the internet to find political and economic ties among Russian elites; identify bots on Twitter to track propaganda campaigns; use Russian electoral data to reveal fraud; follow the Kremlin's efforts to manipulate public opinion and interfere in foreign elections; gather archival data to trace how Stalin-era purges shape voting in contemporary Russia; track political graffiti in Moscow to study protest; and interview top Russian elites to explore how decisions are made in the Kremlin. This research, much of it unknown even to diligent readers, offers some of the best evidence we have of how Russia works. The goal is not just to deepen our understanding of Russian politics but also to add scholarly voices to our national debate on the topic.

If you want to understand Russia better (and who doesn't), the chapters that follow are a good place to start.

WEAK STRONGMAN

1

Information Warrior

I WAS AN INFORMATION WARRIOR before it was cool. Every few years from 1959 until 1992, the United States and Soviet Union each swapped twenty-four "guides" to host standing exhibits about life in their respective countries.[1] Born of the Khrushchev-era thaw in US-Soviet relations, the exhibits were an early example of public diplomacy, and became a critical tool for each country to promote its vision and values. Traveling from city to city every two months, the exhibits allowed Soviet and US citizens a rare face-to-face encounter with their Cold War rivals.[2]

I was one such guide. From November 1987 to January 1989, I worked on the *Information USA* exhibit that displayed fax machines, home computers, CD players, and other information technologies used in daily life in the United States. Each day more than eight thousand Soviet citizens came to the exhibit; we were the first Americans most of them had ever met. A woman in Magnitogorsk, a steel-making town closed to almost all Westerners for the past forty years, exclaimed as she approached my stand, "An American. A real live American. I never thought I would see a real live American."[3]

I was there at a good time. Relations between Moscow and Washington had chilled in the decades after Nikita Khrushchev's fall from power, as had the reception of our predecessors on previous exhibits. But by the time I joined, Soviet leader Mikhail Gorbachev's policy of glasnost, or openness, was in full swing. Intrepid Russian journalists were reassessing many painful moments in Soviet history that had long been off-limits for discussion, from the Great Terror of the 1930s to the corruption of the Brezhnev-era in the 1960s and 1970s. For the first time in its history, the Communist Party allowed and encouraged public meetings to debate reforms to the Soviet system, and our exhibit halls often became sites of pitched political discussions among our Russian guests.

Six days a week, for eight hours a day, we rotated between two hours standing with our props on a small stage answering questions and one hour recovering in our makeshift lounge walled off from the crowds, but not the noise, by black canvas curtains. No topic was out of bounds. Is Michael Jackson popular? Why do you have to pay for college? Why does the United States support the racist regime of South Africa? Are you married? Why not? Why do the women guides wear so little makeup? Which Georgian writers do you read in the United States? If Americans don't have internal passports, how do you catch criminals? We heard it all.

Each guide brought different perspectives to these questions. Most were under thirty (I was twenty-four) and single, but there were few other common traits; we came from all over the United States and had jobs ranging from teacher to movie director to engineer. About half were men, a handful were Soviet émigrés, and one was African American. We trained in Washington for a month learning about our "props," US policy, and the dos and don'ts of being a diplomat before heading to the Soviet Union. We were expected to explain US government policies, but were free to criticize them, and frequently did.

The exhibit filled forty-five tractor trailer–size containers. Every ten weeks we decamped to a new city, and with the help of local workers, put up walls, laid down flooring, and installed lighting in cavernous pavilions that often previously housed displays glorifying the achievements of the Soviet economy. During our stay we were local celebrities, and spent many evenings and rare days off with hosts who were eager to hear about our lives in the United States—and tell us about theirs in the USSR—until the early morning. The job was exhilarating yet exhausting.

With its glossy handouts, video touch screens, and interactive displays, our exhibit stood in sharp contrast to the drab Soviet design of the time. In this preinternet era, our props included not just home electronics but also a range of cultural ephemera, including a video loop of the Talking Heads' "Once in a Lifetime" followed by Cyndi Lauper's "Girls Just Want to Have Fun." What the Uzbek cotton farmers at our exhibit in Tashkent made of David Byrne's convulsions or Cyndi Lauper's hairdo, I can only guess.

As in just about every other exhibit since the program's inception, the most popular prop was a car. In our case, it was a Plymouth Voyager—not the sexiest on the lot, but much more interesting than the Ladas that dotted the roads in the USSR. The second most popular exhibit was a Xerox copier machine, which few had seen since copiers were kept under tight control and had to be registered with the security services. We occasionally got into trouble with the local authorities for copying calls to public demonstrations, historical documents, or forbidden literature from our visitors.

This was not my first trip to the Soviet Union. Caught up in the intrigue and excitement of the Cold War, I studied Russian first in high school in Utica, New York, and later at Middlebury College in Vermont. My first trip overseas was to Moscow in February 1985 as a college junior studying Russian language and literature. I ended up sharing a dormitory with seven hundred students from countries of the socialist camp—East Germany, Cuba, and Afghanistan—and found navigating the local mores about meeting with foreigners no less challenging than learning to conjugate Russian's notorious verbs of motion. Four weeks after our arrival, the suspicious wall-mounted radio that could not be turned off told us that the general secretary of the Communist Party, Konstantin Chernenko, had died and Gorbachev would head the funeral services—a clear indication that he would be the next leader of the USSR.

Life was difficult in Moscow in 1985. I saw ration cards for sugar, witnessed the early days of Gorbachev's attempts to curb vodka sales, and experienced the tension of a particularly difficult moment in US-Soviet relations. Just two years earlier, President Ronald Reagan had deemed the Soviet Union the "Evil Empire" for shooting down a passenger jet near South Korea, while the Soviets accused the United States of warmongering for resuming tests of nuclear weapons. Not everything American was eschewed. One bright spot for Muscovites that year was the ridiculously popular movie "Jazz Is Only for Girls," or as we know it in English, "Some Like It Hot," which sparked a mini revival of Marilyn Monroe in the Soviet capital.

When I joined *Information USA* two years later, I saw more of the contradictions and complexities of a region that would fascinate me for years to come. Each day brought new puzzles. In Tbilisi, the capital of Georgia, a serious-looking young man approached my stand and began, "I know that you have unemployment under capitalism and that it is very bad. We don't have that here. But I also understand that you have something called the 'want ads' where employers advertise to find new workers. How can both be true?" Like many Soviets then and Russians now, they knew that part of what they learned from the media was propaganda and part was true, but they struggled to identify which part was which.

In Irkutsk, a young woman peppered me with pointed questions about US policy in the Middle East. Justifiably unsatisfied with my superficial answer, she sensed weakness. As she started in again with greater ferocity, someone in the crowd announced, "They prepared you very well." Having been called out as a collaborator with the security services, she meekly withdrew amid the crowd's laughter.[4] Battles with provocateurs sent by the local authorities were part of the job.

In Leningrad (now Saint Petersburg), I went with a young Russian to see Oliver Stone's heavy-handed critique of capitalism, *Wall Street*, which received wide play in the Soviet Union with its depiction of the glamorous life of the morally bankrupt investment banker Gordon Gekko. It was obvious, I explained to my friend, why the movie was on so many screens in his country. And he said, "Tim, but you don't understand, when a Russian sees that movie he thinks, if only I could go there" (*Akh, tuda by*).

My education in the nuances of Russia continued as I entered graduate school at Columbia University. I started in January 1989; ten months later, on a tiny black-and-white television in my six-story walk-up apartment on 112th Street, I watched with astonishment as East Berliners climbed over the wall that had divided their country for decades. Communist governments fell that year not just in East Germany but also in

Poland, Hungary, Czechoslovakia, Bulgaria, and Romania. I watched too as the republics of the Soviet Union called for greater independence from Moscow and nationalist protests broke out across the Soviet space. A failed coup by hard-liners in the Communist Party and Red Army in August 1991 ended Moscow's dreams of keeping the multiethnic Soviet Empire together, and scrambled many dissertations underway on relations between the North Atlantic Treaty Organization (NATO) and the Warsaw Pact as the latter no longer existed.

A New Generation

I joined a new generation of Russian and US scholars; trained after the fall of the Berlin Wall, we had unprecedented opportunities to study the collapse of Communism and rise of whatever would take its place. As part of my dissertation research, I worked for two summers in the newly created Russian Securities and Exchange Commission in Moscow. I studied why brokers relied on word of mouth to honor contracts on some capital markets, but turned to big guys with big guns on others. I interviewed bankers and bodyguards, and sometimes had trouble telling the two apart.

Following graduation, I became a professor at Ohio State University and later rejoined Columbia, where I wrote about protection rackets, privatization, corruption, property rights, and more. Russia has provided endless material to study how states and markets work, and more often, how they do not. In 2010, I had a chance to move this work closer to the source when my colleague, the Russian economist Andrei Yakovlev, and I won a large grant from the Russian government to create a research institute at the HSE in Moscow. Our team of a dozen or so Russian, US, and European scholars conducts research at the intersection of politics and economics, surveying Russian lawyers, businesspeople, and the mass public, sorting through government statistics, gathering historical data, writing articles for academic journals, and training young Russians to be hard-nosed social scientists.[5]

And we are not alone. Throughout the last thirty years, through all of Russia's up and downs, academics have produced impressive studies of public opinion, corruption, protest, electoral fraud, propaganda, corporate raiding, and foreign policy. Contrary to the assertion of many observers that Western countries lack expertise on Russia, political science has seen a remarkable flourishing of research on the topic. The flagship journals in political science have been publishing research on Russia at far greater rates than at any time in decades.[6]

Russia has been fertile ground for studying authoritarian rule. Public opinion polls have been far more credible than in other autocracies, and Russia provides more detailed administrative data, including election results, economic information, and social indicators, than do many other authoritarian governments.[7] The country's more than eighty regions offer a tremendous opportunity to compare developments across a diverse landscape. Fearless reporters, academics, and activists in Russia have continued to publish exposés on corruption that would be unthinkable in many other dictatorships. That Russia is an unusually well-educated nondemocracy has also been a great help. Observers of other major autocracies, like China, Egypt, Saudi Arabia, Iran, and Venezuela, face a far more difficult task than do Russia hands.

Many of the most interesting scholars writing on Russia are now Russians. I have been a great beneficiary of this development. In the last fifteen years, I've had as many Russian as American coauthors. The addition of Russian voices to the conversation has broadened the academic debate and encouraged more reflection among non-Russian observers about the biases we bring to the subject.

This research has been part of a broader movement to reassess the workings of authoritarian governments.[8] In the last decade, scholars have made good progress in explaining why nondemocracies like Russia rise and fall, how they survive, why some are more corrupt than others, and why some grow rapidly while others stagnate. Rather than treating autocracies as the mirror image of democracies, these studies identify a host of tensions inherent to autocratic rule that force difficult trade-offs on rulers. There is still much to learn, but we know far more than we did a decade ago about autocratic rule, and many of these lessons are valuable for understanding contemporary Russia.

The Disconnect

Unfortunately, this research has had little impact on public discourse about Russia and its relationship to the rest of the world.[9] Much of this work is unknown even to Russia watchers in academic disciplines outside political science (who, if they are like me, struggle to follow the latest developments in their own discipline, let alone keep up with findings in neighboring fields). Sovietology died long ago in academia, but lives on in popular debate. While there are exceptions, much of this debate lacks balance, depth, and nuance. It is disheartening to see the quality of the discussions around Russia so shallow.

Although less so than in the Soviet period, views of Russia in the West are still highly politicized. Some on the nationalist Right depict Putin's Russia as a defender of the traditional family, white race, and Christian faith, but as Anne Applebaum notes, Russian reality is far from these American dreams.[10] Abortion rates in Russia are twice as high as in the United States, few Russians attend church regularly or read the Bible, and a third of Russian families are headed by single mothers with children.[11] And Russia regularly accepts more immigrants than just about any country but the United States. Some on the Left exaggerate Putin's influence abroad by depicting any decision by the White House that benefits Moscow as evidence that President Donald Trump is just Putin's puppet.[12]

Russia's multipronged effort to influence the US presidential election in 2016 has heightened the politicization of public discourse on Russia. Reactions to this campaign overturned one of the most durable partisan cleavages in US politics as Democrats are now more hawkish toward Russia than are Republicans. These types of rapid changes in public opinion tend to occur on issues where the public has little prior information and can be easily led by politicians. This is only the latest evidence that politics heavily colors popular views toward Russia.[13]

Commentators often fall neatly into hard-line or soft-line camps, and interpret events in Russia through these prisms. A US senator can observe that Russia is just "a gas station masquerading as a country," and a think tanker in Washington can declare that Putin has "Hitler's foreign policy and Mussolini's domestic policy."[14] These comments provoke

equally simplistic charges of "demonizing Putin" and "Russophobia,"
bringing debate to a screeching halt.

Political scientist Tom Pepinsky's colorful characterization of Malaysia will ring true for those of us who sometimes struggle to explain
everyday life in Russia to those unfamiliar with the topic.

> The mental image that most Americans harbor of what actual au-
> thoritarianism looks like is fantastical and cartoonish. This vision of
> authoritarian rule has jackbooted thugs, all-powerful elites acting
> with impunity, poverty and desperate hardship for everyone else,
> strict controls on political expression and mobilization, and a dicta-
> tor who spends his time ordering the murder or disappearance of his
> opponents using an effective and wholly compliant security appara-
> tus. This image of authoritarianism comes from the popular media
> (dictators in movies are never constrained by anything but open in-
> surrection), from American mythmaking about the Founding (and
> the Second World War and the Cold War), and from a kind of "imagi-
> nary othering" in which the opposite of democracy is the absence of
> everything that characterizes the one democracy that one knows.
> Still, that fantastical image of authoritarianism is entirely misleading
> as a description of modern authoritarian rule and life under it.[15]

To be sure, Russia is more repressive than Malaysia, and has become
much more so in recent years, but Pepinsky is not far off the mark. Autocracy in Russia is a subtler beast.

It is just difficult for most people to imagine life and politics in Russia. Moscow is far, and Kremlin politics are opaque. When I started
teaching Russian politics in the mid-1990s, I sometimes joked that if
I told my undergraduates that in Moscow on Tuesday people walk on
their hands, then the students would dutifully jot down in their notes:
"Moscow. Tuesday. Hands." Not that they weren't bright. They were.
Like most people, though, they needed basic information and context
to begin to understand Russia's politics.

But the problem runs deeper than a lack of information and political
bias. Indeed, our two dominant narratives for understanding Russian
politics are helpful, but get us only so far.

Consider interpretations of a pivotal event in modern Russia: the arrest of Mikhail Khodorkovsky as he boarded a private jet in Siberia in 2003. At the time of his arrest, Khodorkovsky was the richest man in Russia thanks to the hugely unpopular privatizations of the 1990s and some savvy business decisions on his part. He was also beginning to play an increasing role in politics by funding opposition parties and think tanks much to the ire of the Kremlin. Authorities accused the forty-one-year-old Khodorkovsky of tax evasion and violating privatization laws. After two trials, he served more than ten years in jail and lost control of the oil giant Yukos to a state-owned rival. While observers agree that the arrest of Khodorkovsky epitomized the reassertion of state control over the economy and curbed the political power of big business, they disagree about the motivations behind it.

One account emphasizes Putin's personal role in the affair. As a former KGB agent, Putin had little interest in building markets and democracy, and sought to lead a revanche by his cronies in the security services that would reassert state power over society. The nationalization of Yukos and its transfer to a company controlled by President Putin's close associate was just one step in this plan.[16] This explanation is part of a broader line of argument that treats Russian politics as an extension of Putin's worldview and stresses his seeming omnipotence over society. If we want to understand Russian politics, we need to begin with Vladimir Vladimirovich Putin.

Another account points to Russia's exceptional history and culture. This view depicts the nationalization of Yukos as Russia reverting to its historical type. Russia's long tradition of fusing state and private property as well as the lack of public support for markets and democracy, doomed efforts to build private companies that could provide a check on state power. As one commentator noted, "What's remarkable about the uproar over President Vladimir Putin's battle with mega-oligarch Mikhail Khodorkovsky, who announced his resignation as head of Yukos Oil from his jail cell last week, is how eerily it strengthens the impression that Russian history is a continuum—no matter how dramatic the break between one era and the next."[17] The "exceptional Russia" argument underscores the gravitational pull of Russia's authoritarian past and culturally ingrained habits that (supposedly) make Russia and Russians distinct as the key to grasping its current politics.

Yet for all the emphasis on the seemingly unique characteristics of Putin and the distinctive aspects of Russia's history and culture, similar expropriations of energy companies via forced sales or contract renegotiations took place in countries as diverse as Algeria, Bolivia, Chad, Dubai, Ecuador, Senegal, and Venezuela in the mid-2000s.[18] Looking more broadly, two researchers who examined all oil-rich countries between 1945 and 2006 found that when oil prices are high in autocracies, nationalizations are much more likely.[19] This pattern indicates that the expropriation of Yukos was driven less by Putin's personality or Russia's historical patterns than by factors common to modern autocracies. As is often the case, events treated as specific to Russia are mirrored in autocracies around the world. To understand Russian politics, we need to recognize the general forces at play in autocracies.

Academics like me are partly to blame for the poor state of our national discussion on Russia. Much of our research appears only in academic journals, and we have not done the hard work of getting these findings out to a broader audience. While there is much great reporting and commentary on Russia, unraveling Russia's increasingly insular politics also requires the kinds of careful counting, focused comparisons, and deep country knowledge that academics can provide.

Academic research brings different strengths than much popular writing on Russia. Journalists have better access to the movers and shakers, and can publish quickly. They are frequently joined by think tankers, politicians, and political activists who have a strong interest in shaping the debate on Russia in one direction or another. Academic research is less timely, but it is more reflective and less partisan than much popular writing on Russia.

There's a reason that popular writing on Russia is indeed popular, and it is easy to argue that much of the popular writing on Russia is better than on many other countries.[20] Masterful writers on Russia employ telling anecdotes, bold investigations, and compelling personal stories that provide richness and detail most social scientists can only envy.[21] These are tremendously powerful tools—sometimes too powerful, as they can be persuasive even when they mislead. Summing up a range of research on "narrative bias," sociologist Duncan Watts writes, "So powerful is the appeal of a good story that even when we are trying to evaluate an explanation scientifically—that is, on the basis of how well it accounts for the data—we can't help judging it in terms of its narrative attributes."[22] We often deem simple explanations and arguments with informative details to be accurate even when they are not. The question is whether these anecdotes, investigations, and personal histories reflect more general developments within Russian society. This is where academic research can help.

One strength of academic research is the ability to gather large data sets that are subject to empirical testing that allow us to grasp broader trends. Arguments that come up short on evidence or logic, or are too partisan, will struggle to make it through peer review. Academic research serves as a necessary complement to, rather than as a substitute for, much of the kinds of deep reporting that dominates the best popular writing on Russia. We need both to get a full picture of what's happening in Russia.

Russia as a Personalist Autocracy

In this book, I pull together much of this exciting new research to offer a different lens for interpreting Russian politics. Rather than viewing Russian politics as driven by an exceptional ruler governing an exceptional country, I highlight common patterns that Russia shares with other autocratic regimes ruled by a single individual. Rulers in these so-called personalist autocracies face a host of common challenges and constraints that differ from their counterparts in democracies and autocracies led by a single party or the military.

In studying personalist autocracies like Russia, it is tempting to focus on the personal quirks and characteristics of the leader—but in doing so, we lose sight of the features these types of autocracies share. While all countries have their own peculiarities, we can learn a good deal about Russia by viewing it alongside other states with similar types of governance: Recep Tayyip Erdoğan's Turkey, Hugo Chávez's Venezuela, Viktor Orban's Hungary, Alberto Fujimori's Peru, and Nursultan Nazarbayev's Kazakhstan among others. Understanding the inherent tensions and constraints of modern autocracies is essential for grasping Russian politics.

Comparing Russia to other countries can help us identify when Russia's politics and economics are driven by factors common to personalist autocracies, and when they are shaped primarily by factors unique to Russia. Where we see commonalities between Russia and other personalist autocracies, we can often attribute them to the political logic of this type of regime, but where we see differences that Russia has with other governments of this type, we can look for other explanations.

As we will see in more detail in chapter 3, three features common to personalist autocracies are especially helpful for understanding Putin's Russia, and each provides a useful counterpoint to conventional narratives on Russia.

First, while commentators focus on the seeming stability of Putin's rule, political life in Russia is inherently uncertain because Russia lacks strong institutions like the rule of law as well as free and fair elections to resolve political disputes that inevitability arise. Absent an electoral calendar and strong institutions to structure political competition, rulers can be removed at any time and typically without agreement on how to choose a successor. These weak institutions do not protect the autocrat after they leave office, making the stakes of losing power in politics in personalist autocracies like Russia much higher than in other types of governments.

Second, autocrats face difficult policy trade-offs. Rulers in a democracy can be removed via the ballot box; autocratic rulers can be removed via an elite coup or mass revolt. Because the dual threats of elite coup and mass revolt can rarely be reduced at the same time, personalist autocrats face inherent policy trade-offs that constrain their power. Policies that enrich cronies frequently come at the expense of the mass public and vice versa. Autocrats face hard choices about rewarding narrow interest groups or pursuing policies with broader benefits, using repression or persuasion against political opponents, and choosing how much to censor the media, cheat in elections, and violate human rights in order to stay in power. Rather than flowing directly from Putin's worldview or Russia's historical legacy, policy choices in Russia are often the result of difficult trade-offs among and between political elites and the mass public.

Third, personalist autocracies have a range of tools—all rather blunt—for managing a modern society. Much popular commentary revolves around Putin as a master of repression to keep society in check. And it is true that crackdowns on free media, intimidation of political opponents, and arrests of human rights activists are part and parcel of political life in Russia. But repression is costly, not always effective, and rarely a first choice. Influential elites and the mass public do not automatically follow the leader but instead need to be convinced to do so, sometimes via fear, yet also via persuasion or self-interest. Autocrats like Putin prefer to rely on personal popularity, economic performance, manipulated elections, and foreign policy successes to stave off elite coups and popular revolts, but these commodities are usually fleeting and beyond the control of the ruler.

From this perspective, a view of Russia emerges that is less focused on President Putin's personality and seeming omnipotence, and less centered on Russia's unique history and culture. Rooting Russia's politics in common patterns of autocratic rule produces a picture of Russia that helps us see the constraints on Putin's power, recognize the difficult policy choices before him, and better understand Russia's politics.

That's not to say that all the research I will present introduces novel findings. Some elements of the common wisdom on Russia are upheld, and others are undermined. The point of social science is not to prove conventional wisdom wrong; it is to examine and test arguments. Because many common assertions about Russia are in tension—Russia's state is bumbling and inefficient, but conducts exquisitely sophisticated cyberattacks; Putin is popular, yet needs to cheat to win elections—these tests are badly needed to untangle these competing claims.

A comparative perspective that draws on academic research can tell us a lot about Russia—but it can't tell us everything. No single approach can. As we will see, this comparative approach sheds more light on Russia's domestic politics than on its foreign policy (although it is helpful there as well) and must be paired with deep knowledge of Russia.

And while it's much easier to do social science work in Russia than in other autocracies, this work still brings great challenges. Many top-flight Russian academics have left for greener and freer pastures. Those who remain in Russia must constantly assess what types of investigations are permissible and what types are not. Studying Russia is a contact sport, and like American football, it has a high rate of injury. Many Russians have paid dearly for their politics, and some academics too have suffered directly for their work. This is a far less dangerous task than being an investigative journalist in Russia, but still one must take care. Studying Russia has become much more difficult in recent years, and current trends— which I'll examine much more in the chapters to come—provide little optimism that the situation will improve in the short run.

———

In the next chapter, I present two approaches to studying Russia that generate much of the conventional wisdom. In chapter 3, I discuss recent research on authoritarian governments that provides an alternative. In successive chapters, I then explore what we know about Putin's popularity, elections, the economy, repression, media manipulation, foreign policy, and cyber campaigns abroad. The final chapter looks at what recent academic research tells us about Russia's future and offers some guidance about how we can improve our national discussion on Russia.

In the pages that follow, you will read about scholarly research that offers some of the best evidence available on many basic questions about Russia. How popular is Putin? Is corruption as high as they say? Why are relations with the United States so bad? Is Russian propaganda effective? Did Russian cyberwarriors swing the 2016 US presidential election? Do elections matter in Russia? These questions are not easily answered, but academics writing on Russia have given them careful consideration. Understanding Russia is more important than ever, and the solid evidence, clear logic, and transparency of academic research can help us cut through the disinformation, misinformation, and simple misperceptions about Russia that cloud our vision. So let's begin.

2

Putinology and Exceptional Russia

There is no Russia today if there is no Putin.

—KREMLIN CHIEF OF STAFF VYACHESLAV VOLODIN, 2014

LIKE MANY RUSSIA WATCHERS, I am occasionally asked to give talks about current events to the general public—to audiences that range from corporate boards to religious groups to book clubs. No matter the group and no matter the topic of the presentation, two questions inevitably arise: "What is Putin really like?" and "Don't Russians just have a different mentality?"

Embedded in these two questions are the assumptions that drive a good deal of the popular discourse about Russia. Some observers emphasize the personal role and worldview of Putin as the key to unlocking Russian politics, and make frequent reference to his temperament, KGB background, and path to power. Other observers highlight the unique features of Russian culture and history, and point to Russia's long experience with czarist and Communist rule.

This chapter assesses these two common views. Like all conventional wisdoms, there is merit in these approaches, but they also mislead in important ways.

Putinology

One approach to contemporary Russia stems from a simple proposition: if you want to understand autocracy, you need to understand the autocrat. Almost by definition, autocrats have an outsize influence on politics in their country and therefore it is essential to have a measure of the leader. In this vein, one of Putin's advisers coined the memorable phrase "No Putin, No Russia." For practitioners of Putinology, "Know Putin, Know Russia" might be more appropriate.[1]

Many scholars have probed Putin's background and career path to find clues to his behavior as a leader. Born in 1952, he grew up in a tough neighborhood in postwar Leningrad as a latchkey kid hearing stories from his grandfather who served as a cook for Joseph Stalin. An aimless teenager, he grew infatuated with the KGB and applied for a job as a spy, only to be turned down for being underage. He graduated from the law department of Leningrad State University in 1975 and entered the foreign intelligence branch of the KGB, where he rose to become a mid-level officer. Stationed in Dresden, East Germany, from 1985 to 1990, he witnessed the fall of Communism in Eastern Europe and famously defended the embassy from Germans seeking access to its files.

He returned to Leningrad in 1990 and became a city official specializing in foreign trade, loyally serving the liberal mayor Anatoly Sobchak, who at the time was one of Russia's most prominent politicians. Putin worked largely behind the scenes, but was accused of overseeing a scheme that sent raw materials and industrial scrap abroad in exchange for food that never arrived and cost the city almost $100 million. A city investigation recommended his dismissal, but Sobchak intervened to save his job. While working for the city, Putin also began to create an inner circle of loyalists who would come to form the core of his team as president and, not coincidentally, become fabulously rich in due time for their effort.[2]

In August 1996, Putin moved to Moscow to take up a post in the presidential administration on the recommendation of prominent liberals in the Yeltsin government. His loyalty to Sobchak reportedly impressed Yeltsin, who in 1998 tapped him to head the Federal Security

Service (FSB, the successor to the KGB) and then serve as acting prime minister in summer 1999—a move widely seen as positioning him to succeed Yeltsin. Backed by a key group of oligarchs and Yeltsin loyalists, Putin was elected president in 2000.

He rode a boom in oil prices and spectacular economic growth to consolidate his power in elections in 2004, and in accordance with the Constitution, stepped down as president in 2008, only to become prime minister, and by many accounts, still exercised powers akin to a president for the next four years. With the economy slowing and protests accelerating, he returned to the presidency in 2012 as an anti-Western nationalist, and used the annexation of Crimea in 2014 to send his popularity skyrocketing and mark Russia's return as a great power.

Reelected for another six-year term in 2018, Putin has struggled to find a new narrative to lead Russia. With enthusiasm for the Crimean annexation fading and the economy stagnating, his popularity has faltered. Putin tries to rally public support by depicting Russia as a "besieged fortress" beset on all sides by enemies, but the public seems more interested in declining living standards and the shock of the global pandemic. To quell public disquiet, he has increased repression and coercion. Facing term limits in 2024, he pushed amendments to the Constitution through the Russian Parliament (the Duma) that allow him to remain in office for two additional six-year terms should he win elections in 2024 and 2030. Rather than rally around Putin, many Russians met the extensions of his term with indifference at best. One survey from January 2020 that gave respondents several possible options for Putin after 2024 found that roughly one-third of Russians wanted him to remain as president, one-third wanted him to remain in government in a different capacity, and one-third wanted him to retire.[3]

Who Is Mr. Putin?

Putin-centered approaches to Russian politics assume that Putin is motivated by a core set of beliefs that are consistent over time, and that he can easily translate these values and beliefs into policy. This leads to a fixation on Putin that dominates much of the analysis about Russian politics. Yet probing deeper, these assumptions are hard to justify.[4]

Some say he is a risk-taker because he surprised everyone with the annexation of Crimea.[5] Others say he is a cautious leader and point to his decision to build massive reserve funds for the state from the oil boom of the early 2000s.[6] Some claim he has a long-term plan to undermine international institutions that he sees as biased against Russian interests.[7] But others posit that he is an opportunist who responds to circumstances as they arise—as in his decision to broker a deal to remove chemical weapons in Syria when President Barack Obama balked at using force against President Bashar al-Assad in 2013.[8] Some argue he primarily seeks personal wealth as witnessed by the enormous riches of his oldest friends (who presumably are willing to share the spoils with him).[9] Others contend that he is at heart a Russian nationalist given his proselytizing of the controversial philosophers Ivan Il'in and Aleksandr Dugin.[10] One of the best biographies of Putin suggests that there are six Putins: the statist, history man, survivalist, outsider, free marketeer, and case officer.[11] Identifying a consistent through line in Putin's values and worldview is more difficult than the conventional wisdom suggests. For Putin, a willingness to adapt strategies to circumstances appears to dominate any deep ideological commitments.

His policy preferences have also changed over time. In economics, Putin is often seen as a statist to his core, yet his policies have veered wildly although a tolerance for corruption runs through his rule. In his first three years in office, he introduced sweeping economic reforms backed by Russia's most prominent liberal economists, including a 13 percent flat tax on income, drastic revisions of the Labor Code, and a revamping of the pension and banking systems. But when it was clear that oil prices would remain high, he left liberal economic policies behind and promoted natural resource development as the key to Russia's rise. After oil prices fell in 2014 and sanctions took hold, Putin turned to the state as the locomotive of economic growth and made taxpayer-funded state projects the cornerstone of his economic policy.[12] Putin's preferences are far more flexible than Putin-centered approaches would suggest.

Attempts to capture the essence of Putin by exploring his intellectual influences typically rest on shaky ground. Historian Timothy Snyder argues that Putin is under the sway of Ivan Il'in, who in the first half of the twentieth century emphasized Russia's unique civilization and cultural superiority, while rejecting liberalism and communism in favor of autocracy and Mussolini-style fascism.[13] Putin may have a soft spot for Il'in, but how do we know that Il'in's writing and not some other factor is shaping Putin's behavior? Putin reads many books and mentions other Russian thinkers far more frequently.[14] Why is Il'in particularly important? Putin's rare Il'in references are generally garden-variety cultural statements and do not touch on his more controversial political positions, yet the notion of Il'in as Putin's intellectual guru persists.[15] Moreover, Putin may like Il'in's ideas because they fit his preexisting beliefs—in which case Il'in's writing are not causing Putin's behavior at all. Consider the counterfactual. If Putin had not read Il'in, would Russian politics look much different?[16] Thinking that we can capture Putin's decision making in a few rules of thumb that are unique to him is not especially helpful because we can usually find evidence to support a wide array of interpretations for his behavior.

Identifying Putin's core values is made difficult by a lack of evidence. In his monumental biographies of Lyndon Johnson, Robert Caro relied on hundreds of hours of taped conversations in the White House, numerous books by close aides, the president's notes, and a six-hundred-page autobiography, but those writing about Putin have little direct access to the man and none to his notes, and his close advisers have little incentive to reveal much of interest.[17] One can mine his many speeches, interviews, and public statements for clues about his beliefs and values, but we should read these with care.[18] When Putin blames the West for Russia's problems and appeals to Russian Orthodoxy as a source of national identity, is this posturing for political purposes or expressing a deeply held belief? My guess is the former, but it is hard to know. Putin's oft-cited biography and public speeches tell us more about Putin as he wants to be seen rather than as he is. Former Kremlin insiders and businesspeople fallen out of favor can provide valuable insights into Putin's decision making, but these accounts merit scrutiny given the political and economic motivations that frequently lie behind them.[19] The dearth of evidence gives much room for speculation about what Putin "must have been thinking" at any given moment—an exercise that is generally fun, but rarely useful.

Sometimes Putinology gets a little silly. Take speculation about Putin's "gunslinger gait." Researchers from Radboud University in Nijmegen, Netherlands, noted that Putin tends to walk with little movement in his right arm and traced this behavior to an old KGB manual that advised agents to retain easy access to their gun, which presumably is on the right hip. One researcher observed that "Putin is a macho leader who kept his gait to show that he is a KGB veteran. We propose that this new gait pattern, which we term "gunslinger's gait," may result from a behavioral adaptation, possibly triggered by KGB or other forms of weapons training where trainees are taught to keep their right hand close to the chest while walking, allowing them to quickly draw a gun when faced with a foe."[20] If only one could identify KGB officers by their unique way of walking.

More seriously, probing Putin's life experience may account for his support for the Jewish community in Russia and perhaps Russia's good relations with Israel.[21] Some of Putin's closest bonds as a child were with his Orthodox Jewish neighbors and Jewish wrestling coach, Anatoly Rakhlin. Putin has long been a supporter of organized Jewry in Russia and donated a month of his presidential salary to kick-start the campaign to build a new synagogue in Moscow. And Jews are well represented within his inner circle of friends and confidants as well as among Russia's business elites. Perhaps as a result, on Putin's watch relations between Israel and Russia have never been better. This is a low bar as anti-Semitism has a long history in Russia, and relations between Moscow and Tel Aviv have rarely been good, but these are notable departures from past practices that can be traced to Putin's formative experience.

Secret Agent Man

One of the most commonly cited influences on Putin's behavior is his KGB background. It is a central theme of his biography *First Person*, which was written as a campaign document to introduce Putin to the

Russian electorate in the 1999–2000 electoral cycle. Observers have used Putin's KGB career and mentality to account for the stealth with which Russian forces seized Crimea from Ukraine in 2014, why Putin prefers repression to accommodation, and his anti-Western outlook.[22] But identifying whether Putin's policy choices are a consequence of his KGB background and not some other factor is not easy. One need not have worked in the KGB to value stealth in military operations, favor repression of political opponents, or be skeptical of the West.

In addition, anti-Westernism seems to be a function of modern nondemocratic rule rather than a feature specific to Putin. When faced with domestic discontent, leaders with backgrounds as diverse as Erdoğan in Turkey, Orban in Hungary, Chávez in Venezuela, and Mahathir Mohamad in Malaysia have also used criticism of foreign interference, fifth columns funded by foreign opponents, and the evils of Western liberal values to rally their supporters.

Relying on his work experience in the KGB to explain policy outcomes is also of little help in accounting for change in policy during Putin's reign. Putin was just as much a former KGB officer during the period 2000–2013 when Kremlin policy toward Ukraine was far more accommodating than it became after the fall of the Yanukovych government in February 2014. His KGB background has not prevented him from cooperating with the United States when it suits his interest. President Putin was the first leader to call President George W. Bush after the terrorist attacks on the World Trade Center in New York City and was instrumental in securing US efforts to provide supplies to NATO soldiers in Afghanistan, ensuring Iranian agreement for a deal reducing Tehran's nuclear ambitions, and reducing US and Russian nuclear weapons in the New START Treaty. He learned English late in life, even singing Fats Domino's "Blueberry Hill" to a stunned international audience in Saint Petersburg in 2010. And as my colleague Kim Marten notes, as late as June 2002, Putin stated that NATO enlargement to include the Baltics was "no tragedy" so long as no new military infrastructure was introduced.[23]

Putin's KGB persona is in part a creation of Putin and his spin doctors. Putin was a midlevel officer in East Germany and left his job in the KGB in the early 1990s. He rose to power less through his KGB connections than through his relationships with liberal politicians like Saint Petersburg mayor Sobchak. His most important promotion came from President Yeltsin, who was naturally skeptical of the security services.[24] Yet the idea of Putin as "Stierlitz," the fictional spy from Soviet-era movies who outwits the Germans during World War II, is a useful one for the current inhabitant of the Kremlin, and a persona that is cultivated with great care by his public relations team.

Putin's background in the KGB is not irrelevant. He draws heavily on advisers from the security services, his view of politics as driven by the basest motives is consistent with a KGB background, and the security services are a key pillar of support.[25] But drawing a line between Putin's work experience in the KGB and his policies is not so straightforward. Many Russians have become cynical nationalists without ever having served in the KGB.

Further, to the extent that Russian politics follows the patterns of other nondemocracies, one can question the importance of Putin's background. For many observers, Putin's KGB background has been critical to the creation of a crony capitalist economy that thrives on stripping assets at home and parking them abroad to the great enrichment of the elites at the expense of the masses. On this view, it is the personal ties and work experience of the KGB that facilitates the illegal capital flight that so plagues Russia.[26] But autocrats without a KGB background are no less skilled in looting their countries, if on a scale more commensurate with their smaller economies. Autocratic elites from Central Asia, the Middle East, and Asia are good at preying on their economies and laundering their reputations abroad even without the benefit of a KGB past.[27]

Similarly, many analysts have credited Putin's long term in office—twenty-one years and counting either as president or prime minister—to his personal guile, ruthlessness, and roots in the security services. This record is all the more remarkable given the many predictions that Putin would be swept aside soon after taking office. Many questioned whether a public official with such a low profile could withstand the powerful oligarchs and regional governors who then held enormous sway.[28] For many of my Russia-watching colleagues, the reaction to

Putin's appointment as prime minister in summer 1999 was, "Wait, which one is he?"

Compared to other rulers in nearby former Soviet republics, however, Putin's time in office is about par for the course. Before dying in office, Islam Karimov ruled Uzbekistan for twenty-seven years, and Saparmurat Niyazov ruled Turkmenistan for sixteen years. Nazarbayev held power in Kazakhstan for twenty-eight years before resigning in 2019. Alyaksandr Lukashenka has ruled Belarus for twenty-six years and counting while Emomali Rahmon has been in power in Tajikistan since 1992. These leaders come from different backgrounds and have different personalities, yet they have all achieved long stays in office.

Indeed, it should not surprise us that Putin pushed to extend his term in office beyond the current constitutional rules. Each personalist autocrat in the former Soviet space has done the same when faced with an approaching term limit, as did Presidents Erdoğan in Turkey and Chávez in Venezuela.[29] Putin's personal characteristics may have helped him carve out a long tenure, but these comparisons with other countries suggest they are far from the full story.

Like a Tub Full of Dough

Putin-centered approaches to Russian politics also assume that President Putin can easily turn his preferences into policy outcomes. To be sure, Putin is the central node in Russian politics, has faced no serious political challenger since returning to the presidency in 2012, and can often pass legislation with few amendments in Parliament, but he also confronts the physical limits of ruling Russia and challenge of governing a modern society. He must rely on close advisers who in turn oversee armies of bureaucrats, each of whom has their own self-interest. He also faces powerful businesspeople more interested in making money than in serving the state. To implement any policy of consequence, Putin must rely on a chain of bureaucrats, businesspeople, and/or spies who may or may not share his preferences, and monitoring his underlings requires time, effort, and resources.

Former leader of the Soviet Union Khrushchev controlled a Communist Party and bureaucratic apparatus with far greater influence over society than does President Putin, but famously described governing Russia to Fidel Castro as follows:

> You'd think I could change anything in this country. Like hell I can. No matter what changes I propose and carry out, everything stays the same. Russia is like a tub full of dough, you put your hand down in it, down to the bottom, and think you are master of the situation. When you first pull out your hand, a little hole remains, but then, before your very eyes, the dough expands into a spongy, puffy mass. That's what Russia is like.[30]

Given the complexity of governing Russia, the Kremlin must delegate some decision-making power and control over implementation of policy to lower levels of government and bureaucracies, with all the inevitable slippage down the lines of communication.

The problem grows when the Kremlin seeks to maintain plausible deniability. Take these three examples. To supply rebels in eastern Ukraine with arms and people, the Kremlin partnered with Konstantin Malofeev, a Russian oligarch who funded a band of private mercenaries that maintained indirect ties to the Russian military.[31] Similarly, the Kremlin not only employs hackers working directly for the security services but also cooperates with hackers working in private-sector front companies that are less directly affiliated with the state.[32] In Europe, an extended network of operatives with obscure links to Russian intelligence agencies reportedly engages in various dark arts—from misinformation to assassinations.[33] Mark Galeotti dubbed the Kremlin's outsourcing of dirty work to groups outside the Russian state a strategy of "adhocracy."[34]

This strategy of extreme delegation exemplifies the limits on Putin's power. The best available evidence indicates that Russian-backed rebels in eastern Ukraine shot down a Malaysian commercial airliner by mistake in July 2014, killing almost three hundred passengers and crew. In addition, the United States quickly identified the hackers of the Democratic National Committee during the US election in 2016 because of their sloppiness.[35] Moreover, that there has been so much written about the Kremlin's "secret" intelligence arm creating havoc in Europe reveals the limits of the organization. It is hard to monitor subordinates directly under your command in the state bureaucracy and even more difficult when ties must remain obscure.

The Kremlin struggles with more mundane tasks as well. On returning to office in 2012, President Putin issued the "May Decrees," a detailed set of targets to increase economic growth, raise bureaucratic efficiency, and support social programs. That the decrees were badly designed to begin with—among other things, they assumed a growth rate of 7 percent a year—is one indication of the weakness of the bureaucracy. Just as striking was the lack of implementation. On the five-year anniversary of the May Decrees, a Putin official noted that the bureaucracy had implemented just 35 of the 179 orders from the May Decrees monitored by his organization. Sergei Mironov, a longtime Putin ally, remarked that the goals of the May Decrees fell far short across the board in living standards, health care, and education.[36] Autocracies have long struggled to elicit honest information from subordinates and monitor implementation of policy by bureaucrats, and Russia is no exception. Putin's much-vaunted "vertical of power" is creaky at best.[37]

One of the most in-depth academic studies of elite politics in Russia drives home the constraints of even a powerful ruler like Putin. Alena Ledeneva, a sociologist from University College London, conducted extensive interviews with a handful of top Kremlin insiders and forty-two experts on elite politics in Russia.[38] She also gathered a host of material on Kremlin decision making between 2005 and 2012. Ledeneva found that rather than ruling by fiat, Putin governs based on a host of informal rules and personal relationships that balance the interests of different elite networks. The members of these networks keep Putin in power as he provides them with benefits in exchange for political loyalty. This *sistema*, in her term, is based on Putin's ability to make deals with different oligarchic groups within the state, but is not rooted in anything specific to Putin per se. She notes, "It is essential . . . not to overstate the personalization of *sistema* in the sense that Putin's *sistema*, which he had shaped by mobilizing his personal networks, is not really controlled by him. Like everyone else, leaders are 'locked' into their networks while relying on them in performing their public functions and satisfying their private needs."[39] To grasp elite politics in Russia, it is more important to understand the rules of the game than the personal characteristics of the ruler.

Putinology makes for an easy tale to tell. A former KGB man behind dark sunglasses seizes power and changes Russia for better or worse. The Kremlin too likes this narrative and encourages this great man version of Russian politics. The tendency to overstate the contributions of leaders is common outside politics, particularly when measuring performance is difficult. Witness the acclaim laid on CEOs in corporate America even with little evidence that their firms' successes are due to the leaders' smarts or hard work.[40] As with the leader of any organization, Putin's specific impact on events and policy needs to be demonstrated rather than asserted, and this is not so easy to do.

This is not to argue that Putin's background and experience are of no consequence, or that any randomly selected Russian who found themselves in the Kremlin would behave like Putin. The debate on whether great individuals make history or history makes great individuals is long and inconclusive. But it is safe to say that our national debate on Russia has overplayed the individual at the expense of other factors.[41] The kinds of easy references to Putin's background or mentality used to support many arguments about contemporary Russia often crumble on closer scrutiny.

Exceptional Russia

Putinologists posit that Russia is shaped by Putin, but others root Russia's current condition in its unique culture and history. Russia is said to be reverting to its traditional role of a great power on the European continent with centralized absolutist rule, a respect for Orthodoxy, and support for a ruler with a strong hand. Putin's Russia is thought to be just the latest cycle in Russia's long historical pattern of expansion abroad and reaction at home, followed by retrenchment abroad and reform at home.[42]

There is much to this view. The past and present are entwined in intricate ways in every country, and in subsequent chapters we will see examples where historical legacies of Soviet central planning, political violence, and everyday repression continue to shape Russia's economy, politics, and society. Moreover, academic research on Russian and Soviet history has flourished in recent years as scholars have provided richness and nuance to topics ranging from serfdom to the Stalinist terror to daily life under Leonid Brezhnev.[43] A deep grounding in history is essential to understanding modern Russia.

But in popular discussions of Russia, observers often take shortcuts that lead us astray. For example, they frequently note that a pattern from Russian or Soviet history is reappearing in Putin's Russia. This may work fine as description, but as an explanation we should know why this particular pattern is emerging and not another one from the past, and why it is emerging now and not another time. To say that Putin is returning centralized political rule to Russia is helpful, but to attribute this centralization to a historical legacy we also need to identify mechanisms linking the past and present, make explicit comparisons between the two, and reject alternative explanations for this centralization. As Mark Beissinger and Stephen Kotkin observe, "Demonstrating the salience of historical legacies proves considerably harder than it looks."[44]

Furthermore, because Russian culture and history is also not all of one piece, observers can rummage around in the great books of Russia in all their richness and diversity to find evidence for and against just about any argument one would like to make. A former head of NATO, for instance, maintains that the best way to understand Russian strategic behavior in international politics is by reading Russian literature: "Want to understand what's really going on in Russia? Read Gogol, Dostoyevsky, Turgenev, Pushkin, Lermontov, Tolstoy, Solzhenitsyn and Bulgakov. That's where you'll find how Russians' really think."[45] As a Russian language and literature major in college, I agree that these are great writers, and I love reading Russian history, but as a social scientist I'm more skeptical. Political scientist Charles King points out that "there is no particular reason to think that Dostoyevsky, for example, reveals something more essential about being Russian—or at least being Russian today—than, say, Russian language hip-hop."[46] If we want to understand how Russians think today, an easier approach is to just ask them in surveys, as I often do.

One common, if frequently implicit, narrative in this vein highlights distinct Russian attitudes and values.[47] Russia is the way it is because that is the way Russians are. In the worst cases, we hear broad generalizations about the "Russian mentality" or "the Russians" without any recognition that Russians' views on most issues of the day are as diverse as the citizens of any country.[48] One can recognize James Clapper's achievements as a former director of national intelligence, but his claim that it is "in Russia's genes to be opposed, diametrically opposed, to the United States and western democracies" is unhelpful at best.[49] Clichés and sweeping statements about contemporary Russia drawn from cultural analogies abound. A headline in the *New York Times* declares, "For Russians, Corruption Is Just a Way of Life," even though Russians dislike paying petty bribes like everyone else.[50] A reporter in the *Wall Street Journal* opines how the "Russian soul" explains the country's current condition.[51] A businessperson from Germany notes in a *New York Times* op-ed, "I've lived in Russia. Sharing is not the Russian way."[52]

In its most explicit form, observers point to a "Homo Sovieticus," a Soviet or post-Soviet person whose attitudes and values are distinct from their peers in other countries.[53] Having lived in repressive conditions under czars and Communists, Homo Sovieticus "is crafty and skilled at doublethink," and "not only tolerates deception, but is willing to be deceived," and is "incapable of understanding complex moral/ethical views and relationships." This Soviet person has "few demands . . . expects nothing good from anyone else," and having lived through the great and small traumas of life under Communism, "just wants one thing—to survive."[54] Homo Sovieticus is passive, conformist, and longs for a strong ruler who will bring order. In this view, Russia's politics are largely a reflection of Russians' values.

Some observers have resurrected Homo Sovieticus as a partial explanation for public acquiescence to Russia's autocratic and nationalist turn in recent years. In 2019, Russian pollster Lev Gudkov and *Moscow*

Times journalist Eva Hartog wrote that "Soviet man has somewhat changed. He's been fed, he's changed his clothes, he's bought a car and owns a home. But he still feels insecure and vulnerable and he's just as aggressive toward his neighbor."[55] One of the best-selling and most acclaimed accounts of Russian politics in recent years invokes this argument. In *The Future Is History*, Masha Gessen argues that due to the horrors of the Soviet system, Russians today have lost "the ability to make sense of one's life in the world" and no longer have the "intellectual tools of sensemaking."[56] Having been "weaned on generations of doublethink and collective hostage taking," the worst features of Homo Sovieticus have returned: passivity, conformity, and an unwillingness to take responsibility.[57]

This approach is common in popular discussions about Russia, but critics note that this reasoning implicitly blames ordinary Russians for their plight, robs them of their agency, and leaves little room for envisioning alternative futures for Russia.[58]

Did the Soviets create a Homo Sovieticus? Are Russians more passive, cunning, and conformist than others? To answer these questions, we need survey data that compare Homo Sovieticus to citizens outside the Soviet Union and Russia. Good survey data from the Soviet period are hard to come by, but studies from the early post-Soviet period cast doubt. Economists Robert Shiller, Maxim Boycko, and Vladimir Korobov conducted surveys in Russia, Ukraine, the former East Germany, Japan, and the United States in the early 1990s. They asked respondents about risk-taking, private initiative, and attitudes toward markets, and found that "while some differences in attitudes do seem to occur across countries, it is rather misleading to refer to homo sovieticus as a distinct breed of person."[59] Similarly, political scientists Ada Finifter and Ellen Mickiewicz surveyed more than two thousand Soviet citizens in 1989 and found a familiar pattern: those groups expecting to benefit from political change—the young, the educated, Russians in Russia, urban residents, and males—were more likely to support those changes.[60] This pattern is long established in countries with and without a Soviet past.

Based on surveys in the 1990s, political scientist James Gibson found that Russians exhibited less tolerance toward dissenting views than did others, which is consistent with the Homo Sovieticus view. But he also discovered that Russians were no less trusting of others, socially isolated, or unsupportive of democracy. Indeed, he studied rates of trust between people in more than 40 countries in the 1990s and found that Russia landed solidly in the middle of the pack.[61]

Most recently, an international team of researchers dropped seventeen thousand wallets in 355 cities in 40 countries to test patterns of civic honesty.[62] Russians ranked fifteenth in the rate at which they returned "lost" wallets without cash to their owners—a figure slightly higher than Americans and the British, and on par with Canadians. Russians returned wallets with small but internationally equivalent amounts of cash at about the same rates as Americans, British, and Canadians. Far from being morally stunted after decades of Communism, Russians were about as honest as the average North American.

Recent data also report levels of trust that do not reflect a deep societal trauma. Researchers Anton Sobolev and Alexei Zakharov studied data from more than 50 countries in the most recent round of the World Values Survey, and found that while Russians are much less likely to join civic groups than one would expect for the country's level of development, they are no less trusting of other citizens than the average respondent in other countries.[63] Indeed, they are more trusting of their fellow citizens than the average Pole, South Korean, or Spaniard.

A closer look also belies Russians' supposed political passivity—a key feature of Homo Sovieticus. When given the chance to take part in competitive politics in the 1990s, Russians voted at higher rates than did their US counterparts. Turnout in presidential elections in 1996 and 2000 was almost 70 percent in Russia and just 50 percent in the United States. And Russians largely rejected the political party most closely associated with Homo Sovieticus—the Communist Party of the Russian Federation, which has never received more than 25 percent of the vote in seven parliamentary elections since 1993. Moreover, as in other countries, Russians voted in ways that largely aligned with their interests: pensioners tended to vote for leftist parties, and private businesspeople tended to vote for rightist parties. Interests, rather than deep-seated cultural patterns induced by living through Communism, seemed to guide Russian voting patterns.[64]

Even in the current period when the costs of engaging in politics has increased dramatically, protests against government policies are a frequent part of the political landscape. Russia's Center for Economic and Political Reform notes that about twenty-five hundred protests took place in 2018. About half of the protests had less than a hundred people, and most focused on local issues, but a few were large and directly targeted toward the Kremlin.[65] One can always point to an anomalous survey result (often due to a poorly worded question) that underscores political passivity or support for order over democracy (as if the two were opposites), but on balance there is just not much evidence that the behavior of ordinary Russians in politics has been all that damaged by the Soviet past, as awful as that past was.

To be sure, living under Communism left an imprint on some popular attitudes. In perhaps the best study on the topic, political scientists Grigore Pop-Eleches and Joshua Tucker took advantage of massive surveys across more than fifty countries between 1990 and 2009, and found that the longer a respondent lived under Communism, the less supportive they were of democracy and free markets relative to citizens in countries that did not experience Communism.[66] These are not the same traits as those defining Homo Sovieticus, but Pop-Eleches and Tucker show something distinctive about the impact of Communism on how people see the world. At the same time, they find that the effect of Communism on popular views was similar for Poles, Uzbeks, Romanians, and Russians, so it seems that Russians are not uniquely shaped by the Communist legacy.[67]

It is also best to keep the impact of these cultural traits on politics in perspective. Social scientists have long been skeptical about sweeping arguments that "national character" or a single personality type determines a country's politics. The notion that a personality type reflects a society is hard to justify because differences in attitudes among citizens within a country are typically more diverse than those between citizens in different countries. Every country has multiple political cultures that can change over time and situation. Privileging one without accounting for others is problematic. I can attest that my Russian coauthors are no less (ir)responsible than my American ones.[68]

Moreover, history has not been kind to arguments linking cultural values to a country's type of government. For many years, observers contended that Catholic, Asian, and non-Arab Muslim-majority countries had value systems that condemned them to authoritarian rule, but the experiences of France, Germany, Spain, Japan, India, and Indonesia, among others, suggest the limits of a link between democracy and cultural values.[69] The current crisis of democracy in countries like the United States and Britain thought to have value systems supportive of democracy also gives one pause about this assertion.

To the extent that Russians' attitudes and values are distinct, they are better explained by their immediate situation than by anything inherent or specific to Russian or Soviet culture. The types of public conformism and private opposition to power, passivity in the face of injustice, and moral adaptability at the core of Homo Sovieticus are common tools for marginalized groups facing arbitrary rule.[70] In Italy, the ability of the weak to use cunning and cleverness to evade its dense bureaucracy is known as *furbizia*.[71] The anthropologist James C. Scott finds similar forms of evasive tactics before authority among rice farmers in Malaysia, lower castes in India, Polish workers under martial law, and slaves in the US South.[72] Anyone who has ever worked for a horrible boss might recognize these "weapons of the weak." Gudkov and Hartog, the most sophisticated Russian proponents of Homo Sovieticus, note, "Russians today simply reflect and respond to their circumstances. In a different situation, they'd behave differently."[73]

Popular opinion in Russia in recent years has become more nationalist, anti-Western, and supportive of traditional sources of authority like the military, security services, and Orthodox Church, but this has more to do with current events and government efforts to shape popular opinion than with deep-rooted attitudes and values specific to Russians.

Common Flaw: Overlooking and
Underplaying Society

The Putinology and exceptional Russia arguments found in much popular discourse stem from different premises, but each downplays the agency of Russian society. The former leaves society out of the picture and focuses on Putin, his worldview, and the circle of elites around him, while the latter posits a Russian society that is trapped by its past with little capacity to change course.

No country reinvents itself overnight, but Russian society has certainly changed since the fall of the Communist Party. Half of Russians today were eight years old or younger in 1991, meaning that direct experience with the USSR or Cold War is limited. Most Russians have little personal familiarity with the hallmarks of Soviet rule: the planned economy, blanket restrictions on foreign travel, Communist Party cells in the workplace or schools, and extremely limited access to foreign media. Gone too is a state-sponsored ideology in every sphere of life. Students, workers, and managers no longer suffer through interminable lectures on the holy trinity of Marx, Engels, and Lenin.[74] My students at the HSE in Moscow think little of having an American lecture them on politics and economics—an idea that would have seemed odd to their parents and inconceivable to their grandparents when they were in school.

Like all post-communist countries, Russia experienced a historic decline in economic growth and living standards in the 1990s. But thanks to a spectacular rise in oil prices and sharp devaluation of the ruble in 1998, the economy boomed shortly after Putin took power and nearly doubled in his first two terms in office. This oil-fueled growth led Andrew Kuchins to dub President Putin "Vladimir the Lucky" in the tradition of "Peter the Great" and "Ivan the Terrible."[75] Russian GDP per capita grew to around $27,500 at purchasing power parity by 2018.[76] This placed Russia a bit below Hungary at $28,300, a bit above Argentina at $20,800, but well above China at $16,800, adjusting for local prices.[77]

And these changes are more than just oligarchs buying bits of Manhattan, Miami, and Mayfair. During the great boom, poverty fell from around 25 percent of the population to around 14 percent even as it has increased in the last six years as the economy has slowed to a crawl. Shopping malls have sprung up around Russia to serve its new middle class, and Russians have taken advantage of their newfound wealth to travel. In 2017, Russians made about forty million foreign trips with just under half of these trips to the former Soviet Union and three hundred thousand to the United States.[78] To put these changes in perspective, I think of a French language teacher I met in Uzbekistan in 1988. She was a Francophile to her core, which was all the more remarkable in that she had never been to France. Even more depressing, she had little hope of ever seeing the City of Lights. In her living room, she had a three-dimensional map of Paris that she knew as well as the streets of her native Taskhent. Her disappointment was apparent when I revealed that I had never been to France.

The coronavirus has hit Russia hard, but male Russians are also not dying off at a young age as they did in the 1990s. Thanks to frequent binging on cheap vodka and wide tobacco use, male mortality in Russia plummeted from sixty-four in 1990 to just fifty-nine in 2000—a stunning decline for a country at war, let alone one at peace. Two studies trace this decline to changes in the real price of vodka over two decades.[79] As the economy rebounded and the real price of vodka rose, however, so did male life expectancy, growing to sixty-six in 2019.[80] Male life expectancy in the city of Moscow, at seventy-three, is now about on par with that found in middle-income countries, even as it lags elsewhere in Russia. Female life expectancy across Russia experienced a much smaller decline and now stands at seventy-seven. The eleven-year gap between male and female life expectancy in Russia is larger than in any other country in the world.

Cell phone and internet use has surged in the last twenty years. Almost all Russian adults have cell phones, and 70 percent have smartphones.[81] About two-thirds of Russians report getting their news from internet and social media sources.[82] This is a far cry from my first visit to Moscow in 1985, when making a three-minute phone call to the United States required ordering it seventy-two hours in advance, traveling to a special telephone/telegraph office in another part of Moscow, and paying ten dollars a minute for the pleasure.

No society changes completely in a generation, and one can certainly find legacies of Soviet rule in ways big and small. Russia's population is much better educated than most middle-income countries in part due to the legacy of Soviet institutions and practices. Some parts of the Russian state, like the police and FSB, have undergone only superficial reform and retain many Soviet-era practices.

Moreover, many Russians still live in cities developed by Soviet planners with little regard for economic efficiency or personal comfort. Clifford Gaddy studied the hundred coldest North American and Russian cities, and found that Russia has thirty cities with more than a half-million people and a mean January temperature of minus 8 degrees Celsius, while the United States has only one. These Russian cities are far more remote and colder than one would expect to find in a country that did not experience Soviet central planning.[83]

And pockets of Russia are being left behind. Data from the Russian state statistical agency indicate that majorities living in small villages lack access to centralized sewer systems, as do 10 percent of Russians living in cities.[84] About every fourth Russian still lacks some of the basic accoutrements of modern life.[85] In fall 2018, almost half of Russians said that they had enough money for food and clothing, but would struggle to buy a durable consumer good like a television or refrigerator.[86]

Historical legacies persist to be sure, but the bigger picture points to social change rather than continuity. Or as one of my Russian colleagues noted recently, "When I tell my twenty-year-old son about what we went through in Soviet times, he just looks at me like I'm crazy." Recognizing these changes in society is important not only for gaining an accurate picture of Russia today; these shifts also have important implications for how Russia is governed. Authoritarian rulers do not need majority support from society to stay in power, but depicting society as passive and lacking in agency overlooks the crucial role that social groups play in both buttressing and threatening authoritarian rule.

––––––

Rather than treating Russia's most recent autocratic turn as rooted in Putin's KGB past or a return to Russia's thousand years of dictatorship, we can trace it to a more familiar and recent pattern of modern autocratic rule. As long-standing democracies become increasingly dysfunctional and less attractive as a model, an outsider comes to power in a highly unequal middle-income country. Facing a disorganized opposition, the ruler rides an economic boom to popularity, which he then uses to dismantle courts and legislatures, intimidate the free press, and discredit political opponents as foreign agents. With some nuances for local context, this story would be familiar to observers of Turkey, Venezuela, and Hungary, to name just a few. Many popular narratives lead us astray by failing to consider the ways that features common to autocracies shape Russia's politics—a topic I turn to next.

3

The Autocrat's Dilemmas

All absolute governments must very much depend on the administration;
and this is one of the great inconveniences of that form of government.

—DAVID HUME, *THAT POLITICS MAY BE REDUCED
TO A SCIENCE*, 1741–42

IF A FOCUS PRIMARILY on Putin's worldview or Russia's unique culture can often lead us astray, how should we understand Russia? I suggest we explore the type of government Russia embodies, and how this shapes its politics. More specifically, I treat Russia as a personalist autocracy—a common type of nondemocratic government led by an individual rather than a party or organization. Personalist autocracies share a host of common features that help us better understand much of Russia's politics. With its size, nuclear weapons, and legacy as a superpower, Russia is an unusual autocracy in foreign affairs, but at home, Putin faces the same trade-offs that many autocratic leaders confront.

By drawing on a range of cross-national studies that identify the distinctive patterns of personalist autocracies, this chapter puts Putin's rule in comparative context and introduces three themes that will reappear in the chapters that follow. It also shows why Putin is a weak strongman. Unrivaled in domestic politics, he is also constrained by the inherent limits of autocratic rule.

Russia as a Personalist Autocracy

How can we identify autocracies? No government calls itself an autocracy. Even Kim Jong-un's North Korea is formally known as the Democratic People's Republic of Korea. Many autocracies adopt the trappings of democracy, such as a limited free press, semifree elections, multiple political parties, and occasional protests against the government, but are widely seen as autocratic. And politics in countries considered democratic frequently veer considerably from the idealistic versions propagated by their leaders and high school civics textbooks.[1]

For scholars, the lack of free and fair elections to select the national leadership is a defining feature of autocracies. Countries that hold elections on a relatively uneven playing field or do not allow some share of the adult population to vote, or do not permit multiple candidates to run for office without obstruction, are considered autocracies. This inevitably requires some judgment calls, but the large data sets that academics use to study autocracies show a high degree of agreement.[2]

While all autocracies lack free and fair elections, they are remarkably diverse on other dimensions. Fujimori's Peru saw considerable political competition, while Brezhnev's Soviet Union did not. Saddam Hussein's Iraq relied on repression and violence, but Janos Kadar's Hungary had a lighter touch. Ayatollah Khomeini's Iran regulated the daily life of its citizens, while Francisco Franco's Spain left the private sphere alone.

To gain some clarity, scholars usually divide autocracies into one of three broad types.[3] Some autocracies are led by a single political party that controls major personnel and policy decisions. While other parties may be permitted, they play supporting roles at best. Examples include the Communist Party in China, the Institutional Revolutionary Party that ruled Mexico from 1929 until 2000, and the People's Action Party that has dominated politics in Singapore since the mid-1960s. Single-party regimes were by far the most common type of autocracy during the Cold War and now represent about 40 percent of all autocracies.

A second type is led by the military. Often taking power via coup against civilian rulers, military-led autocracies typically vest power in a small number of senior officers that rule as an informal group. Brazil in the 1960s, Turkey in the 1980s, and contemporary Thailand are good illustrations. While military dictatorships were common during the Cold War, only a handful remain today.

Finally, personalist autocracies, like Russia, concentrate power in the hands of a single individual. While personalist autocracies frequently have parties, legislatures, and influential militaries, key decisions over personnel and policy are taken by one person. Other indicators of a personalist autocracy include a reliance on an informal inner circle of decision makers that grows narrower over time, the appointment of loyalists rather than specialists to critical positions in the government, the creation of new security organizations responsible to the leader, appeals to popular support as opposed to procedures to legitimate the ruler's authority, and the appointment of family members to crucial posts.[4] While Putin has kept his family members from the levers of power, these other indicators ring true for contemporary Russia.

Contemporary examples of personalist autocracies include the governments of Erdoğan in Turkey, Nicolas Maduro in Venezuela, Rodrigo Duterte in the Philippines, and Orban in Hungary. The former Soviet space has proven to be especially fertile ground for this type of government. At the moment, personalist autocrats rule Belarus, Azerbaijan, and the five Central Asian republics as well as Russia. On a global scale, the share of personalist autocracies recently surpassed one-party regimes as the most common type of autocracy.

Most personalist autocracies emerge via coups, rigged elections, or other nondemocratic means, but others are created when a democratically elected leader takes office, and then undermines courts, parties, legislatures, and the free press. Venezuela provides a good example. Elected democratically in 1998, Hugo Chávez slowly eroded the powers of the legislature, packed an enlarged constitutional court with supporters, and cracked down on the media and political opposition.[5] By 2005, he had turned the longest-standing democracy in South America into a personalist autocracy. Russia too fits the model as Putin did not come to power via a coup but instead was elected in a flawed though relatively free and fair election in 2000, only to expand his power in subsequent years bit by bit.[6]

Personalist autocrats do not rule entirely on their own. Even rulers like Putin who control policy and make top personnel decisions need support from other elites, who provide advice, head the agencies that implement policy, run the factories that generate revenue for the state, and most important, oversee those who wield the weapons of repression. Managing these elites and their subordinates is a major challenge for personalist autocrats.

In addition, personalist autocrats confront the challenge of managing the mass public. Some personalist autocrats muster little popular support and must rely heavily on coercion to stay in office. But others garner considerable and genuine approval. Often this popularity is rooted in economic booms fueled by natural resources, generous foreign aid, or foreign policy success, but whatever its source, it comes in handy. Personalist autocrats such as Chávez in Venezuela, Evo Morales in Bolivia, and Putin in Russia used their personal popularity to subvert formal institutions, and justified their expanded power not so much by adhering to democratic procedures but rather by invoking the popular will. They claimed, not without some justification, that their enhanced powers were just an expression of public sentiment.

While personalist autocracies differ on many dimensions, they all concentrate power in an individual as opposed to an organization. Yet this hardly makes personalist autocrats omnipotent. Digging deeper, we can identify three underlying dilemmas inherent to autocratic regimes in general and personalist autocracies in particular that shape politics in fundamental ways. Each of these trade-offs highlights the essential constraints that autocratic rule poses for rulers like Putin.

Weak Institutions

First, personalist autocracies tend to have weak political institutions such as legislatures, courts, and independent bureaucracies. This makes it easier for autocrats to take power in their own hands and become a personalist ruler, but also makes it harder for them to govern once in office.[7]

When autocrats come to power facing organized groups like the military or a strong party that can credibly threaten to remove them from office, they are compelled to share greater power and wealth with these organizations.[8] Elites in military and one-party regimes can keep rulers on a short leash. In Mexico, the Institutional Revolutionary Party limited presidents to a single six-year term—a policy that lasted decades. In the USSR, the Politburo of the Communist Party removed Khrushchev from power and compelled his successor, Leonid Brezhnev, to rule by consensus.

Where elites cannot act collectively via a party or state bureaucracy, however, autocrats can usurp far greater power for themselves by bargaining with each member of the elites separately. Individual elites can rarely remove the autocrat by themselves, and because elites compete with each other for influence, the autocrat's threats to dismiss them should they become too greedy or ambitious are especially persuasive. Another potential member of the elites is always waiting to take their place. Without strong organizations to check them, autocrats are well positioned to take power in their own hands and become personalist rulers.

This distinction is critical to understanding the emergence of personalist autocracy in Russia. On taking office in 2000, Putin faced powerful oligarchs, but the oligarchs lacked an organization they could use to limit the power of the president. Putin also had to grapple with influential regional governors, but their nascent political party, Fatherland–All Russia, could not represent the diverse interests of these regional elites and soon fell apart, spurring the concentration of power in the Kremlin. In addition, the oil boom that doubled the size of the Russian economy from 1998 to 2008 gave Putin great spoils to distribute to individual oligarchs and governors, who were then in little mood to form organized groups to check his power. Finally, because Putin had roots in the security services, these organizations could have confidence that he would protect their interests, and he has done just that over the last twenty years even when they have made painful blunders. Indeed, turnover at the top of Russia's various security services has been far lower than in other parts of the government. Kremlin insiders who are dismissed from a top post almost always find a sinecure elsewhere in the bureaucracy. Putin's skillful management of conflicts among the elites has been key to his longevity.[9]

Weak institutions can help an autocrat seize power, but they also heighten political uncertainty and raise the costs of losing power because they cannot resolve the deep clashes over policy and principle that inevitably arise in politics. Rulers in democracies can rely on high courts or elections to address political conflicts, but Putin cannot turn to the Constitutional Court because judicial decisions may be ignored by powerful people with powerful guns, and he also cannot turn to voters in a fully free and fair election or risk losing his status as an autocrat. Without a political calendar punctuated by free and fair elections, he can be removed from power at any time. Autocrats often fall in the same way that people go bankrupt according to Ernest Hemingway: gradually, then suddenly.[10]

This deep level of uncertainty is amplified by the absence of strong institutions to prevent the ruler from changing policies on a whim. Investors, citizens, and bureaucrats alike have good reason to expect policy to change, and all make decisions in the shadow of this uncertainty.

Even governments like Russia's that appear stable from a distance or boast rulers who have been in power for years cannot escape this fundamental problem. Gleb Pavlovsky, a former Putin adviser, captures this sentiment. Interviewed in January 2012 shortly after large protests rocked Moscow, he observed that "in the Kremlin establishment, there has been an absolute conviction that as soon as the Kremlin is shifted, or if there is some mass popular pressure, the appearance of a popular leader, then everybody will be annihilated. . . . [There is] a feeling of vulnerability. As soon as someone is given the chance—not necessarily, the people, maybe the governors, maybe some other faction—they will physically destroy the establishment, or we'll have to fight and destroy them instead."[11]

The costs of losing office are acute in personalist autocracies like Russia.[12] After losing power, leaders in military regimes can retreat to the barracks and heads of one-party dictatorships can retire to a post in the party, but personalist autocrats have no soft landing pad. They enjoy their wealth and influence only if they hold office. Once they give up power, they are vulnerable to their successor, who is not likely to abide a formerly powerful potential rival. Because of this threat, personalist rulers like Putin have strong incentives to resort to extreme measures to prevent a transfer of power.

And the data bear out this fear. Three political scientists collected data about the rulers of all nondemocracies from 1946 until 2008. They found that personalist leaders were especially likely to fall via "irregular means" such as coups, protests, and revolts, and were unlikely to transfer power via a constitution. Seventy percent of rulers in personalist nondemocracies lost office through so-called irregular means versus 47 percent for military dictatorships and just 19 percent for one-party regimes.[13]

In addition, rulers in personalist autocracies who lose power suffered far worse fates than did their counterparts in other types of nondemocracies. Eighty percent of personalist rulers who lost power ended up in jail or exile, or dead, while similar figures for rulers in military and one-party autocracies were 41 and 25 percent, respectively. These perils are not lost on rulers, who must constantly be on the lookout for threats both big and small. As political scientist Milan Svolik notes: "Autocrats who manage to die in their bed have made a notable achievement."[14] Because political institutions to resolve disputes are so weak, politics in Russia are rife with mistrust, threats, and violence. The Putin team will cling to power for the same reason that all personalist autocrats do: the fear of what comes next.

The great vulnerability and uncertainty of nondemocratic rule extends to businesspeople who fear being expropriated by their rivals in collusion with the security services, state officials who could be dismissed by the Kremlin at any time, and even top fashion models, who, I'm told by a friend who runs in these circles, usually juggle two or three wealthy paramours to hedge their bets against political risk.

Facing this uncertainty, it is hardly a surprise that capital flight from Russia is great. Having few guarantees that their rights will be respected should the leader change their mind or fall from power, businesspeople are reluctant to take risks by making the kinds of long-term investments that drive economic growth. Indeed, cross-national research by political scientist Joseph Wright suggests that since the end of World War II, personalist autocracies have experienced slower rates of economic growth and more volatile policies than other forms of autocracies.[15] Russia's slow economic growth since the end of the oil boom is rooted in part in its weak institutions.

The Dual Threats

Second, rulers also often face a trade-off between satisfying those in their inner circle and pleasing the public. Whereas rulers in democracies fear losing office via elections, rulers in nondemocracies face threats from two sources: the political elites via coups, and the mass public via protest.[16] Unfortunately for the autocrat, these dual threats can rarely be addressed in isolation. Placating popular protest with larger social programs may require cutting defense spending and thereby make a palace coup more likely, while cutting social spending to boost the security services may increase the chances for a revolt from below. To stay in power, rulers must balance these two competing threats.

Consider relations between the ruler and their elites. Research from all nondemocracies from 1945 until 2012 shows that rulers are far more likely to be replaced by a member of the elites who previously supported them than by a popular revolt.[17] Coups, forced retirements, and arrests have felled dictators great and small. Because violence and threats of violence are frequently trump cards in these power struggles, the security services are key players in any autocratic regime.

Autocrats and the elites who support them work in a setting of mutual distrust and dependence. Autocrats seek to maximize power and spoils for themselves, while elites try to do the same. Rulers depend on elites to stay in office, and therefore cede to them some power and wealth, but elites are also a source of danger for autocrats when they can threaten to remove them.[18] At the same time, elites benefit from their proximity to the ruler, but fear giving away too much power and wealth because they are vulnerable to dismissal by the ruler.

To date, Putin has largely avoided direct elite challenges to his rule. He has muted elite conflict and used Russia's resource-fueled economic boom to distribute benefits to regime insiders, a loosely knit group of top state officials and businesspeople, including some with long-standing personal ties to him. Putin has allowed elite cronies and lower-level state officials to become quite wealthy by tolerating high levels of corruption. This is a common strategy for keeping regime insiders on the ruler's side in personalist autocracies. Cross-national studies show that since World War II, personalist autocracies have exhibited higher rates of corruption than other forms of autocracy.[19]

In addition to threats of elite coups, rulers in nondemocracies confront a threat from below in the form of mass protests and revolts. Most relevant for Russia is the example of the "color" revolutions in other former Soviet states that saw nondemocratic rulers brought low in nearby Georgia in 2003, Ukraine in 2004, and Kyrgyzstan in 2005. Few topics more reliably enrage the Kremlin than the possibility of a popular uprising, and many argue that the large protests against corruption and electoral fraud in 2011–12 sparked the Kremlin's more repressive policies in the years that followed. Russia's elites are not well organized and have largely been co-opted by the Putin team, but because the mass public is relatively wealthy, urban, and well educated, threats from below have been front of mind for the Kremlin. It not just that Putin has had to address large-scale protests in 2005, 2011–12, and 2017–18 but also that the regime has been preoccupied with preventing protests throughout his time in office.

Fortunately for the autocrat, their elite and mass opponents too face many challenges in seeking to replace the leader. They need to identify and rally supporters while also agreeing on a potential successor. This is a challenge because opposition groups often have conflicting interests that autocrats are keen to exploit. Furthermore, opposition groups may all agree that they would prefer someone else in power, but they would also prefer that other individuals bear the costs of protesting and risking their lives in order to remove the leader from power. Individuals organizing against an autocrat deal with the constant threat of informers in their midst and must constantly be on guard against infiltration. The opposition needs to accomplish these tasks in secrecy and under threat of punishment as well.

To prevent popular dissent from coalescing into an organized movement, autocrats have a range of tools. The "tragic brilliance" of autocracy is that it uses the individual self-interest of its opponents against them.[20] Autocrats can dangle enticements of higher pay, greater access to policy makers, and new jobs to co-opt potentially influential public figures, and thereby use individual self-interest to undermine organized opposition.[21] They can also wield the stick to dissuade mass protests if need be. Once a nondemocratic ruler concentrates political power in their own hands, they are difficult to unseat, as Russian opposition leaders have come to learn.

Indeed, cross-national research since World War II indicates that personalist autocrats stay in power longer than rulers in military-led regimes, if not longer than rulers in single-party autocracies. We often find the paradoxical situation of a personalist ruler who manages a long stay in office, but only by pursuing policies that inhibit economic growth and weaken the bureaucracy—two key tools of state power over the long run.

Opposition leaders face numerous obstacles to taking power in personalist autocracies, but any ruler who ignores these threats is not long for office. That Putin has avoided a direct challenge by the elites and deftly channeled pressure from below does not make these threats any less important. Many observers emphasize the seeming security of strongman leaders, but to get under the hood of nondemocratic regimes like Russia, it is crucial to explore the origins and severity of mass and elite threats, and understand how the autocrat tries to address them.

To do so, we must trace how events and decisions shape the relative power of the ruler, regime elites, and the mass public. Sometimes rulers get lucky and experience fast economic growth via oil booms or generous foreign aid, and thus can deliver benefits to their elite cronies and raise living standards for the mass public. But typically they have to make hard choices about rewarding their elite cronies or the mass public. And these choices become more important during economic downturns when the ruler has fewer spoils to distribute to cronies and confronts an increasingly restive public. For example, after a decade of dismal economic performance, economic growth turned sharply negative in summer 2020 due to low oil prices and the shock of the coronavirus. President

Putin's approval rating fell to its lowest level since taking office in 2000, and infighting among the elites appeared to be on the rise as government largesse declined.[22]

Blunt Tools: To Repress or Not to Repress

Third, autocrats face a trade-off about using repressive or nonrepressive means to manage the political opposition. All autocracies use coercion, and Russia is no exception, but some types of autocracies rely on it more than others. One recent study of all autocracies from 1950 to 2010 found that personalist autocracies like Russia are more likely to repress their publics than better-institutionalized autocracies led by a strong party or military.[23] This insight fits the Russian case. Putin's rule has become more personalist since he returned to the presidency in 2012, and we have seen much stricter limits on political protests and harsher treatment of political opponents in subsequent years.

But using coercion is not as easy as it seems. Any security agency that is powerful enough to put down a popular revolt is also powerful enough to overthrow a leader.[24] Autocrats must balance the benefits of creating a strong security agency that prevents mass revolts or a weak one that prevents coups. There is no free lunch that allows them to address both challenges simultaneously.[25]

Coercion is also costly for the ruler, who must pay the agents of coercion to do their jobs and pay for the weapons needed to put down a popular revolt. Each dollar spent on increasing the means of coercion is a dollar not spent on the ruler, their family, or their cronies. It is not a dollar spent too on providing the public goods that promote broad-based economic growth for the mass public.

Moreover, repression sometimes backfires by emboldening protesters who smell weakness rather than strength when a ruler resorts to the truncheon. Rulers that repress political opponents and their followers also risk raising the profile of opposition leaders who are then well placed to elicit sympathy from the broader public. Recognizing this possibility, opposition figures sometimes provoke overreactions by the authorities to gain support from those outside their movement, as US civil rights marchers well understood.[26]

Finally, the security services face the possibility of retribution by the new regime should their efforts to support the incumbent in a crisis fail. In power struggles among elites, the security services want to avoid the worst outcome of having to put down a popular revolt that ultimately succeeds in removing their boss. The fear of a change in power may compel security services to hedge their bets by remaining neutral in an elite struggle. The last days of East Germany provide an extreme but telling case of the limits of coercion. Confronting mass demonstrations in October 1989, Erich Honecker, the longtime leader of the Politburo, ordered the head of the Stasi, the much-feared secret police, to repress protesters who had gathered in the capital, but was told, "Erich, we can't beat up hundreds of thousands of people." When Honecker persisted, the head of the Stasi threatened to leak a file detailing Honecker's sex life, lavish lifestyle, and collaboration with the Nazis. And with that, the East German government fell.[27]

Because coercion is costly, autocrats frequently prefer to use other tools to legitimate their rule and stay in power when possible. They manipulate the media, rig elections, and bribe officials, while also trying to engineer economic growth and policy successes that will appease the masses and prevent coups. But employing these nonrepressive tools often requires the cooperation of social groups that inevitably want something in return—like increased political rights, better governance, and improved living standards. Hence the dilemma of relying on these tools to stay in power.

———

Viewing Russia as a personalist autocracy shifts our attention from the unique features of the leader and Russian culture to the stuff of politics. How do politicians claim credit for policy successes and shift blame for policy failures? How do economic shocks like oil booms create new winners and losers? How do interest groups battle for a larger piece of the pie? How do term limits shape succession struggles, or elections and public opinion polls reveal information about the strength of the ruling elite and potential challengers? When do opposition groups cooperate or not cooperate with each other, and under what conditions do the fractious security services threaten or support the ruler? In trying to understand Russia, we should move beyond psychoanalyzing Putin, and explore the shifts in power among and between the ruler, the elite, and the mass public that drive politics in autocracies like Russia.

In addition, this approach suggests the value of recognizing differences within autocracies. Politics in personalist autocracies follow patterns distinct from those in military and one-party regimes. Personalist rulers like Putin typically face greater costs for losing office, are more likely to lose power by coups or revolts than by constitutional means, and are more likely to rely on repression than are rulers in military or single-party regimes.[28] To be sure, no two personalist autocracies are alike. Russia is better educated and wealthier, and has a larger footprint in global politics than most personalist autocracies. It takes a deep knowledge of the country to understand the limits of the approach, but we can learn a lot about Russia through this prism.

Whatever the type of autocracy, it is better to be a popular than unpopular autocrat. This is particularly true for personalist autocrats who claim a mandate from the popular will rather than from democratic procedures. A genuinely popular personalist autocrat can increase their power without having to persuade the security services to repress political opponents or cut checks to keep supporters in the fold. I explore Putin's personal popularity in the next chapter.

4

Better to Be Feared and Loved

PRESIDENT PUTIN'S POPULARITY

What can a girl sing about? She can't sing that Putin is great. That would be stupid and it wouldn't be funny. But she can sing that everything around her sucks, and she needs a man like Putin.

—ALEXANDER YELIN, LYRICIST FOR THE HIT SONG
"A MAN LIKE PUTIN"

IN DECEMBER 2019, President Putin began to address the question on the minds of all Russia watchers since 2012.[1] The Constitution required Putin to step down as president after his second consecutive six-year term in 2024, but would he stay or go? On January 20, 2020, Putin submitted proposals for amendments to the Constitution that among other things, gave greater clout to the Parliament, granted precedence of Russian law over international law, and expanded the power of the State Council. The latter proposal led many to speculate that Putin would step down as president in 2024 to head a newly empowered State Council.[2]

For six weeks, a working group in Parliament refined the proposals and charted a different course. On March 10, Russian Duma deputy Valentina Tereshkova, a former cosmonaut who is best known as the first woman in outer space, proposed an amendment that would nullify

President Putin's two most recent terms and reset his term limit clock to zero—a move that would open the door for him to rule until 2036 should he run for office and win elections in 2024 and 2030.[3] Shortly after her remarks, President Putin made a surprise appearance before the Duma, where he backed Tereshkova's proposal. Within a week, the Parliament and regional governments ratified the amendments, and the Constitutional Court approved the changes.[4] Like every other personalist autocrat in the former Soviet Union who has faced term limits, President Putin too found a way to extend his stay in office.[5]

Throughout the discussion of these amendments, Putin insisted that the changes be ratified in a nationwide vote by the Russian public even though this was not required by the Constitution.[6] Putin said that he "considers it necessary to conduct a vote by citizens on the entire packet of amendments to the Constitution. And only according to the results of the vote could a final decision be made."[7] To this end, the amendments also included popular measures like mandatory increases in pensions, a more generous minimum wage, defining marriage as only between a man and woman, and strengthening the status of the Russian language.[8] The up or down vote on the entire packet of amendments took place from June 25 to July 1, 2020, and passed easily.

To be sure, the Kremlin had many levers to ensure popular approval of the amendments, and by many measures, the vote was the most irregular of any in Russia in the last twenty years, but why create the headache of a popular vote when it was not needed?[9] Why would Putin care at all about public opinion? After all, he is an autocrat who does not need majority support to stay in office.

Personal popularity serves at least two goals for an autocratic ruler. It deters elites who might be interested in challenging the ruler. Regime insiders who only see high levels of support for the ruler may think twice before seeking to replace them. To overthrow the ruler and take power, they need to be confident that other elites and at least some of the masses will support them. In the absence of a free press and fair elections, public opinion surveys that convince others that the ruler is genuinely popular can be an important signal that the public will oppose any efforts to displace the autocrat.

In addition, great popularity reduces incentives for the masses to mobilize against the ruler. If a leader is so loved, why would citizens believe that their compatriots would rally to overthrow him? Niccolò Machiavelli famously wrote that if a ruler has to choose between being feared and being loved, they should choose the former, but being loved and feared is the better option.[10] The importance of popularity for nondemocratic rulers is ironic because they do not hold free and fair elections that would allow them to claim legitimacy based on popular support.

This point is not lost on personalist autocratic rulers today.[11] Among others, Erdoğan in Turkey, Chávez in Venezuela, and Orban in Hungary have all translated some mixture of economic growth, nationalist rhetoric, and appeals to an increased foreign policy stature into considerable popularity for at least some period. For example, shortly after taking office, Venezuelan president Chávez parlayed his personal approval rating of around 80 percent into a referendum to call a constituent assembly to redraw the Constitution. Within months, the assembly put forward a new Constitution that allowed presidents to be elected to consecutive terms, increased presidential terms to six years, and expanded executive control over the military.[12] Translating temporary personal popularity into expanded formal powers is a common pattern in personalist autocracies.

Putin too has enjoyed high approval ratings for much of his tenure. During his first twenty years in office, his approval ratings averaged a hefty 76 percent and peaked at 89 percent in the wake of the annexation of Crimea. Only in summer 2020 in the midst of a global pandemic and sharp economic contraction did his rating fall into the high 50s.

Putin's approval ratings have also been high relative to other public figures in Russia. When asked in December 2012 to name someone who could replace President Putin as President of the country, the most common response was Dmitry Medvedev at 14 percent.[13] This gap in popularity and name recognition gives President Putin a valuable asset among the Russian political elites: only he has demonstrated that he can solve the problem of maintaining popular support for the regime. The absence of another popular figure to coalesce around makes breaking with Putin all the more difficult for the elites and masses.

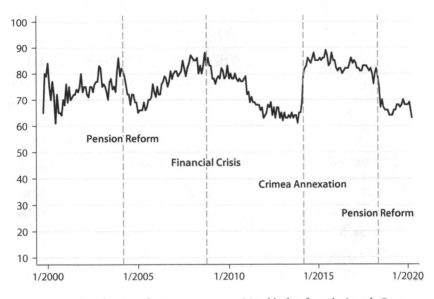

FIGURE 4.1. Putin's approval ratings, 2000–2020. Monthly data from the Levada Center.

Popular discussions of presidential approval ratings frequently point to Putin's personal charisma and public image, or patterns deep in Russian history such as a preference for a "strong ruler" and an abiding anti-Western sentiment that a ruler can easily exploit.[14] Historian Perry Anderson captures both of these sentiments by linking Putin's popularity to his "image of firm, where necessary, ruthless authority. . . . Historically the brutal imposition of order has more often been admired than feared in Russia."[15]

Scholars find surprisingly little support for either view. There is good evidence that Putin's approval ratings are not driven by his personal characteristics or deep historical patterns of state-society relations but instead by more prosaic factors, such as the performance of the economy, and foreign policy success, such as the annexation of Crimea. In addition, diving deeper into the data also reveals that Putin's approval ratings as president have been high for much of his term, but by other more nuanced measures his support is more prosaic than commonly depicted in the press. Putin has been a popular leader, yet is far from a superman (see figure 4.1).

How Can We Know Whether Putin Is Popular?

But wait, if Russia is an autocracy, then why should we believe President Putin's approval ratings? Aren't respondents too scared to give an honest answer? Aren't survey companies too intimidated to report bad news?

This view is widespread. Appearing on CNN, author Ben Judah offered the following perspective on Russian polling:

> So what that opinion poll is, is not a poll of approval but it's a poll of fear. An opinion poll can only be conducted in a democracy with a free press. In a country with no free press, where people are arrested for expressing their opinions, where the truth is hidden from them, where the media even online is almost all controlled by the government—when a pollster phones people up and asks, "Hello, do you approve of Putin," the answer is overwhelmingly yes.[16]

President Obama also weighed in on the veracity of President Putin's approval ratings: "I mean, if you control the media and you've taken away everybody's civil liberties and you jail dissidents, that's what happens. The pollster calls you up and says 'do you support the guy who if you don't support him he might throw you in jail?' You say 'yes, I love that guy.'"[17] Similar perspectives are often encountered in the Russian press, and some have suggested that even the Kremlin itself does not believe the polls.[18]

Fortunately, for autocrats (and researchers) the quality of public opinion polling in Russia is quite good for a nondemocracy. About a half-dozen firms regularly conduct surveys across Russia. Some, such as VTSIOM and FOM, are more Kremlin friendly, and are akin to "house" polling firms in US politics that work primarily for Democrats or Republicans. But others, such as GFK, Bashkirova and Partners, and especially the Levada Center, are more independent. A number of firms also conduct regular online surveys, similar to those run in other countries. Scholars using survey data from these Russian survey companies regularly publish articles in the top journals in economics, political science, and sociology.

Cross-national evidence from the World Values Survey attests to the quality of surveys in Russia too. Using data from more than fifty-nine surveys conducted in nondemocracies, political scientists Xiaoxiao Shen and Rory Truex find that Russians are about as willing to answer sensitive questions as respondents in other nondemocracies.[19] Scholars studying China and the Middle East face far greater difficulties in conducting the type of high-quality face-to-face polls that are regularly done in Russia.

Survey firms in Russia work frequently with academics, but by far the largest client for many survey companies is the Kremlin, and its polling operations are formidable. Kremlin-friendly polling firms conduct massive weekly and quarterly surveys, and the data are not released to the general public. The questions on these surveys are quite informative about the Kremlin's concerns. Many questions focus on support for the president and the willingness to protest.

For the Kremlin, there is some advantage in having independent survey firms. Without a benchmark provided by an independent polling firm, the Kremlin might wonder whether its house firms are accurately reporting their findings or simply telling the Kremlin what it wants to hear. The Putin administration appears to recognize this dilemma and often conducts polls simultaneously using several pollsters to increase their accuracy, but this strategy is costly.

As Russia has become more repressive in recent years, however, concerns about the quality of its polling have increased. Most worrying has been the treatment of the Levada Center, which is widely regarded as the best independent polling firm in Russia. For many years, the Kremlin tolerated the work of the Levada Center, but in recent years it has faced increasing harassment.[20] In September 2016 on the eve of a parliamentary election, the Russian government labeled the Levada Center a "foreign agent" in line with restrictive legislation on funding for nongovernmental organizations (NGOs) that engage in political activity. To get around this law, the Levada Center quickly established a new for-profit company, Levada Marketing Research; since it was not an NGO, it was not burdened with the requirements of operating as a foreign agent in Russia. This change does not appear to have had much effect on quality, and the Levada Center retains considerable respect, but it does reveal the vulnerability of independent public opinion firms in Russia.[21]

Is Putin's Popularity Real?

Over the years, I have partnered with the Levada Center on many surveys, and we have often discussed the problem of eliciting honest answers to sensitive questions. When I told the center's staff about the "list experiment," a technique that gives respondents the possibility to answer sensitive questions truthfully, they intuited the logic immediately and with warm admiration said, "That is a sneaky question" (*Eto khitrii vopros*).

It goes like this. A list experiment is a survey question that provides respondents with a list of items and asks them to tell the interviewer how many of these items apply to them. They are not asked which specific items on the list apply to them. The distinction between "which" and "how many" items apply to them is critical. Because respondents only give a numerical answer, the interviewer does not know how the respondents feel about any specific item on the list. This gives the respondent confidence that the interviewer cannot determine how they would respond to the sensitive item on the list. Scholars have used this technique to study sensitive topics such as race relations in the United States, corruption in India, and support for opposition groups in nondemocracies, so my three coauthors—Scott Gehlbach, Kyle Marquardt, and Ora John Reuter—and I thought it might be helpful for exploring popular support for the leader of Russia.[22]

In a national survey in January 2015, we divided the respondents according to random chance into two groups. In the "control" group, the respondents saw a list of three former leaders of Russia: Joseph Stalin, Leonid Brezhnev, and Boris Yeltsin. In the "treatment" group, respondents saw the same three names plus Vladimir Putin. All the respondents were then asked the same question: "Take a look at the list of politicians and tell me for how many you generally support their activities?"

We found that in the control group with just three names on the list, the respondents on average supported 1.18 of the politicians mentioned. In the treatment group, with four names including President Putin, the respondents supported 1.98 politicians. Because 1.98 minus 1.18 equals 0.80, we found that 80 percent of the respondents supported Putin. This number is quite close to the 86 percent of respondents who reported that they support Putin in a direct question in the same survey. Moreover, because public opinion polls always include a margin of error in the responses, we could not rule out the possibility that there is no difference in the responses using the list experiment and direct question.[23] In other words, people were not lying when they expressed their approval for Putin.

Because we did not want our finding to rise or fall on responses to a single question in the survey, we also asked the respondents later in the same survey about their support for a list of three contemporary politicians rather than for three historical leaders of Russia and saw similar results. To further assess the credibility of our findings, we repeated both survey questions three months later and found almost no change in the results.[24] Results from four survey questions conducted over three months provide good evidence that the respondents were not dissembling when they were asked about support for Putin. In contrast to the view that Putin's approval ratings are inflated, we find good evidence that they are not. More generally, Putin's popularity does not appear to be the result of fear of repression for expressing opposition in a survey.

Other evidence supports our conclusion. Foreign companies have conducted surveys of presidential approval in Russia and found results similar to those conducted by Russian-based firms. Polls by the Associated Press and Gallup find approval ratings well in line with those done by Russian firms at the time.

In addition, Russians are often quite critical of other parts of the government. The Parliament, courts, and especially police are frequent targets of public ire. Russians are also quite willing to disapprove of other politicians, even ones in the government, who receive far lower approval ratings than does Putin. Kremlin-backed policies too are not beyond the pale of criticism. Despite the broad popularity of the annexation of Crimea, a majority of Russians in 2015 were willing to tell pollsters that they opposed sending Russian troops to Ukraine, and more than 80 percent of Russians were willing to express opposition to incorporating eastern Ukraine into Russia.[25] The public uses public opinion polls to rail against corruption, inequality, and Russia's notoriously bad roads as well.

But Why Is Putin Popular?

That President Putin's approval ratings are real, however, does not explain what drives them up and down. While folk wisdom emphasizes Putin's personal characteristics and Russians' supposed desire for a "strong hand" that would deliver order in the country, two factors stand out on closer scrutiny of the data.

First, as in most other countries, the underlying state of the economy predicts support for the president. Using monthly public opinion polls from the Levada Center from 1992 until 2008, political scientist Daniel Treisman assesses a wide range of factors commonly cited as sources of Putin's popularity and finds that perceptions of the performance of the economy were largely responsible for President Putin's approval ratings during much of his time in office. He notes, "Wartime rallies, media effects and image did play a part at times. . . . However, Russians' perceptions of economic conditions have been consistently more important."[26] In addition, he finds that Russians' perceptions of the economy were tightly linked to the actual state of key economic indicators such as real wages, pensions, and wage arrears.

Other scholars who have tracked Putin's approval rating in recent years also find that voters whose economic fortunes have improved are more likely to support Putin.[27] In this way, Russians are like the citizens of many countries. They reward politicians in good economic times and punish them in bad economic times—regardless of the politician's personal traits.

This finding is even more striking because it holds for President Yeltsin's nine years in office as well. In the 1990s, a declining economy weighed heavily on Yeltin's approval ratings while a near doubling of the size of the economy during Putin's first two terms fueled a sharp increase in support. Putin is popular for the same reason that Yeltsin was not: the economy. This suggests that factors unique to Putin, including his macho photos and spearfishing publicity stunts are less important for his personal popularity than more mundane factors like the state of the economy.

The reliance on the economy to maintain Putin's popular support must be unsettling for the Kremlin as Moscow's ability to shape global energy prices is limited, particularly with the rise of shale gas and prospect of low energy prices for the near future. Far from being able to manipulate public opinion about his approval ratings with ease, Putin must rely to a good degree on the vagaries of international commodity prices. And the Kremlin recognizes this link. Concerns about popular reaction to economic downturns are an important consideration for policy makers and provide a significant constraint on the ruler.

Second, looking beyond economic fundamentals, foreign policy success, as epitomized in the annexation of Crimea, offers another explanation for presidential approval. Following the annexation, Putin's approval ratings shot up from the mid-60s to the high 80s and remained in the 80 percent range for four more years.

For many Russians, the annexation of Crimea was more than just an increase in their options for a summer vacation, but also marked the reemergence of Russia as a country to be reckoned with in global politics. Public support for the annexation of Crimea (or as it is known in Russia, the reincorporation of Crimea into the Russian Federation) remained high in just about all demographic groups. Those who had previously abandoned Putin now supported him in large numbers following the annexation of Crimea along with the continued hostilities involving Russian and Ukrainian forces in eastern Ukraine.[28]

Political scientists Samuel Greene and Graeme Robertson document how the Putin team tapped the public's deep-seated emotional attachments to Russia's role as a great power to increase its support. They maintain that the "collective euphoria over events in Ukraine as played on Russian state television led to an emotional outpouring of pride, hope and trust in Russia's leaders."[29] Greene and Robertson find that many Russians who rallied around the Kremlin also reported that petty corruption was declining (despite objective evidence), Russia's economic future was rosy (despite the imposition of sanctions), and their personal economic situation in the 1990s was better than those who did not rally around the flag (despite there being no objective differences). The annexation of Crimea made Russians feel better about their lives on many levels, even those unconnected to the event.

The annexation of Crimea bolstered popular support for the government, but identifying the precise size of its impact posed a challenge. The annexation was quickly followed by economic sanctions—a policy that is often cited with sparking a nationalist backlash that increases support for the sanctioned ruler. Indeed, some argue that sanctions against Russia were having just such an effect.[30] Anthony Scaramucci, an adviser to President Trump, observed, "I think the sanctions had in some ways an opposite effect because of Russian culture. I think the Russians would eat snow if they had to survive. And so for me the sanctions probably galvanized the nation with the nation's President."[31]

How could we know whether the increase in support for Putin was due to the annexation of Crimea or imposition of sanctions? The two events occurred almost at the same time, and each assertion seemed plausible. The answer also had implications for policy. If the sanctions were primarily serving to increase support for the Russian government, then it is harder to support arguments in their favor.

To probe whether support for the Russian government was due to the annexation of Crimea or economic sanctions, I conducted surveys in Russia in November 2016 and January 2017.[32] To my surprise, reminding respondents that the United States had levied sanctions against Russia had no discernible effect on their support for the Russian government. By contrast, reminding them about the annexation of Crimea increased support for the government by about 30 percentage points on a five-point scale. Almost three years after the annexation of Crimea, reminding the respondents of this event produced a sharp increase in support for the Russian government, while reminding Russians of the US sanctions did not.

We should interpret the impact of the Crimean consensus carefully.[33] Putin's high approval ratings following the annexation should not be attributed to an abiding anti-Westernism rooted deep in the Russian psyche. The Kremlin began to drum up anti-Western sentiment in earnest following large protests in late 2011. This campaign included accusations by Putin that the US State Department and Hillary Clinton in particular organized and paid protesters with the goal of destabilizing Russia. This period also saw the passage of laws restricting foreign ownership of media outlets in Russia, and an attempt to position Russia as an alternative to an immoral West that no longer respected the traditional family or valued organized religion. Yet these anti-Western broadsides had little effect on Putin's approval ratings, which lingered in the mid-60s through 2012 and 2013. It was only with the imposition of economic sanctions that anti-Western feelings in the general public surged—a response that likely occurs in all sanctioned countries.[34] Indeed, a majority of Russians had generally positive attitudes toward the United States in the decade prior to the annexation of Crimea, and attitudes toward the West have tended to rise and fall in predictable ways in response to events.[35]

Nor should we see the annexation as a diversionary war created by the Kremlin to rally support for a failing leader. Putin's approval ratings were in the mid-60s in February 2014, and Kremlin insiders at the time were far from panicking about this figure.[36] Putin was sufficiently confident in his position that two months before the annexation, he pardoned regime critics Khodorkovsky and the members of Pussy Riot, the balaclava-clad oppositionists whose protest in a Moscow church created a viral sensation and popular backlash that the Kremlin skillfully exploited.[37] Russia had just finished hosting the Sochi Olympics, which were widely seen as a success. And according to one former Putin adviser, the Kremlin "could not have known" how large the surge in support would be, but it was a "welcome surprise."[38] The annexation of Crimea certainly boosted support for the Kremlin, but there is not much evidence that the move on Crimea was driven by a need to shore up Putin's weakness.

The annexation of Crimea resonated deeply with a Russian public proud of the Kremlin's newly credible claim to great-power status.

Moreover, the public greatly appreciated that the annexation occurred with little cost in Russian lives. Putin's control over the media and the sheer audacity of the annexation of Crimea go a long way in accounting for the surprising duration of the rally around the flag effect. This may explain why Putin's approval ratings remained high for the next four years, even as economic growth slowed and support for other governing institutions tumbled. Far from being inscrutable, or due to factors unique to Russia or Putin himself, Putin's approval ratings are largely driven by the same things that propel executive approval in other countries: economic performance and perceived policy success.

What Do Putin's Approval Ratings Mean?

Observers have paid much attention to Putin's approval ratings. It is important to put them in context, though. Other, more detailed questions about Putin's popularity paint a less rosy picture than do his approval ratings. For many years, the Levada Center has asked respondents what factors they associated with President Putin, ranging from "disgust" to "rapturous admiration" with six categories in between. If we look closely at figure 4.2, which depicts responses to this question starting in 2000 collapsed into five categories, we find that about 30 percent "rapturously admire" or "are fond" of Putin, another 30 percent "can't say anything bad about him," another 30 percent say they are "neutral" or "can't say anything good about him," and less than 10 percent in the top area express "antipathy" or "disgust."[39]

These are impressive figures, but also not as extraordinary as his approval ratings would suggest. The results bring Putin back within the realm of other popular politicians in other settings. As noted above, Putin is not the superman that pro-Kremlin commentators would have one believe. He is a popular politician.

Russians also have few illusions about Putin. Surveys over the last half decade routinely show that less than one-quarter of Russians believe that Putin governs in the interest of the middle class, with most believing that he governs in the interest of the security services and oligarchs.[40] Moreover, when asked in an open-ended question to name

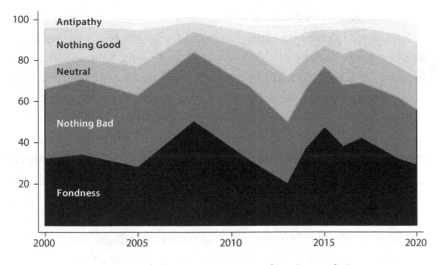

FIGURE 4.2. Putin feeling thermometer. Data from the Levada Center.

a politician they trust, 70 percent of the respondents named Putin in 2016, but no more than one-third did so in each month in 2019, and even fewer did so in 2020.[41]

While Russians appreciate the economic growth and foreign policy successes of the Putin era, they also recognize the value of changing leaders from time to time. Even when Putin was at an 80 percent approval rating in the second half of 2007 and faced the upcoming end of his second term, most Russians preferred that someone else become president in 2008. In July 2011, then prime minister Putin only led then president Dmitry Medvedev by 5 percentage points in a hypothetical presidential race.[42] Similarly, a poll in 2020 found that about half of Russians reported that they would like Putin to stay in power after 2024, and about 40 percent would like him to leave politics.[43]

Russians have even fewer illusions about other parts of the government. They express little trust in public institutions such as the government, police, Duma, or courts. They have not become immune to corruption scandals and unexpected changes in policy. After anticorruption activist Alexei Navalny published an exposé in spring 2017 about Prime Minister Medvedev's wealth and luxurious lifestyle, Medvedev's approval rating fell by 10 percent in the next month.

As in most countries, most Russians are not especially interested in politics. Several studies found that Russians have long since abandoned hope that the government will help solve their problems. Samuel Greene, a professor at King's College London, observed that Russia has remained politically stable even in the face of steep drops in living standards since 2014 because of a "particularly disengaged relationship between Russian citizens and their state." In his view, Russians recognize the failings of the state and are well aware of Putin's shortcomings, but have developed ways to cope with the many dysfunctional governments that they have seen through the decades. Whether experiencing the economic chaos of the 1990s or the clawing back of civil liberties in the 2000s, Russians continue to rely heavily on friends and family to find jobs, earn a living, and solve their daily problems. They turn to the state and politics primarily when all other options have failed. As Greene argues, "The general quiescence [of the Russian public] coexists with a deep-seated antipathy toward the country's ruling elite."[44]

———

Taken together, recent research is hard to square with popular depictions of relations between Russians and the state. Rather than being indifferent to public opinion, the current residents of the Kremlin pay it considerable heed. Russia is an autocracy, and its leaders are not accountable to the public in any strict sense, but the Kremlin devotes significant attention and energy to monitoring and shaping public opinion.

Instead of mobilizing in a wave of nationalist fervor to back their leader, Russians have rather ambivalent attitudes toward the state and few illusions about Putin, even though large majorities have approved of his activities for most of his first twenty years in office. Yes, Putin has had high approval ratings for much of his term, and they are more or less accurate, but by other measures Putin's popularity is more prosaic. And Putin fatigue appears to be setting in; in summer 2020, his presidential approval ratings sagged to their lowest levels since he took office.

Moreover, his approval ratings are largely driven by factors we understand relatively well—economic performance and rally around the flag effects—rather than personal charisma, reverence for the czar, or Russians' supposed preference for a strong leader.

Looking ahead, whoever runs the Kremlin will struggle to replicate Putin's approval ratings from the past twenty years. Putin benefited from a historic surge in oil prices and the high-reward, low-risk annexation of Crimea—two factors that are unlikely to be repeated. Leaders also cannot simply bequeath their popularity to a successor. Witness the disastrous transfer of power in Venezuela from the relatively popular Chávez to the much-disliked Maduro. High approval ratings have been a key feature of Putin's formula for ruling, and likely helped to stave off elite defections and challenges from the masses, yet whoever occupies the Kremlin in the coming years will likely find it more difficult to use public approval to increase their power.

The Kremlin uses approval ratings to justify Putin's rule—but when it comes to a politician's popularity, more important even than approval ratings are election results, especially when the election is free and fair. Campaigns, debates, and missteps frequently produce surprises in honest elections, and that is precisely why rulers in autocracies avoid them. The stakes are high because election results can lead directly to a loss of office.

Approval ratings allow you to judge support for a single politician, though not to compare candidates, which is the essence of an election. While you may approve of a candidate, you may approve of another candidate more, but that distinction will only be reflected in an election.

I turn to elections—which potentially can be a far more consequential way to express approval of the president—in the next chapter. As with presidential approval ratings, we will see that elections in Russia are more than meets the eye.

5

The Surprising Importance of Russia's Manipulated Elections

Yesterday, Vladimir Putin won reelection with 76% of the vote. . . .
Congratulations to President Putin for making up a realistic number.

—STEPHEN COLBERT, "GUESS WHO WON
RUSSIA'S ELECTION?"

IN LATE SUMMER 2016, Amuragrocenter—one of the largest soybean-processing plants in far eastern Russia—announced plans to hold a "Day of Health" on September 18. Flyers hanging throughout the plant invited workers to join the celebration for a healthy meal and take part in a discussion of good dietary practices, followed by music and dancing. Management also encouraged workers to include their spouses and other family members. For workers themselves, attendance was mandatory, and there was one other requirement: they were told to bring their absentee ballots to the meeting so that they could vote in elections to the Russian Parliament scheduled for that day under the watchful eye of their employer. The implied threat was not lost on the employees. A worker at the plant told a reporter, "They are forcing workers to vote for one party, they are saying 'you want to work, then attend.' People don't like it, but no one wants to lose their job."[1]

This form of voter intimidation is far from an isolated incident in Russia. In the 2011–12 election cycle, the vote-monitoring organization Golos gathered reports of election violations. Fifty-seven percent of all reported violations involved employers, and of these, 83 percent involved voter intimidation via threats of dismissal, cuts in pay, or declines in working conditions. Voter intimidation was by far the most commonly reported electoral violation.[2]

When we think of elections in autocracies, these kinds of outrageous abuses of voting rights come to mind. Although autocratic regimes engage in objectionable practices during elections, they also use strategies common to democratic elections. Operating in this gray area requires much more effort than just stuffing ballot boxes on Election Day, and it raises the odds of an unpleasant outcome—but it allows autocrats to maintain a veneer of legitimacy too and gives them some ground to claim a popular mandate.

This patina of legitimacy is valuable in Russia because elections are popular and fraud is not. In "The Myth of Mass Support for Autocracy," political scientist Henry Hale reports that in 2008, 89 percent of Russians agreed that the state needed a leader "with a strong hand to solve its problems," but 96 percent thought that the "people should choose this leader," and 87 percent of Russians thought that the leader should be chosen in "free, fair, multicandidate elections."[3] In other words, Russians preferred a strong leader elected by democratic means—hardly a unique desire. A 2016 survey found similar levels of support for free and fair elections, and reported that just 8 percent of Russians consider it acceptable to limit television appearances by opposition candidates.[4] After reviewing a range of evidence, political scientist Ellen Carnaghan finds that support for stability and order in Russia is often mistakenly seen as support for authoritarian rule.[5] Russians want good governance from their leaders, not restrictions on free speech, assembly, or elections.

And Russian voters—even supporters of the pro-government party, United Russia—do not like election fraud. In a study from 2018, political scientists David Szakonyi and Ora John Reuter found that supporters of United Russia were more likely to believe that elections in Russia are free and fair. No surprise here. Informing these pro-government respondents about specific instances of electoral fraud, however, significantly reduced their propensity to support United Russia. Blatant election fraud is costly for autocrats not just because it may spark protests by the opposition but also because it reduces support for the government among its core voters who also oppose fraud.[6] Simply canceling elections without a good reason or using only the crudest forms of electoral fraud risks a popular protest, and would nullify Putin's claim to be governing in the name of a majority.

Indeed, autocrats who cheat less can earn "honest majorities" by winning elections that have elements of fairness. In doing so, they can more easily claim a popular mandate. If voters are willing to go to the polls and vote for the incumbent in large numbers with limited coercion and fraud, then rivals will think twice about challenging the leader or taking to the streets. Autocrats who believe that they are popular and can win elections have real incentives to cheat less in an election, thereby demonstrating the ability to create an honest majority to deter potential challengers.

But here is the familiar rub. The more free and fair the election, the greater the risks for the ruler. Political scientists Grigore Pop-Eleches and Graeme Robertson studied all nondemocracies in the post–Cold War era, and found that election years were significantly more likely to produce political liberalizations than were nonelection years.[7] They also found, not surprisingly, that elections that were more free and fair were more likely to weaken autocratic rule. Cheat too little and risk a defeat at the polls, but cheat too much and spark a popular backlash or elite challenge.

Autocratic elections involve more than an all-powerful ruler dictating the final tally or a passive public meekly accepting the results. They signal the strength of the ruler and opposition. Elections are often less about choosing who will hold power (they are rigged enough that we usually know that in advance) than about gauging the popularity of the incumbent and their party relative to potential rivals. Turnout levels, the margin of victory, and the amount of fraud needed to achieve victory can tell us a good deal about the relative strength of the incumbent and challengers.

This chapter explores how the Kremlin has managed the inherent trade-offs of autocratic elections. Recent research shows that the Kremlin uses fraud in ways both big and small—but fraud is not the whole story. The Kremlin also recognizes the risks of excessive cheating, and tries to generate "honest support" and emphasize the legitimacy of electoral outcomes. The mix of these two strategies has changed over time, however. Following an unpleasant surprise in 2011, the Kremlin has made elections increasingly biased in its favor and left less to chance—even at the expense of electoral credibility. Without the ability to appeal to "honest majorities" generated by elections, the Kremlin has made increasing use of coercion. By choosing to make elections less free and fair, the Kremlin reveals its weakness rather than its strength.

Balancing Fraud and the Appearance of Legitimacy

Looking across the globe, elections under authoritarian rule have become increasingly common. Since 2000, all but five nondemocracies have held formal elections, and three-quarters of these elections included multiparty competition. These elections range from the wholly manipulated, as in North Korea, to the rather competitive elections of Kenya under Daniel Arap Moi.

By definition, autocratic elections are not free and fair. Dictators frequently resort to crude forms of electoral subversion. They stuff ballot boxes with votes for the incumbent party, ban opposition candidates from running for office, and when all else fails, miscount and misreport vote totals. Rare is the autocratic election without grossly inflated reports of turnout and votes for the ruling party from at least some electoral districts.

But some autocratic elections are more free and fair than others. To demonstrate their authentic strength and gain an element of legitimacy, autocrats often adopt seemingly democratic rules, but subvert them in ways that expand executive power and undermine liberal democracy. By using tactics that are formally legal, yet violate the spirt of the law, autocrats try to create an impression of fairness even as they tilt the electoral playing field in their favor. These tactics do not eliminate electoral risk, but they do load the dice in favor of the autocrat.

One strategy is to borrow the least democratic elements of democratic elections. For example, autocrats can adopt high electoral thresholds for parties to win seats in parliament. The democratic rationale is that this makes it easier to form a government; in Sweden, for instance, parties must receive at least 4 percent of the national vote to receive any seats in Parliament. Autocrats take this a step further. Turkey under Erdoğan has the highest electoral threshold of any country in the world: parties must clear a 10 percent threshold before gaining any seats. This comes in handy. In 2003, Erdoğan's party won 34 percent of the popular vote yet 67 percent of the seats in Parliament because votes for parties that did not clear the threshold were wasted.

Autocrats can also draw electoral districts with the stated goal of increasing fairness and unstated goal of expanding the seat share of ruling party candidates—a practice all too common in the United States. Venezuelan president Chávez perfected this art. In a remarkable feat of electoral engineering, Chávez's party won 53 percent of the vote but 93 percent of the seats in the Venezuelan Constituent Assembly in 2003.[8] In 2014, Orban's Fidesz party in Hungary received fewer votes than when it lost elections in 2002 and 2006, but the party ended up with a supermajority thanks to gerrymandering.[9]

Another strategy is to cancel elections for regional officials on the grounds of improving efficiency and ensuring that lower levels of government implement the policies of the central government. This is the policy in France, where the central government appoints regional prefects. The comparison was well wide of the mark, but in 2004, Kremlin officials cited just such an example to justify canceling gubernatorial elections.

Other tactics that autocrats can borrow from democracies include limiting free speech on the grounds of protecting the rights of vulnerable groups, adopting strict requirements for candidates to get on the ballot (supposedly in order to ensure that candidates are viable), and disenfranchising voters by dropping them from registration lists in the name of ballot security. In specific circumstances, each of these practices can be defended as serving larger democratic goals, but dictators often resort to them when circumstances are least appropriate. Moreover, in democracies these elements are frequently counterbalanced by other institutional features that mute their antidemocratic effects. The gerrymandering of electoral districts in the United States is conducted at the state level, which dilutes its effect on national politics. In contrast, autocrats typically stitch together the least democratic elements of tolerably democratic systems to create an illiberal monster.[10] At various times, Russia has combined high electoral thresholds, gerrymandered electoral districts, appointed governors, six-year presidential terms, and strict requirements to run for office to limit political competition.

In addition to using crude falsification and subverting democratic practices, autocrats adopt many tactics that are the bread and butter of democratic elections. Dictators too engage in get out the vote efforts, hold campaign rallies, and conduct opposition research to discredit their opponents. They publish party platforms to try to sway voters, seek endorsements by popular citizens, and use microtargeting to get their message out on different social media platforms.

For instance, the Kremlin oversees a massive polling operation, runs sophisticated political advertisements, and backs incumbents who emphasize their ability to bring home pork for their districts. It also recruits candidates with an eye toward winning elections. Loyalty to the Kremlin is a necessary but insufficient condition to get the backing of the ruling party as the pro-government United Russia favors candidates with name recognition and financial resources that it can use to turn out voters.[11]

The Kremlin also tries to identify popular policy positions and adopt them as its own. Henry Hale and fellow political scientist Timothy Colton found that in Putin's first two terms, considerable swaths of the population professed sympathy for policy positions espoused by United Russia. They note that while Putin's personal role and various types of fraud shape voter choices, "United Russia has an independent basis of support grounded in values, perceptions of policymaking success, and emerging party attachments that are distinct from loyalties to Putin personally."[12] United Russia's star soon faded, but its early success reminds us that not all votes in Russia are based on fraud, fear, or undying support for Putin.

In its efforts to convince voters of the legitimacy of elections, the Kremlin highlights the shortcomings of established democracies as well. It touts that speech in Russia is freer because is it not limited by "political correctness," points out the hypocrisy of US support for repressive regimes like Saudi Arabia, and underscores the outsize role of money in US elections. The goal is less to convince Russians that their elections are a democratic ideal than to create the impression that all elections are flawed in fundamental ways and the shortcomings of Russian elections are just a feature of real existing democracy.

Why do autocrats go through all this effort? Why not just steal elections with fraud? Creating the image of democracy via elections is important because autocrats like Putin, Chávez, Erdoğan, Orban, and others claim to be governing in the name of the people rather than promoting an abstract ideology as did autocrats in the twentieth century. To do so, they cannot simply cancel elections or rely heavily on the crudest forms of electoral fraud. Instead, autocrats seek to combine elements of fraud with more democratic components of elections to tilt the playing field in their favor, but not so much that they lose an election or spark a backlash. Doing so allows them to claim that their legitimacy derives from winning elections. As Kim Lane Scheppele, an expert on Orban's Hungary and astute observer of modern autocrats, argues,

> Portraying themselves as democratic constitutionalists is absolutely essential to their political legitimation; what is missing . . . is any respect for the basic tenets of liberalism. They have no respect for pluralism, minorities, or toleration. They do not believe that public power should be limited or accountable. In short, liberalism is gutted while they leave the facades of constitutionalism and democracy in place.[13]

The Kremlin's Menu of Manipulation

How do we know that elections are manipulated in Russia? No election is completely free and fair; I stood in line for three hours in Ohio in 2004 at a voting place within sight of the state capitol building. Russian officials often dismiss instances of electoral manipulations as mere irregularities that occur in all elections, and claim that Russian elections are within the bounds of the rough and tumble of democratic politics in middle-income countries.

Russian and Western reporters frequently point to specific cases of ballot-box stuffing, multiple voting by groups that travel between polling places, and harassment of opposition candidates in impressive detail. Moreover, the willingness of ordinary Russians to share their experiences of election fraud suggests that it is quite common. But without more systematic research, it is hard to generalize from these individual examples of electoral manipulation. Are they isolated or widespread? Are they systematic? Are these just sour grapes stories from the losers of the election? Fortunately, scholars have developed means to explore these questions, and Russia has been a key case in this discussion.

Several teams of Russian- and US-based social scientists have pored over election results using forensic techniques that detect unusual patterns in voting data that may indicate fraud. One trick is to identify reported vote totals that deviate from what one would find if results were reported honestly. For example, if there is no tampering, then it should be about as likely for an electoral precinct to report a 49 or 54 percent vote total for a party as a 50 or 55 percent vote total, but it turns out that the bunching of the number of vote totals that end in zeros or fives is much larger in Russian elections than in other countries' elections, which suggests some rounding up.[14] Moreover, that vote totals are rounded up in favor of pro-government candidates and parties rather than for all candidates and parties provides good evidence of tampering.[15]

The Russians appear to have caught on and may be "giving us the statistical finger," according to Kirill Kalinin and Walter Mebane, two election forensic experts. They contend that the reported results from the 2016 parliamentary elections were so squeaky clean that they reeked of manipulation.[16] Due to a mathematical quirk known as Benford's law, in a naturally occurring distribution of numbers between zero and one hundred, zeros, ones, or twos should be slightly more likely to occur than sevens, eights, or nines. This means that in a perfect world, if you took the average of the second digit of the vote count reported across all precincts, the result should be 4.187, which is exactly the number that we find in the Russian parliamentary election in 2016 down to the third decimal place. Since all research involves some small amount of error, achieving precision of the degree reported in this election is highly suspect. Kalinin and Mebane observe that the "statistics are perfect. The Russians appear to be telling folks like us that they have pretty good skills at faking vote data. . . . They know we're watching. We know they are watching. . . . Apparently, they aren't simply faking all the votes. Instead, they appear to add just a few [millions]."[17]

Another team of researchers used a clever technique to detect ballot-box stuffing in the parliamentary elections of 2011. Russian social scientists and the Russian NGO Citizen Observer sent small teams of election observers to 156 randomly selected electoral precincts in Moscow.[18] Because the observers were assigned to electoral precincts randomly, monitored and unmonitored precincts were essentially identical in factors that might account for differences in vote totals, such as the precinct's wealth, voter demographics, and ease of access to polling places.

Nonetheless, these researchers found that in precincts without monitors, vote totals for United Russia were about 11 percentage points higher than in monitored precincts and reported turnout was about 7 percentage points higher than in monitored precincts.[19] This is strong evidence of skulduggery as the ruling party did better and turnout was higher in the unmonitored than in the monitored precincts.

Not all electoral subversion takes place on Election Day, and not all types of vote fraud can be easily detected by observers. As election monitors have become more popular, rulers turn to less easily detected forms of electoral subversion such as using employers to subtly and not so subtly coerce their workers to vote. Employers can threaten to withhold paychecks, promotions, and perks unless workers can show that they turned out to vote.

With two coauthors, I studied how this works. We conducted a survey shortly after the parliamentary election of 2011 and found that one in four workers in Russia experienced some pressure from their employers to get them to vote.[20] Not surprisingly, this practice was more common among state bureaucrats. Almost 40 percent of workers in the state bureaucracy reported some pressure from their boss to go to the polls, but 22 percent of private-sector workers also experienced this form of voter mobilization. Some of these efforts by managers may be innocuous, but given weak worker protections in Russia, a little pressure from the boss may go a long way. We followed up in subsequent elections in 2016 and 2018, and discovered similar results.

Our research on voter mobilization in Russia also revealed some surprises.[21] Across the globe, one of the most common forms of electoral subversion is vote buying. From Argentina to Nigeria to Indonesia, brokers acting on behalf of political parties trade small gifts to get voters to the polls. Brokers typically target poor voters with packets of rice, bags of sugar, or small cash gifts to ensure that voters not only get to the polls but vote the right way too.[22]

In Russia, however, vote buying of the classic "bag of sugar for your vote" variety is much less common than other forms of electoral subversion. According to a national survey we conducted, only about 7 percent of voters in Russia in the 2012 electoral cycle were targets of vote buying. We conducted a similar survey in Indonesia, and found that 25 percent of all voters reported receiving a gift or payment from a party in the 2014 parliamentary election. Crowdsourced electoral violations collected by the election watchdog group Golos also reported low levels of vote buying in Russia.[23]

What accounts for the difference? One reason is that it may be cheaper to intimidate than to buy voters in Russia. The best targets for vote buying—the large underclasses that one often finds in the countryside or slums in poorer countries—are simply a much smaller group in Russia than in, say, Nigeria. Vote buying can be targeted to students, pensioners, and the extremely poor, but it is much more expensive to buy votes among the bulk of the population that is employed. John F. Kennedy's facetious response to questions about the role of his father's wealth in his political success captures this logic: "I have just received the following wire from my generous daddy. It says, 'Dear Jack, don't buy a single vote more than is necessary. I'll be damned if I'm going to pay for a landslide!'"

Perhaps the most damaging form of electoral subversion is simply banning viable candidates or parties from running for office. This is more difficult to study, but appears to have increased over time. In the first decade of the 2000s, liberal opposition parties, like Yabloko or Right Cause, faced an uneven playing field and the usual dirty tricks of incumbents.[24] By the 2016–18 election cycle, the Kremlin only faced "perennial candidates and handpicked shadow-boxers."[25]

To give some sense of how the Kremlin manages the risks inherent in autocratic elections, I focus on the December 2011 parliamentary election and its consequences for subsequent elections.[26] A closer look at elections over the years depicts a Kremlin trying to balance the uncertainty of cheating less and generating honest support against the benefits of cheating more and winning in rigged elections, and increasingly siding with the latter.

The Great Fraud Machine Misfire of December 2011

In the 1990s, national elections in Russia were competitive, open, and uncertain. From the strong showing of Vladimir Zhirinovsky's Liberal Democratic Party in parliamentary elections in 1993, to the failure of the pro-government Our Home Is Russia Party in parliamentary elections in 1995, to Yeltsin's unlikely surge in the presidential elections of 1996, and the rise of Putin in 2000, each election in the 1990s produced surprises. This type of uncertainty is an important, if insufficient, indicator of democracy.[27] Elections were rife with manipulation by both the Yeltsin government and local Communist Party barons, but they also saw opposition candidates receive access to the media, hard-fought campaigns, and intense and unfettered public debate about the direction of the country.

The Duma and presidential elections that brought Putin and his party to power in 1999 and 2000 had many democratic elements. No major parties were barred, and competition was fierce. Putin won 54 percent of the vote, and his party won roughly one-quarter of the seats in Parliament. The Organization for Economic Cooperation and Development (OECD) monitored the presidential election of 2000, and reported, "In general, and in spite of episodic events that sometimes tested the system's capacity to uphold the principles of fairness and a level playing field, the presidential election was conducted under a constitutional and legislative framework that is consistent with internationally recognized standards."[28] In nonbureaucratic speak, the election was more or less free and fair even if there were instances of manipulation.

Since 2000, however, the playing field has grown ever more skewed in favor of pro-government candidates. In the next two election cycles of parliamentary and presidential elections, in 2003–4 and 2007–8, candidates and parties critical of the Kremlin faced higher barriers to get on the ballot, less access to media, and increased levels of vote fraud.[29] Bolstered by Russia's booming economy, Putin's high personal popularity, and the usual dirty tricks of autocratic elections, the pro-government United Russia dominated these elections, with smaller shares of seats going to its "frenemy" parties: the Communist Party of the Russian Federation, which boasts of lineage to the Communist Party of the Soviet Union; the Liberal Democratic Party, which is neither liberal nor democratic; and Just Russia, which was created from whole cloth by the Kremlin. These parties provide only token resistance, are easily cowed or bought by the Kremlin, and crowd out more independent opposition.

The inequities in these elections produced much grumbling among the political opposition, yet did not translate into popular protest. Two sets of surveys by foreign researchers indicated that many Russians felt that the election results in 2007 included falsifications, but also largely corresponded to political realities in the country.[30]

In the parliamentary elections of 2011, though, the Kremlin's great electoral machine misfired. Voters across the spectrum spurned the ruling party, and United Russia's vote share fell from 65 percent in 2007 to 49 percent in 2011. Even with the usual levels of fraud and all the advantages that go with being an incumbent, the pro-government party failed to receive a majority of votes.

The rejection was sweeping. Researchers found that United Russia voters in 2007 who were less educated, strong supporters of democracy, or lived in large communities, led a "defection cascade," and were especially likely to take their vote elsewhere in 2011.[31] In the largest cities in the industrial heartland, vote shares for the pro-government forces fell from the mid-60s to the mid-30s. And these were just the formal results, which were surely inflated.

Among other factors, Putin fatigue contributed to the rejection of the governing party. Several months prior to the parliamentary elections, then prime minister Putin announced that he would run for president in March 2012—a move that was greeted without much enthusiasm among most Russians and considerable dismay among the opposition. Voters who favored a change in leadership likely used the parliamentary elections to express their opposition to Putin by voting against United Russia.

Even before the polls closed, videos of ballot stuffing and multiple voting flooded the internet. Spurred on by a belief that the elections were rigged and sensing weakness in the government, opposition politicians cried foul, and social media spread the word. About five thousand protesters took part in a demonstration approved by the city government on the day after the election. Police detained about three hundred protesters who attempted to approach the Kremlin. On December 6, a much smaller unsanctioned demonstration was met with violence by the police, who detained more than six hundred protesters.[32] On December 7, protesters received permission to conduct a demonstration on Bolotnaya Square (Swampy Square) three days later.

On December 10, sixty thousand people gathered to protest the election results, making it the largest opposition protest in twenty years.[33] The scale of the protest surprised many. Days before the election, one prominent commentator remarked, "A lot of people are unhappy with the authorities, and they are out to vent their anger against Mr. Putin's party . . . however very few people are actually likely to go to the street to take any form of action to challenge the election results when they are publicized."[34] Another popular commentator described it this way: "I flew out of Russia last Sunday. I arrived last night in order to attend the protest. And in the span of a week when I was away I flew back to a new country. Two weeks ago it would have been impossible to imagine."[35]

From midday until late evening, opposition activists from the Left and Right took to the stage to demand new elections and an end to corruption, but did not take more radical measures. They did not call for occupying downtown Moscow or engaging in violence. Opposition crowds chanted for a "Russia without Putin," shouted that "Putin is a thief," and railed against United Russia as the "party of crooks and thieves." This moniker stuck. Ten months later, surveys showed that one-third of Russians associated United Russia with this phrase.[36]

The protest was large, but it occurred with only minor clashes between protesters and state security. Protesters and journalists noted the peaceful nature of the demonstration as well as the lack of conflict between police and protesters. One reporter observed, "The organizers and participants of the meeting in Moscow said that the civility [*vezhlivost'*] and goodwill [*dobrozhelatel'nost'*] of the members of the police was unprecedented." A correspondent for *Kommersant'* witnessed dozens of protesters thanking the police for keeping order. Participants even gave members of the security forces hot coffee in plastic cups and flowers.[37]

State television reported on the protest largely without bias, but omitted some protesters' call for Putin to resign. Eight days after the protest during his annual radio call-in show, Prime Minister Putin noted that protesters had the right to express their views, but that they needed to obey the law and avoid putting Russia's hard-earned political stability at risk. He also accused them of being paid by foreign governments.

Protesters returned in even larger numbers on December 24. Despite the bitter cold, a hundred thousand people marched through Moscow with few arrests or disruptions in what was the largest opposition demonstration in modern Russia. Outside Moscow, protests broke out as well, but on a much-smaller scale. Researchers identified 428 protests for free and fair elections outside Moscow in the six months after the Duma elections, as Russians expressed their opposition to vote fraud, corruption, and in some cases, Putin's pending return to the presidency. These regional protests had an impact. One study found that Russians who were exposed to the protests were less likely to vote for Putin in March 2012.[38]

The Kremlin responded to the poor showing of United Russia and subsequent protests in 2011 by making changes that gave the appearance of respecting democratic principles, while slanting the playing field even further against the opposition. In balancing between generating honest and dishonest support, the Kremlin shifted greatly toward the latter.

Rather than sending in the troops against the demonstrators, the Kremlin organized counterprotests. The Kremlin made good use of its administrative resources to privilege the pro-Putin rallies. It bused supporters to fill stadiums with counterdemonstrators in support of President Putin. Some of these counterprotesters were paid, and others were coerced to attend—an option not available to anti-government protesters. If the opposition had to rally at the appropriately named Swampy Square in a hard-to-reach section of downtown Moscow, the pro-Putin rallies took place in major parks and stadiums on nonworking days. The Kremlin scheduled a rally on the Day of the Defenders of the Motherland at the massive Luzhniki stadium in central Moscow. One-hundred and thirty-thousand Russians attended the festivities featuring celebrities, food and drink, and dancing all paid for with state funds.[39] The countermobilization of pro-Putin supporters received far greater exposure on national television than did the anti-government protests as the Kremlin hoped to generate a patriotic wave against protesters who aimed "to destabilize Russia" and "acted upon the orders of foreign powers."[40]

In response to charges of ballot-box stuffing, the Kremlin installed webcams that allowed anyone to follow the action in each of Russia's more than ninety thousand polling places for the March 2012 presidential election. This might have given the appearance of reducing an obvious form of vote fraud, but likely just moved the fraud off camera.[41] The Kremlin replaced Vladimir Churov, the widely discredited head of the Central Election Commission who was known as "The Magician" for his ability to make votes appear and disappear, with a less odious yet still pliable figure.

The Kremlin reintroduced elections for regional governors in 2012, but also made it difficult for opposition candidates to win office. Candidates for governor were required to obtain the backing of a majority of deputies in the regional legislature, and because United Russia controlled the legislature in every region in the country, the chances for an outsider to be elected were slim.

As it has done in every election since 2000, the Kremlin changed voting rules too. Given United Russia's unpopularity, the government made half of the seats in Parliament determined by majority vote in single-member districts rather than have all seats assigned according to party lists. In creating boundaries for these new districts, the Kremlin created a presidential commission to study the experience of other countries.[42] To dilute the urban (and often less pro-Kremlin) vote, the Kremlin appears to have learned from the example of Texas. As in the capital of Austin, Russia's new single-member electoral districts frequently combine urban and rural districts, and run well beyond city limits into the countryside. By joining more pro-government voters in rural districts with fewer pro-government voters in city centers, the Kremlin watered down opposition votes.

Taking no chances, the Kremlin also restricted independent watchdog groups from monitoring elections in polling places. New legislation required independent election observers and journalists to declare which polling stations they planned to attend two weeks prior to the elections. These maneuvers gave election officials plenty of lead time to concentrate electoral fraud in unmonitored precincts.

Not only was the playing field tilted in favor of United Russia, the parliamentary elections of 2016 took place in a favorable environment as the Kremlin was still basking in the glow of the annexation of Crimea. While United Russia won 54 percent of the vote and obtained a supermajority in the Duma, only 48 percent of voters bothered to cast a ballot. The turnout was just 35 percent in Moscow, and even in recently annexed Crimea, the turnout was only 49 percent. What one reporter called "the most boring election of 2016" revealed not the power of the Kremlin but instead the depth of public apathy toward the governing party in Russia.[43]

This result spurred the Kremlin to mount an aggressive campaign to turn out the vote in presidential elections in March 2018. Having barred the most serious independent candidate from running for office, President Putin faced little opposition, but the Kremlin feared that voters might stay home.

To boost turnout, the Kremlin allowed regions to add referenda on local issues to the ballot. It pressured private employers and state officials to get the workers under their command to the polls. The Kremlin moved the date of the presidential election to March 18, the four-year anniversary of the annexation of Crimea. In Moscow, the head of the Moscow Election Commission set the goal of "visiting every apartment in the city," noting that this had not been done since elections in Soviet times. In Nizhny Novgorod, the regional Ministry of Industry reportedly sent a recommendation to industrial plant managers that it was not acceptable to use force and they could not mention particular candidates, but they should seek to secure "practically 100 percent participation of their workers, the members of their families, and military veterans" by holding rallies as well as calling workers at home.[44]

Despite the lack of fervor for the incumbent or hot-button issues on the agenda, the Kremlin managed 68 percent turnout in the official reporting, and Putin received 77 percent of the vote. That the Kremlin devoted so much attention, effort, and political capital to the most recent round of national elections even when the result was not in doubt indicates the importance that it attaches to getting elections right.

The Dangers of Heavy-Handed Fraud

Local elections also raise dilemmas for the Kremlin. In September 2019, Moscow held elections for the city Duma, a body of forty-five members with few formal powers. But given the declining popularity of United Russia, the long-stagnant economy, and few other opportunities for Muscovites to voice their views, the elections took on a significance far beyond the body's meager formal status.

The authorities took no chances and sought to keep independent opposition candidates off the ballot. Most prominently, they barred Navalny, the longtime anticorruption activist who rose to prominence in 2011 by labeling the pro-government United Russia "the party of crooks and thieves."

In addition, the requirements for getting on the ballot posed a challenge. Candidates running in one of Moscow's forty-five electoral districts had to collect signatures from at least 3 percent of their constituents. In most cases this was around five thousand potential voters. But if the Moscow City Election Commission (MCEC) declared more than 10 percent of these signatures to be fraudulent, candidates were barred from running. Candidates had to thread the needle of collecting enough valid signatures to get over the five thousand threshold, but still have fewer than 10 percent be declared invalid. Not surprisingly, candidates from United Russia and its faux opposition parties satisfied these demands with ease, yet the most viable independent opposition candidates were declared ineligible by the MCEC on the grounds of having too many fraudulent signatures.

Opposition candidates challenged the decision, and accused the MCEC of forging signatures and altering ones gathered by the candidates.[45] The MCEC voided the list of Lyubov Sobol, a lawyer from Navalny's anticorruption organization, in part by declaring the signature of her own law school professor invalid. Sobol went on a hunger strike to protest the decision.

Opposition candidates also organized protests on most weekends in July and August. At the height of these protests, more than sixty thousand people—many of them under thirty—took to the streets, making these the largest demonstrations since 2012. The authorities responded with greater force against protesters than in the past. They detained several thousand protesters, and while they quickly released most of them, the authorities charged about two dozen with crimes carrying potential sentences of ten to fifteen years. They searched the homes of opposition politicians and cracked down on Navalny's anticorruption organization by levying heavy fines against it. The harsh response did little to remedy the situation as the public again took to the streets to demonstrate in support of those arrested for protesting.

In the end, United Russia achieved a small majority of seats on its own and a large majority in concert with the "official" opposition parties. These elections to a body with little formal power did not threaten to bring down the Kremlin. They did, however, underscore the larger lesson: blatant electoral subversion that denied candidates access to the ballot provoked large protests, much to the dismay of a government that touts bringing stability to Russia as its greatest achievement.

Elections in Russia are subtler affairs than is commonly understood. Depictions of Russian elections as solely determined by fraud and a Russian populace cowed into supporting government candidates are part of the story, but only get us so far. The Kremlin uses a range of tactics, from outright fraud to more nuanced techniques to get voters to the polls, and often struggles to meet its marks. As Timothy Colton points out, 62 percent of participating voters cast ballots against United Russia in 2003, followed by 36 percent in 2007, 51 percent in 2011, and 46 percent in 2016.[46]

Like all autocrats, Putin faces a thorny trade-off when choosing to rig elections. Too much fraud and too little fraud both pose risks. Election results and the amount of fraud needed to achieve them shape the expectations and strategies of the two groups most threatening to the regime: elites and the mass public. A strong showing of sincere support at the polls may deter elites from a coordinated challenge against the ruler and inhibit mass mobilization by the public. A weak showing as revealed by massive fraud, low turnout, or a smaller than expected vote share reveals vulnerability. An autocratic ruler who mismanages the trade-off between cheating too much and revealing weakness or cheating too little and actually losing the election puts their position in peril. Fraud is a much blunter tool than many realize.

To date, the Kremlin has managed this trade-off well, and Putin has avoided the fate of other personalist autocrats felled by popular revolts after botched elections, but the increasingly skewed electoral playing field diminishes his ability to claim a genuine popular mandate. Putin's 2004 and 2012 electoral victories were due in large part to a strong economy, and his 2018 reelection owed much to the annexation of Crimea. But in 2020, United Russia looked like an increasingly spent force, and Putin himself is aging; should he decide to run for the presidency in 2024, Putin will be seventy-one.

Just as autocrats subvert elections to stay in power, they try to manipulate the economy to the same end. But as we will see in the next chapter, distorting the economy for political ends raises a host of challenges and difficult trade-offs.

6

Neither as Strong nor as Weak as It Looks

RUSSIA'S ECONOMY

Russia in 10 years will be one of the 5 largest economies.

—VLADIMIR PUTIN, QUOTED IN *VESTI*, 2007

In the next 10 years, Russia will be one of the 5 largest economies.

—VLADIMIR PUTIN, QUOTED IN *VESTI*, 2011

Russia will be among the 5 largest economies in the next two to three years.

—VLADIMIR PUTIN, QUOTED IN *VESTI*, 2012

Our goal is to make Russia one of the top 5 global economies by 2024.

—VLADIMIR PUTIN, QUOTED IN *RT*, 2017

Russia Ditches Goal of Becoming Top 5 Economy by 2024.

—*MOSCOW TIMES*, JULY 21, 2020

RUSSIA'S BANKING SECTOR is a problem.[1] While a handful of top banks that dominate the market, like Alfa-Bank, Bank VTB, and Sberbank, have improved their service and corporate governance in recent years, Russia has long had many "washing machines": banks that exist to launder money, hide income, and enable risky transactions that put depositors at risk. These banks deliver vast benefits to narrow groups of bank owners who typically have good connections with the authorities.

But they also raise the likelihood of a banking crisis that can spark protests by depositors and drain government coffers with bailouts. Banking crises are politically dangerous because they do not just hurt regime insiders linked to these banks; they also raise the prospects of popular unrest from those who lose their savings.

Enter Elvira Sakhipzadovna Nabiullina, a former academic economist with few ties to Putin's inner circle who has headed the Russian Central Bank since 2013.[2] Under her supervision, the Central Bank has skillfully managed the price of the ruble, kept inflation in check through several shocks, and reduced the number of banking licenses from 982 in 2012 to 484 in January 2019.[3] For her efforts, *Euromoney* named her Central Bank Governor of the Year in 2015, and the *Banker* named her Central Banker of the Year for Europe in 2017.

But she does not have an easy job. Banks with good political connections are hard to close even if they pose risks for the economy. In June 2017, the Russian Central Bank revoked the license of Bank Yugra, one of the country's thirty largest banks, for failing to pay debts, misreporting its financial condition, and transferring assets from the bank to its owners.[4] The majority owner of Bank Yugra was Alexei Khotin, one of the hundred richest Russians, who just happened to be the "main sponsor of the Night Hockey League in which the star player and top goal scorer is President Vladimir Putin."[5] The general prosecutor of Russia took the unusual step of publicly disputing the claims of the Central Bank and calling for the reinstatement of Bank Yugra's license. The Russian Central Bank had to appeal to prosecutors six times to press charges against the bank for siphoning assets without avail before finally revoking its license—a decision that was upheld in a Moscow court in 2018. Khotin was put under house arrest in summer 2019. Surely other dodgy banks with better connections have escaped the reaches of the Central Bank.

This example highlights a central dilemma of Russia's political economy that is familiar to students of comparative autocracy. Distort the economy too much with sweetheart deals for your friends and economic growth will slow, with all the inherent risks of provoking popular discontent. Remove the distortions, however, and risk losing the support of key political allies who benefit from these distortions in the economy. Managing the Russian economy is more akin to a balancing act than simple theft (although there is plenty of that as well). Maintaining this balance is much easier when the economy is booming, but a challenge as the economic pie shrinks. With many hungry elites to feed and a mass public to satisfy, Putin has far from a free hand in the economy.

The bias toward regime cronies that marks autocratic rule has real consequences. The evidence is not clear-cut, but on balance autocracies tend to grow more slowly than democracies.[6] Autocracies experience more volatile economic performance and are more likely to get stuck in long periods of stagnation.[7] One area where autocracies outperform democracies is in faking their data on economic growth. One study of 179 countries between 1990 and 2008 showed that the difference between the official economic growth data reported by the government and the intensity of nighttime light usage—a common proxy for economic development that is much harder for the government to fudge—was higher in autocracies than democracies.[8]

And among autocracies, personalist regimes tend to perform worse than single-party ones. Personalist autocracies are less able to survive economic shocks and have higher rates of corruption than do other types of autocracies.[9] The political logic of personalist autocracies hinders economic development in large part by skewing the playing field toward regime insiders. For example, expropriations and the sale of private firms to owners supportive of the autocrat have been a key feature of economic policy in Hungary, Turkey, and Venezuela in recent years. Journalist Rory Carroll points out that Chávez's policies of nationalization, currency controls, and cronyism created a class of "Boligarchs," a pun on Chávez's beloved Simon Bolivar, while Balint Magyar, a former Hungarian politician, describes in great detail how Orban and his close associates took over hundreds of firms to create what he calls a "mafia state" in Hungary.[10] Beyond expropriations, each of these personalist autocracies has seen dramatic increases in perceived corruption following their autocratic turn.[11] Draining the swamp is not on the agenda in personalist autocracies.[12]

This chapter focuses on distortions introduced by political connections, hostile corporate takeovers, and corruption. These topics are difficult to study given their innate opacity. Few who engage in these activities are willing to talk, and those who do usually have incentives to misrepresent their actions. Businesspeople often inflate their political connections to impress investors while downplaying them to law enforcement. Former regime insiders or political activists frequently have an ax to grind and selective memories. Occasionally we get lucky and find a paper trail as in the Panama Papers, which among other things, revealed that Sergei Roldugin, a cellist and old friend of Putin, had amassed a fortune of $2 billion without any obvious source, leading many to speculate that he was merely holding these funds for his now high-placed friend.[13] Despite the challenges, academics have developed a range of tools to help us understand these important topics. But I begin by presenting some background on the Russian economy.

Russia's Economy since 2000

Russia's economy under Putin can be divided into two periods. From 2000 to 2014, Russia experienced one of the greatest economic booms in its history. Thanks to a ruble devaluation in August 1998, impressive economic reforms in the early 2000s, and high oil prices, the size of the Russian economy doubled in less than a decade. The global financial crisis in 2008–9 hit Russia hard, but growth rates quickly turned positive even if they fell short of previous highs. During the boom, the Russian government courted foreign investment, joined the World Trade Organization, and put aside more than $500 billion in reserve funds. It also went on a buying spree that dramatically increased the role of the state in the economy. Ownership in the important oil sector went from 10 percent to more than 80 percent.

Living standards in Russia soared. Car sales doubled between 2006 and 2009, and travel abroad became far more common. Homeownership increased as mortgages became affordable for an increasing number of

Russians. Even as the number of billionaires soared, the poverty rate was cut in half between 1999 and 2012.

Public infrastructure too improved. A good example comes from Ulyanovsk, a city of six hundred thousand that is best known as Lenin's birthplace. In 1988, the authorities began building a bridge to stretch more than three miles across the Volga River, but funds soon dried up, and for almost two decades, frustrated drivers could see the half-built structure in the middle of the river that did not reach either shore as they jockeyed for space on a crowded bridge in terrible traffic jams. Thanks to high oil prices and good macroeconomic policy, the government found funds for the project and the new structure now known as the President's Bridge was completed in 2009.

Since 2014, however, the Russian economy has been a bust. A sharp drop in oil prices in 2014–15 led to almost two years of negative growth. Growth returned in 2016, but only on the order of 1 to 2 percent. Real incomes in 2019 for the average Russian remained below the levels of 2014—and are falling as COVID-19 wreaks havoc on the Russian and global economy. Observers expect a sharp decline in 2020, with future prospects for growth quite limited.

During the bust, foreign direct investment dried up as economic sanctions imposed against Russian elites deterred many corporations from working with their former partners.[14] In response, Russia levied countersanctions against European and US companies that banned many agricultural products favored by the emerging Russian middle class. The severing of trading ties increased Russia's economic isolation, and spurred an exodus of foreign businesspeople and their families from Moscow. Traditional Russian breakfast staples like *grechka* replaced boxed cereals at Moscow's Marriot Tverskaya, a brunch spot once popular with expatriate families.

Having abandoned early policies of liberal economic reforms and oil-led growth in the boom period, Putin responded to the bust with a program of state-led development centered on twelve "national projects" ranging from infrastructure to digital innovation to agriculture that were supposed to use massive state spending to wake the economy from its slumber. But the national projects have been a disappointment,

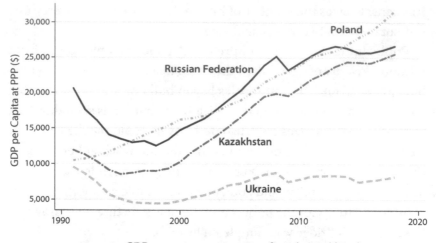

FIGURE 6.1. GDP per capita over time. Data from the World Bank,
World Development Indicators.

in part because the government has been unable to spend its massive
surpluses despite Putin's entreaties to do so.[15] The central government
expresses concern that the funds will be embezzled by officials in the
bureaucracy, and some bureaucrats are wary that they will be accused
of corruption if the projects fail.

Observers often attribute factors unique to Russia to account for its
economic performance. Over the last thirty years, though, patterns of
economic growth have been similar to, if somewhat worse than, another
nearby oil-rich personalist autocracy, Kazakhstan, which began the
transition poorer than Russia on a per capita basis, but became about
as wealthy by 2018. More broadly, economic growth in Russia has been
worse than in Poland and much better than in Ukraine. Figure 6.1 reports changes in the level of GDP per capita over the last thirty years in
current US dollars.

As Russia enters the global recession induced by COVID-19, it has
impressive financial reserves, little inflation, and low unemployment,
but is plagued by weak rule of law, vast corruption, and an excessive reliance on volatile international commodity prices. Even if the economy
recovers quickly from the shock of the pandemic, prospects for economic growth for the next decade are dim.[16]

For many observers, the Russian economy is a basket case. A prominent banker noted, "Russia is an economic pipsqueak—apart from its nukes and its ability to make cyberwarfare, it certainly is not a bear."[17] This goes too far. At market exchange rates, which is a common way to compare these things, Russia's economy produced goods worth about $1.6 trillion in 2019—about as much as produced in Canada and South Korea. By this measure, Russia's economy was the twelfth largest in the world. Taking into account local prices, Russia's economy was the sixth largest at $4.3 trillion, behind Germany at $4.4 trillion and ahead of the next five largest economies: Indonesia, Brazil, France, the United Kingdom, and Mexico.[18] Russia is a solidly middle-income country where per capita income is on par with Greece, Turkey, and Latvia.[19] A World Bank study from 2019 that focused on accumulated wealth rather than on income found that the average Russian was about 1.7 times wealthier in 2017 than in 2000, but was still only about one-quarter as wealthy as the average resident in a developed economy.

Like Brazil, Mexico, Malaysia, Argentina, Venezuela, and other resource-rich middle-income economies, Russia struggles to manage the volatility of international commodity prices that are central to the state budget, has an inefficient state sector, and lacks the strong state institutions to promote competition and protect property rights found in upper-income countries.

But these problems are exacerbated by Russia's political system. Like all politicians, personalist autocrats have to balance special interests against the general interests of the mass public. Democratic rulers aim to satisfy the median voter, and one-party-led regimes aim to satisfy the median member of the party, but rulers in personalist autocracies aim to satisfy a much smaller group of regime insiders while also producing enough growth to keep the masses at bay.

A good example comes from Russia's energy sector, which delivers great benefits to regime insiders while also being a critical source of funds for state social programs. In 2017, oil and gas provided one-quarter of the GDP, 39 percent of the federal budget revenues, two-thirds of foreign earnings from exports, and almost a quarter of the overall investments in the national economy.[20] Russia ranks first, second, and third in the export of gas, oil, and coal, respectively. The most prominent companies in the oil and gas sector, Rosneft' and Gazprom, are majority state-owned, but their shares also trade on international markets.[21] The federal government reaps the benefits of booms in oil prices as revenue generated above a fixed price reverts to the government budget rather than to the companies.

Gazprom is one of the largest gas companies in the world, and for many years, was the single-largest contributor to the federal budget.[22] Much of this revenue comes from the export of gas to Europe, where Russia is the lowest-cost provider thanks to its proximity and pipelines. Gazprom's owners and management make up a powerful lobby in favor of increasing exports as a way to boost the company's revenue. The perks of holding a high position in Gazprom are legendary. Popular Russian singer Semyon Slepakov even penned an ode to Gazprom in which he pleads to become a shareholder and promises to be a model Gazprom citizen by spending his birthday on the French Riviera, building three homes on the Park Avenue of Moscow, and buying a thirty-meter yacht so he will blend in with the other Gazprom shareholders.

At the same time, Gazprom literally keeps the lights on in many Russian cities by providing gas to utility companies at below-market prices. It props up employment by subsidizing loss-making firms that would otherwise have to lay off workers.[23] Reducing these subsidies to firms would benefit Gazprom's bottom line, but would raise electricity costs and spike unemployment, thereby generating political instability. Gas prices are a sensitive topic in many countries, especially in Russia, and the Kremlin faces the challenge of balancing the demands of energy barons against those of the general public.

Indeed, the energy sector is crucial for other social programs. Russia's social safety net is patchy, but the public is sensitive to cuts in these programs. Pensions are small yet regular, and adjusting them is difficult. Rounds of pension reform in 2005 and 2018 sharply reduced President Putin's approval ratings. The poverty rate crept up from 12 percent in 2012 to around 14 percent in 2017, but it is still a far cry from the 29 percent rate of 2000.[24]

The Russian state provides free health care and spends about 3.5 percent of the total state budget to this end, but the quality of service is uneven, and public opinion polls suggest great dissatisfaction.[25] To receive better service, citizens pay relatively small bribes to health care professionals. Surveys indicate that only the police are more likely to receive bribes.[26] In funding health care, Russia faces demographic problems common in Europe: an aging population (the median age in Russia is thirty-eight), which increases demand for health care, and a shrinking workforce of those who pay into state health care programs. To compensate for these shortcomings, spending on private health care has increased over the last decade and now accounts for about one–third of total health care spending. In addition, about a half-million Russians travel abroad for medical treatment.[27]

Russia's response to the coronavirus highlights some of the pathologies of autocratic rule. As with elections, official statistics about the pandemic tell a narrative favored by the Kremlin, but are met with some skepticism by experts. Russia uses a nonstandard method of tallying coronavirus deaths that many believe leads to undercounting. In addition, health officials are reluctant to report bad news to governors, and governors are equally reluctant to report bad news to Moscow. As a result, many coronavirus deaths have likely gone unreported. One indication is that in May and June 2020, excess fatalities were three times higher than the average monthly death tally over the last five years (26,3600) even as the reported coronavirus figures were just 9,303.[28]

In addition, because Russia lacks free and fair elections to legitimate its rule, the Kremlin relies on other ways to bolster its claim to power, such as outcompeting wealthier and more technologically advanced countries in the race to produce a vaccine against the coronavirus. In August 2020, the Kremlin announced the creation of a coronavirus vaccine well ahead of other countries, but the World Health Organization and other experts sharply criticized Russia for moving its vaccine to market before completing standard tests for effectiveness and safety.[29]

The Russian public has treated pronouncements from the Kremlin about the coronavirus with its usual dose of skepticism. A survey from August 2020 found just 38 percent of Russians reported that they would be willing to use Russia's vaccine if it was free and voluntary, and more than half thought the vaccine was not ready for use despite assurances from the Kremlin.[30] The Kremlin's public relations efforts run against a deep strain of skepticism toward vaccinations in Russia. A global survey of 140 countries from 2018 found that while eight in ten respondents agreed that "vaccines are safe," only one in two Russians held this view. Russia was among the countries most distrustful of vaccinations.[31]

The quality of health care in Russia leaves something to be desired, but education has been a relative bright spot. Russia spends only about 6 percent of the state budget on education. This figure is on the low end among the developed economies of the OECD, and is on par with spending in Japan, the Czech Republic, and Hungary. But education is a valuable asset for Russia: 58 percent of Russians between the ages of twenty-five and thirty-four have completed higher education. Only Korea and Japan score higher on this measure among the forty-seven advanced countries of the OECD.[32] The chief economist of the European Bank for Reconstruction and Development noted that "even adjusting for the quality of education, Russia is much more educated than other countries at its level of income."[33] And while Russia fell short of its ambitious goals of putting five universities in the top one hundred universities in the world by 2020, its top universities have made gains in the last five years in the QS university rankings.[34]

The problems of balancing the interests of regime insiders and the general public are also made more severe by Russia's great inequality. The data are far from perfect as the ultrarich often hide their wealth. One study found that Russians held as much wealth in offshore accounts as they do in onshore accounts in Russia.[35] But by some measures, Russia is among the most unequal countries in the world, in part due to the large number of millionaires and billionaires given its level of wealth. In 2013, Credit Suisse reported that Russia had 112 billionaires—second only to the United States at 326.[36] In 2016, economist Thomas Piketty and his team of researchers found that the share of income held by the top 10 percent in Russia was as high as in the United States, and about 50 percent larger than in France. Moreover, the share of income held by the top 1 percent in Russia was about twice that found in Poland, Hungary, or the Czech Republic.[37]

Political scientist Daniel Treisman crunched the numbers from the *Forbes* ranking of the richest people in the world over the last fifteen years. He found that Russia has more billionaires than one would expect given its level of wealth, but also that the vast majority of them earned their wealth in the boom years of the 2000s rather than from the privatizations of the 1990s, and that most billionaires owed their wealth to sectors outside energy like real estate, telecoms, agriculture, and finance. Treisman discovered that the volatility of the wealth of Russian billionaires was far higher than for billionaires in other countries like the United States, China, and Germany.[38] In addition, the sources of volatility changed over time. If political pressure tended to push people off the *Forbes* list in the early 2000s (think Khodorkovsky and Yukos), in the last decade Russian billionaires were much more likely to succumb to global market conditions and economic sanctions. That outright expropriations of large firms are less frequent may be due to a greater willingness of high-net-worth individuals to accommodate state officials rather than risk losing their assets. Many wealthy and superwealthy individuals who have found themselves on the wrong side of the Kremlin have left Russia in the Putin years.

The World Bank estimates Russia's level of inequality using the Gini coefficient at 0.38, about 10 points higher than Finland (0.27) and Poland (0.30), about 15 points lower than Brazil (0.53) and Colombia (0.51), and about the same as in the United States (0.41) and Turkey (0.41).[39] Given the difficulty of measuring inequality, these figures are rough at best, but indicate that Russia's income inequality is pronounced.

Russia's inequality is not only great between individuals; it is also great across Russia's regions. Moscow and Saint Petersburg have benefited most from economic growth—often on a spectacular scale. And in any large city, there are now a range of decent hotels and Airbnb options abound. There are Jaguar dealerships in every city with more than a million residents, indicating that high-end wealth is not limited to Moscow.[40]

But economic growth has not transformed the small towns and villages where about one-third or so of Russians live. From the mountain villages of North Caucasus to the small towns of central Russia and Siberia, these depopulated areas, frequently with large numbers of pensioners, live according to the agricultural calendar rather than the booms and busts of the national economy.[41]

Despite having a well-educated populace, a good mix of industry and agriculture, a large internal market, and much reasonable (if often ignored) policy advice, Russia has been mired in slow growth for a decade. In 2018, the average Kazakh became just about as wealthy as the average Russian.[42] Russia's economy is driven far more by international commodity prices and geopolitical events, like the imposition of sanctions and the pandemic, than by sound policy or technological innovations. On its own, it generates little economic dynamism.

The Political Economy of Autocracy

Russia's economic stagnation is rooted in part in its cronyism. Without a level playing field, economic rewards go not to the most innovative and efficient but to those who are best connected to the autocrat. Many studies have documented the vast wealth of individuals in Putin's inner circle. Some of these ties go back to the cooperative Ozero and Bank Rossiya in Saint Petersburg in the mid-1990s, when Putin was a vice governor of the region. Of the seven founding Ozero members outside Putin, three—Vladimir Yakunin, Yuri Kovalchuk, and Nikolai Shamalov—have regularly appeared on lists of Russia's richest compiled each year by the Russian version of *Forbes*, as do other Putin associates from this period such as Arkady and Boris Rotenberg and Gennady Timchenko.[43]

Political scientist Natalia Lamberova and economist Konstantin Sonin used open sources to study twenty-four members of Putin's inner circle who had close familial or personal ties to Putin prior to his move to Moscow. Compared to other members of the superwealthy on the *Forbes* list, members of Putin's inner circle saw their income grow far faster, particularly when oil prices where high. The effects were enormous. Lamberova and Sonin estimate that when oil prices were above $70 per barrel, members of the inner circle reaped $800 million a year more than other Russian members of the *Forbes* list.[44] When oil prices were low, however, members of the inner circle saw their incomes fall further than did other superrich Russians. Personal connections at the highest level appear to be a double-edged sword and depend a good deal on energy prices. This kind of cronyism is common in personalist autocracies, where rulers and their close allies enrich themselves at the expense of taxpayers and other elites, but given the size of the economy in Russia the opportunities for enrichment are much larger.

We know a good deal less about personal connections beyond the superwealthy in Russia. These kinds of political connections are difficult to study not only because they are opaque but also because business-people who develop strong connections with politicians may be good at running firms. Many of the same skills associated with developing political connections are associated with success in the marketplace too: ambition, preexisting wealth, location, and educational ties, among other things.

David Szakonyi found a clever way to unpack this problem. He began by scouring the web to gather publicly available financial data on twenty-seven hundred firms between 2003 and 2012. Then he examined all twelve thousand candidates who ran for office in regional parliaments during this period, and compared the performance of firms whose director ran for office and won a seat versus those whose director ran and lost in a close race. This comparison helps to rule out a host of other possible explanations related to the individual traits of the businessperson and the firm.

He found that firms with CEOs who won a seat in the regional legislature boosted their company's revenue over a term in office by 60 percent and their profitability by 15 percent relative to those firm owners who also ran for a seat and lost. These businesspeople/politicians excelled in large part because they were better able to access state procurement contracts. They were about 40 percent more likely to win a contract from the state budget than were firms whose managers ran and lost in the election. Moreover, these results hold not just for United

Russia deputies but also businesspeople/deputies in other parties. Holding a seat in a regional parliament in Russia is lucrative.[45]

Michael Rochlitz, Evhenia Mitrokhina, and Irina Nivzolina took a different approach, studying how even the mention of support from United Russia can influence the response of the bureaucracy. They contacted more than 180 local government investment agencies across seventy regions in Russia. These agencies are designed to be nonpartisan and independent, and have a purely economic function: to attract potential investors to the region as well as support businesses in the region with advice and information.

Between December 2016 and June 2017, the researchers sent short emails to these agencies in which a fictitious businessperson named Alexander Shabolov expressed an interest in investing and asked for some basic information about government support in the region. The researchers randomly varied features of Shabolov's firm such as its political affiliation and nationality.[46] For example, some emails mentioned that the investor had a relationship with the pro-government United Russia, while others noted ties to the Communist Party of the Russian Federation, the nationalist Liberal Democratic Party of Russia, or Yabloko, a long-standing liberal opposition party that had not earned seats in Parliament since 2003.

These agencies were responsive: 57 percent of them replied. But investors describing a relationship with United Russia were about 11 percentage points more likely to receive a response than were other firms, while those mentioning a relationship with the opposition party Yabloko were about 16 percentage points less likely to receive a response. In other words, switching the political affiliation of a potential investor from the opposition party Yabloko to the government party United Russia on average increased the chances of receiving a reply by about 30 percent. Mentioning other parties had no effect.

Rochlitz, Mitrokhina, and Nivzolina also found that the regional bureaucrats discriminated against investors representing a firm from China, but not against investors from firms in the United States or Germany. Investors from firms with ties to China were 6 percentage points less likely to receive a response than were other investors.[47] This is somewhat surprising given that Germany and the United States had placed sanctions on Russia in 2014, and the Russian government was touting the importance of building economic ties with China.

This experiment is stylized, and one can question the economic importance of receiving inquiries about government programs, but it gives a good sense of how political connections can skew the playing field in everyday business practices far from the spotlight or electoral arena.

Corporate Raiding

These kinds of connections also play a role in the politically motivated expropriations of private firms that are a common feature of personalist autocracies in Hungary, Turkey, and Venezuela.[48] Known as *reiderstvo* in Russian, these corporate raids are often hostile in the literal sense of the word.[49] One typical pattern is for a private firm to bribe state security officials to raid the premises of an economic rival and arrest the owner until they agree to sell the firm at a reduced price. By arresting firm owners (frequently) on dubious charges, filing suits in friendly jurisdictions, and bribing state officials to take their side, corporate raiders can often take over firms and strip their assets for themselves. As one practitioner of this dark art noted, "These are not raids. We do not take enterprises away. We minimize their market value by means of various instruments. As a rule, these are voluntary-coercive measures using administrative levers. However, people usually figure out where we come from," he said, before adding that his firm employed relatives of high-ranking officials in the presidential administration and FSB.[50]

A professor at the Russian Academy of the Ministry of Internal Affairs put the scale of these "voluntary-coercive measures" in perspective: "In 2007, out of 211,000 criminal cases involving economic crimes only 16 percent were brought to court. It is obvious. These charges were used as a means of blackmail."[51] According to one report, between 2000 and 2009, about 15 percent of Russian businesspeople faced criminal charges for financial crimes.[52] Running a business in Russia is not for the faint of heart.

Prominent examples of hostile takeovers include the expropriation of Yukos, the largest oil company in Russia in 2003, and the forced sale of the oil company Bashneft' in 2016. Both companies ended up as part of Rosneft', the oil giant run by longtime Putin associate Igor' Sechin. These instances are well known, but many firms in Russia operate under threat of expropriation by the state, a rival, or some combination of the two on a daily basis. Each year about a hundred thousand business-people are charged with economic crimes, and the number of such cases increased by about one-third in 2019. As the economy stagnated, cor-porate raiding took on new momentum.[53]

To get some sense of the scale of the problem, my colleague Andrei Yakovlev and I surveyed company managers at more than nine hundred firms across Russia in December 2011, and found that one in eight thought it was "very likely" that their firm would be taken over by the state or a rival using illegal means in the next two years. And only half of the firms considered this scenario to be "very unlikely."

From a research point of view, we got lucky when halfway through our survey, the ruling party had the surprisingly poor showing in the Duma elections discussed in the last chapter. This allowed us to exam-ine how businesspeople responded to the political shock of United Rus-sia's poor performance by looking at the responses of firm managers interviewed just before and after the elections. We found that managers in the most vulnerable types of firms interviewed mere days after the election were about 10 percentage points less likely to say that their firm would be taken over by the state than those interviewed just days before the election. Businesspeople viewed the poor showing of United Russia as a sign that state pressure on their firms would decline.[54]

The economic effects of *reiderstvo* are difficult to measure, but re-searchers have found that firms that expect to be the target of a raid invest at much lower rates than other firms, and this lack of confidence in their property is a major drag on the economy.[55] As a result of these kinds of threats and other forms of bureaucratic harassment, many Rus-sians prefer to park their wealth (and often their bodies as well) outside Russia. By one estimate, capital flight from Russia amounted to $250 to $300 billion between 2014 and 2018.[56] In the year 2018 alone, Russia saw a net outflow of $68 billion thanks in part to economic sanctions, but also to Russia's weak property rights.[57]

The Kremlin's efforts to compel oligarchs to bring their piles of cash back to Russia have had mixed success at best. In 2014, the Russian Parliament passed a law on "de-offshoring," thereby forcing Russian taxpayers to declare their interest in offshore companies so that they can be liable for taxes in Russia. This is a common practice, but was new to Russia, where taxpayers did not have to declare these foreign holdings. One survey of three hundred wealthy Russians found that in response to the law, as many as 40 percent of those with offshore holdings had given up residency in Russia and preferred to live abroad for at least half the year rather than report their overseas holdings to Russian authorities. In discussing this issue, the dean of the Moscow School of Management at Skolkovo, Andrei Sharonov, asserted, "The first thing entrepreneurs say is that there is a big sense of mistrust: mistrust toward each other, mistrust toward the state."[58] In another sign of insecurity, Russian oligarchs keep more of their wealth in cash in US dollars than do the wealthy in any other developed country according to a report in *Bloomberg*.[59]

The Russian government has acknowledged the problem. Even President Putin admonished officials in the security services for engaging in "extortion masquerading as state service."[60] The Kremlin has taken small steps by creating an ombudsperson who collects data on hostile corporate takeovers, but protecting private firms by strengthening the courts, reducing the power of the security services to jail businesspeople before trial, or making ownership more transparent would hurt the interests of powerful businesspeople in league with state officials who benefit from hostile takeovers. And Putin has sided with the latter. Despite expectations that he would grant a sweeping amnesty for many of the more than a hundred thousand businesspeople in jail for economic crimes according to a plan adopted by his predecessor, Putin freed just thirteen hundred in 2013 under this plan.[61]

Corruption

We can also view Russia's corruption through this frame. Corruption benefits narrow groups that typically support Putin, but imposes costs on society. Scholars often divide corruption into grand corruption, involving high-level officials engaged in bribery, theft, or abuse of power, and petty corruption, involving low-level officials who request small bribes for avoiding traffic tickets, getting permits, or receiving government services, such as health care or education.

Grand corruption in Russia is illustrated by an old joke. Economic ministers from two countries meet in private. From her office window, the first says, "See that bridge over there? Twenty percent went right into my pocket." A year later the second finance minister hosts the first. From her office window, she points to a river and asks, "Do you see that bridge?" The first finance minister replies, "What bridge?" And the second finance minister answers, "One hundred percent went right into my pocket."

Grand corruption in Russia is massive, and cases of pure theft are not hard to find, but Russia is more like country one above. Private companies inflate their costs on state contracts, yet they usually deliver a product at the end of the day.[62] Roads get built, but they are expensive in large part due to kickbacks to government officials for receiving contracts. One study from the World Bank found that the cost of building a road is three to six times cheaper in Finland than in Russia despite the almost identical climactic conditions.[63]

This logic is especially true for high-profile projects like the World Cup, Sochi Olympics, or the new bridge connecting Crimea to Russia. For the Sochi Olympics, Russia built a thirty-mile road for over $5 billion. The geographic conditions were challenging, but for the same price one could have paved the road with an eight-inch layer of foie gras.[64] That the head of the state agency in charge of construction at the Sochi games was replaced four times in six years—with each dismissal followed by charges of embezzlement and abuse of office—gives further evidence of grand corruption on this prestigious project. At the same time, stadiums, roads, and hotels were built, and the Olympic games in Sochi were largely considered a success despite many predictions of failure.[65]

More mundane examples exist as well. On the back of the oil boom of the 2000s, developers and the city government built Moscow City, a cluster of skyscrapers that includes the tallest building in Europe.

Construction companies grew rich, but the project struggled for years. At Moscow City's nadir, office space in one of the skyscrapers was used as a youth hostel.[66] It has turned around in recent years, but not after experiencing massive losses. White elephants like these that reward the politically connected by misusing taxpayer funds are common in autocracies. One academic study found that nondemocracies are much more likely to build new skyscrapers and use them less efficiently than are democracies.[67]

Like grand corruption, petty corruption exhibits a familiar trade-off between producing benefits for insiders and costs for the mass public. Noah Buckley of Trinity College Dublin took advantage of a remarkable set of nationwide surveys of more than 180,000 respondents between 2001 and 2016 that ask Russians about their experiences with petty corruption. Surveys on petty bribery are always suspect because respondents may be less than forthcoming, but Buckley uses a variety of techniques to establish the veracity of the data. Because petty corruption is widely discussed in the media, often goes unpunished, and is acknowledged even by state officials, respondents may be willing to talk about it in general terms. Buckley found that about 15 to 20 percent of the respondents were willing to report giving small bribes in any given year. Wealthier, more educated respondents as well as business owners were more likely to report giving bribes, while those who voted for United Russia reported giving fewer bribes. To the best we can determine, most bribes in petty corruption are small (less than half of a monthly salary), but larger bribes are not uncommon. The respondents reported that the police and traffic police were most likely to ask for bribes, with state officials in health care and education not too far behind.

Buckley discovered an interesting political pattern in the data too. In years when governors were scheduled to have their appointment renewed—either by election or presidential appointment—respondents in the governor's region reported less petty corruption than in other years. It seems that Russian governors curtail petty corruption in appointment years to reduce the possibility of a public scandal that might hurt their chances of retaining their position, but allow insiders in the bureaucracy to earn more from corruption in nonappointment years.[68]

The government is aware of the high cost of corruption, but its attempts to address the problem have been half-hearted. These efforts give the appearance of battling corruption, and have some effects at the margin, but fail to address the root problem because doing so would anger key constituents within the state.

For example, in 2009 the government passed legislation requiring Duma deputies and other high officials to report their annual wealth using a standard form. This is a common anticorruption measure. Duma deputies duly complied and reported their income, although doubts remained about the veracity of many of the reports. Journalists began writing articles about the sudden increase in wealth of the spouses of Duma members as many members of the Parliament apparently transferred wealth to their spouses to avoid declaring it. In 2013, the Duma passed new legislation requiring Duma deputies to report the wealth of their spouses and underage children as well. Forced to choose between money and marriage, 102 of Russia's 450 Duma deputies divorced their spouses in the next legislative session before the law would take effect. Thirty deputies divorced in the last two months before the legislation went into effect. For comparison, only seven divorces occurred in the entire prior legislative session, suggesting that many Duma deputies chose money over marriage.[69] Of course, many of the post-2013 divorces were in name only. In 2016, legislators from the Communist Party of the Russian Federation proposed legislation compelling the former as well as current spouses of Duma deputies to report their income. They also tried to broaden the definition of marriage to include those who divorced legally yet "remained in marital relations," but the legislation went nowhere.[70]

Duma deputies also like to fake their educational credentials. An anonymous watchdog group in Russia known as Dissernet.ru takes advantage of the requirement that all PhD dissertations in Russia be made public. It scrubs the web and other sources to root out academic fraud, and found that one in nine members of the Russian Parliament had plagiarized parts of their dissertation or had fake academic degrees.[71] Researchers at the Brookings Institution in Washington, DC, also found that parts of Putin's master's thesis on resource management were taken word for word from other sources.[72] Ironically, Putin borrowed from a textbook written by two US scholars.[73]

As a codirector of our research institute at the HSE, I have felt the consequences of the government's attempts to reduce corruption and kickbacks. About a decade ago, the government instituted an online bidding system for all state entities—including the HSE—designed to reduce sweetheart deals between buyers and sellers by increasing transparency. In many countries, state procurement is an opaque and corrupt activity dominated by kickbacks to sellers and inflated pricing. As a state organization, our institute bids out all large purchases via this online system. Whether it reduces corruption is an open question, but it requires an enormous amount of paperwork, time, and effort. One lesson I've learned is that being honest in a corrupt system is a real headache, in part because government attempts to reduce corruption increase paperwork for those of us who follow the rules.

———

There is a saying among Russia watchers that Russia is neither as strong nor weak as it appears, and nowhere is this more apt than in the economy. The economy moves—sometimes sharply—with shifts in energy prices and geopolitics. But of its own accord, it produces neither booms nor busts. This muddling through is rooted in the politics of autocracy, which lead rulers to balance the conflicting interests of their cronies against those of their citizens, with the former usually having the upper hand.

As a result, Russia's economic outlook is far from rosy.[74] The macroeconomy is in good shape and has been for much of the Putin era, but with oil and gas facing increased challenges from renewable energy sources, powerful insiders well placed to block much-needed structural reforms to the economy, and few obvious sources of economic growth for the long term, Russia will fall further behind its rivals. The Putin administration not only needs to address the economic crisis induced by the 2020 pandemic but also find new sources of economic growth going forward; otherwise, the political problems of satisfying both elite cronies and the mass public will grow more challenging over time.

My only one-on-one meeting with an oligarch illustrates this favoritism. In summer 2012, one of Russia's richest people invited me to his residence in Barvikha, the toniest suburb outside Moscow, to discuss his plans to create a research center on international conflict, perhaps in cooperation with Columbia University. The oligarch's driver picked me up in the center of town, and we made our way past Moscow's nondescript residential districts. Shortly after crossing the city line, the greenery thickened, traffic jams dissolved, and the road grew smooth. On the right, we passed a small auto dealership offering Maseratis, Porsches, and Bentleys, and a strip mall of stores featuring Gucci, Ralph Lauren, and Dolce & Gabbana before approaching the estate. With its high gates, over-the-top decor, and an army of staff that seemed to appear from nowhere, the residence was just what one would expect.

About halfway through dinner, my host took a phone call. He said it was the new minister of industry, who had just been appointed earlier that day, calling to check in and pay his respects as if it was perfectly natural for high state officials to do so after taking office. After dinner, we retreated to the garden for tea and sweets, and took in the splendor of Moscow's long summer nights. On leaving at 10 p.m., I bumped into the governor of the region that was home to the oligarch's major economic asset as he was coming to pay my host a visit. Would that the Russian state was so solicitous of all its citizens.

7

Hitting Them with Carrots

THE ROLE OF REPRESSION

In Russia, we use carrots and sticks. When we are done hitting them with sticks, then we hit them with carrots.

—A RUSSIAN JOKE

OVER THE YEARS, Russia has seen high-profile murders of business-people, journalists, and the occasional vice governor, but none shocked like the killing of Boris Nemtsov on a bridge steps from the Kremlin just before midnight on February 27, 2015. A former governor and vice minister under President Yeltsin, Nemtsov had not held political office since 2003 and had become an outspoken critic of the Kremlin. With a small following of liberal activists, Nemtsov organized regular protests against the Kremlin, and had become a vocal opponent of the annexation of Crimea and Russia's role in the war in eastern Ukraine, but his efforts were finding little traction in a Russia enthralled by its new status on the world stage. Nonetheless, on March 1, more than fifty thousand demonstrators marched in central Moscow to protest his murder.

Rumors soon swirled. He was killed because he was preparing a report on Russian involvement in the war in Ukraine—an involvement denied by the Kremlin. He was killed by the former warlord turned governor of Chechnya, Ramzan Kadyrov, who had been a frequent target of Nemtsov's criticism. He was killed by the security services as a message to Putin to take a harder line on the political opposition. In June 2017, a Moscow court found five men from Chechnya guilty of Nemtsov's murder, but the investigation did not uncover who had organized the assassination.

Shortly after the murder, followers built a makeshift memorial of flowers, candles, and testimonials on the bridge where Nemtsov was killed. From time to time, it is removed in the middle of the night, but supporters quickly rebuild the memorial where it stands to this day.

This kind of crude repression is front and center for many commentators. When thinking of Russia's strongman president, visions of a tough guy in a judo belt come to mind whether you want them to or not. This is no coincidence as the Kremlin relies heavily on references to masculinity to bolster Putin's rule.[1] This has led many popular commentators to trace Putin's longevity in power to simple repression. In this view, Putin's power comes at the barrel of a gun, or more often, in subtle forms of everyday intimidation and coercion.

Relying on repression and coercion to stay in power, however, is trickier than the conventional wisdom suggests. Choosing the right level of coercion against political opponents—from brutal forms of repression like mass arrest and executions to subtler forms of coercion like denying promotions, pressuring family members, and arresting opponents for short stays in jail—is no easy task. Too much or too little can produce catastrophic results for the ruler. In addition, relying on coercion typically strengthens the security services, which also present a constraint on the ruler.

Moreover, research indicates that coercion begets more coercion because it typically fails to address the problems underlying political opposition such as corruption, bad economic performance, and distrust in the government.[2] Coercion is a central element of political life in autocracies like Russia, but it is a blunt instrument that involves hard trade-offs for rulers.

To explore this topic, I begin by describing Russia's security agencies before discussing the two most prominent ways that the Kremlin manages political opposition: targeted coercion and autocratic legalism. I then focus on two examples of how the Kremlin balances the costs and benefits of coercion, and conclude by arguing that Putin's increased reliance on repression in recent years is more a result of the failure of other tools for staying in power than of Putin's personal background or Russia's autocratic history.

The *Siloviki*

To understand repression in Russia, it is helpful to know the players. Putin oversees a range of security agencies that have mixed motives. They have a common interest in supporting the Kremlin, keeping the opposition off guard, and protecting Russia against foreign foes, but they also have overlapping agendas, and compete with each other for access to state funds, influence with the Kremlin, and opportunities to shake down private businesses. The competition between agencies helps to prevent the emergence of a single rival to Putin. While many observers recognize the influence of the siloviki (members of the various state security agencies) and their consistent worldview, the big guns do not speak with one unified voice, and have no leader apart from Putin.[3] One feature in common is that these organizations are among the least reformed from the Soviet period, and some are headed by officials who served the Soviet regime prior to 1991.[4] They are also, to varying degrees, unaccountable to the broader public and other parts of the state, such as the Parliament and government.

Putin frequently taps elites with security backgrounds for posts in other parts of the government. About one-quarter of the governors, 20 percent of the presidential administration, and around one-quarter of the heads of state-owned companies are affiliated with the security services in one way or another.[5] The insertion of security officials into various state organizations has served to both weaken the state agencies that now face political oversight and distract the security services from their core missions.[6] Russia is not a military autocracy, like Myanmar or Augusto Pinochet's Chile, but there is little doubt that the security services are key pillars of Putin's support.

The successor to the KGB, the FSB, has pride of place. Not only is the FSB Putin's former employer, but it has great reach into Russian society and maintains an active presence abroad. The FSB oversees counterintelligence, border security, counterterrorism, surveillance, and internal security, while also playing lead roles in the struggle against organized crime. In addition to its legal activities, its agents have been linked to the doping scandal at the Sochi Olympics, cyberhacking against targets in the United States, and crackdowns on NGOs and independent journalists alike. More than just an intelligence-gathering organization, the FSB is considered a military organization under Russian law. Only two men have headed the FSB under Putin. Nikolai Patrushev, who self-servingly hailed the FSB as a "new nobility" that was "united in its sense of service," headed the agency for Putin's first eight years in office before being replaced by Alexander Bortnikov in 2008. Gaining credible evidence on the scope and scale of Russian security agencies is a challenge as they do not publish their budgets or declare their number of employees (although conservative estimates suggest at least two hundred thousand) but the FSB is the most prominent in Russia's internal politics.[7]

The FSB has deep roots in its predecessor and regularly invokes the "heroic" deeds of KGB agents of the past, yet it also operates in a different political environment. The KGB was constrained by the powerful Communist Party of the Soviet Union, which oversaw its operations at every turn, but the FSB faces no other institution that can rival its reach, power, and access to the top leadership.

The Ministry of Defense has undergone a resurgence in recent decades from its low point in the 1990s. It is headed by Sergei Shoigu, one of Russia's longest-serving elites and a much-discussed possible successor to President Putin in the past. The Ministry of Defense oversees Russia's armed forces, which have not only become better equipped in recent years but have gained valuable field experience in Georgia, Syria, and Ukraine too. Its position within Russia has also improved, and the army has become one of Russia's most trusted organizations.[8] The Russian military is involved in everything from counterterrorism to arms sales to nuclear weapons, and competes with the FSB on intelligence gathering, particularly outside Russia. Its military intelligence wing, the GRU, was the lead spear in the election interference operation against the United States in 2016, and has been linked to the poisoning of the Skripal family and a British citizen in the United Kingdom in 2018.[9]

One prominent newcomer is the National Guard. Created in 2016 for the specific purpose of putting down mass revolts within Russia, the National Guard has around three hundred thousand troops at its disposal and reports directly to the president.[10] Some have argued that this praetorian guard was created not only to put down popular revolts but also to discipline potentially disloyal elites.[11] That one of Mikhail Mishustin's first acts as prime minister in January 2020 was to double the pay of those in the National Guard and police responsible for protecting social order gives some idea of their importance.[12]

The Interior Ministry underwent a cosmetic reform in 2011; its main achievement was changing the name of its officers from the militia to the police. Since 2012, the ministry has been headed by career police officer Vladimir Kolokoltsev, who oversees more than one million officers. The police are distrusted by the public and enmeshed in economic crime.[13] The Procuracy oversees criminal investigations and is responsible for ensuring state compliance with the law. These two functions give the Procuracy great leverage both inside and outside the state even as it lacks the armed troops of other security agencies. One competitor to the FSB on economic crime is the Investigative Committee, which has about twenty thousand employees. It was created in 2011 to specialize in gathering evidence and battling corruption, and was quickly accused of engaging in corruption itself.[14]

The heads of these security services are joined by the president, minister of foreign affairs, prime minister, and heads of the two branches of Parliament to form the twelve permanent members of the Security Council, the most powerful body in Russia. The permanent members of the Security Council are among Putin's closest advisers and typically have long ties to the president. In 2020, the average tenure of a permanent member of the Security Council was 8.3 years. Those in charge of economic and social policy in the Russian state come and go, but those who control the big guns in Russia are hard to displace.

The security organizations report to the president, but the Kremlin cannot monitor all the activities of these sprawling agencies, let alone easily direct them. As Russian journalist Mikhail Zygar remarked, "They [those in the Kremlin] would never say, 'Please steal those billions of dollars or please murder those journalists.' They would say, 'Do what you have to do. You know your obligations; please fulfill them.'"[15] Given the vagueness of these kinds of instructions, mistakes occur. Moreover, with this level of ambiguity, security officials have great leeway to pursue their own interests even when they may conflict with those of the Kremlin.

Targeted Coercion and Autocratic Legalism

Authoritarian regimes like Russia vary in their use of repression and coercion. Saddam Hussein in Iraq resorted to electric shocks, beatings, and murder, while Alberto Fujimori in Peru relied far more heavily on bribes than bullets to stay in power.[16] Some regimes like East Germany are repressive without utilizing large-scale violence or mass arrests, whereas others threaten all sectors in society with arbitrary violence as in the Cultural Revolution in Maoist China.

The Soviet epoch offers a range of repressive strategies. As a graduate student, I was a house sitter for two summers for John Hazard, a legendary Columbia University professor who studied at Moscow State University's law department from 1936 to 1938 at the height of the Stalinist purges. During this three-year period, roughly 1 million Soviet citizens died at the hands of the state in a frenzy of nearly unpredictable and unimaginable political violence.[17] One night over dinner, Hazard described how the law school students arrived in the lecture hall one day to find a new professor reading from his predecessor's notes. The new professor said nothing about his predecessor's departure. No one knew precisely why the professor had been arrested or where he had gone, and no one dared to ask given the risk of suffering the same fate.

By the Brezhnev era, repression had become far more predictable. The Soviet state persecuted political dissidents who called for greater rights for ethnic minorities or urged the Communist Party to abide by its international commitments to respect human rights, but most citizens avoided this fate by giving up basic freedoms of speech, association, and travel in exchange for small increases in living standards and a welfare state that provided basic necessities.

The legacy of Soviet-era repressions continues to shape Russian politics today. Yuri Zhukov and Roya Talibova at the University of Michigan sorted through data on the Stalinist terror of the 1930s and political participation in Russia in the 2000s, and found an unusual pattern: electoral districts that suffered the greatest losses during the Stalinist terror exhibited lower rates of voting in every national election in Russia between 2003 and 2012, even controlling for other factors.[18] The Stalinist terror casts a long shadow.

Similarly, a study I published with three colleagues of Muscovites' relations with the local police also found that the social costs of state terror and coercion can be long lived. We surveyed Moscow residents in 2012 and explored their willingness to report various types of everyday crimes, such as petty theft and burglary. Some groups were told that they would be given a small reward if the tip was accurate, but this financial incentive had little effect on responses. Others were told that they would be granted anonymity and this slightly increased reporting rates. A final group was told that it was people's civic duty to report crimes to the police. To our surprise, this prompt reduced the respondents' willingness to report some types of crimes—perhaps reflecting a negative reaction to the reliance on informers who worked with the police during the Soviet era.[19]

Two forms of repression are prominent in Putin's Russia. Targeted coercion is the most straightforward, and occurs when state officials use violence and threats of violence for political ends against specific individuals or groups. Targets may include political activists, aggrieved citizens, or businesspeople who refuse to cooperate. Nemtsov is a good example, but consider also Alexander Litvinenko, poisoned in London via tea laced with polonium; Sergei Magnitsky, the Russian accountant who died in police custody after uncovering a large tax fraud by the Russian security services; Lev Shlosberg, a journalist and regional Duma deputy from Pskov in northwestern Russia who was beaten by unknown thugs after identifying the tombstones of Russian soldiers killed while fighting in eastern Ukraine; or Natalya Estemirova and Anna Politkovskaya, a crusading human rights activist and reporter, respectively, killed in Chechnya and in Moscow more than a decade ago. The details in cases like these differ, and the details matter. Some cases are rooted in politics, and others in economic disputes, and they vary in the intensity of their links to the Kremlin, but all demonstrate the impunity with which state officials can abuse their authority.

Targeted coercion is directed not only against regime opponents in society but also political elites within the state. Given the opacity of elite politics in Russia, studying this topic is a challenge, yet not impossible. Four researchers gathered data on more than 1,000 mayors in Russia's largest cities between 2012 and 2018, and found that 10 percent were arrested during their term, with corruption being the most common charge. Opposition mayors were four times more likely to be arrested than were United Russia mayors, suggesting the political roots of these arrests. But that is not the whole story. Because United Russia mayors were much more common than opposition mayors (771 versus 139), the majority of arrests actually involved pro-regime mayors, some of whom may have fallen afoul of their superiors.

What features made mayors more likely to be arrested? Opposition status to be sure, but the researchers also found two surprising results. First, prior work experience in the state administration or security services had little effect on the likelihood of being arrested. Political connections generated by working within the state did not help protect against mayoral arrest. Second, mayors who were more popular as measured by their margin of victory in elections were much less likely to be arrested, controlling for a range of factors. The authorities appear reluctant to bring charges against popular mayors, perhaps fearing a public backlash. This may be why so many cities in Russia have switched from elected to appointed mayors in recent years.[20]

While high-profile acts of targeted repression garner the most attention, researchers find that marginal groups are especially likely to suffer violations of their rights at the hands of the police and other security agencies. Russian sociologist Ella Paneyakh studied thousands of prosecutions in Russian courts, and discovered that it is the poor, less well educated, and less well connected who were most vulnerable to the everyday predations of Russian state officials. She argues that arresting and sentencing individuals with fewer resources to fight back is less headache for police, prosecutors, and judges who need to hit their numbers to satisfy their superiors.[21] For the average law enforcement official, the weak are much more tempting targets than the powerful.

Autocratic Legalism

In addition to targeted coercion, the Kremlin relies on what scholars call "autocratic legalism"—the use, abuse, and nonuse of the law to promote autocratic ends. This tactic has become a mainstay of modern autocratic regimes from Hungary and Venezuela to Turkey and Kazakhstan.[22] Rather than ban troublesome NGOs, autocrats may prosecute them on tax violations, and argue that it is only following the law and doing what any government would do.[23] Instead of shuttering opposition newspapers, autocrats may dissuade firms from advertising in these papers, thereby starving the paper of revenue.[24] Autocrats may not ban opposition candidates from running for office, but rather require them to overcome absurd bureaucratic hurdles while arguing that all countries have rules for getting on the ballot. As opposed to jailing political opponents, they may open lengthy investigations that sap their foes' time and energy.[25] They may not disband high courts but instead purge disloyal judges on technicalities and stack the court with their supporters.[26]

The essence of autocratic legalism can be summed up in the phrase attributed to Peruvian strongman Oscar R. Benavides Larrea: "For my friends anything, for my enemies, the law." A striking example of this tactic comes from the southern republic of Chechnya, where Ramzan Kadyrov, a former warlord turned governor, pitilessly represses political opponents, the media, and human rights groups while also being lauded by the Kremlin for bringing stability to the region.[27]

Kadyrov not only manipulates formal Russian law but also use sharia law and Chechen customary law known as *adat* to boost his powers. Political scientist Egor Lazarev studied how Kadryrov does it. Despite the repressive environment of Chechnya, Lazarev managed to interview state justice officials, religious leaders, and local elites, conduct a survey of twelve hundred respondents using local interviewers, and gather data on more than a hundred thousand court cases in Chechnya. In great detail, Lazarev depicts how women took on new social roles during the Second Chechen War from 1999 to 2009. With Chechen men in hiding or on the run from Russian troops, Chechen women often became breadwinners for the family, played critical roles as interlocutors between Chechen families and various armed groups, and interacted frequently with state officials. After the war, many of these newly empowered women turned to state courts to defend their rights—far friendlier venues for women than the sharia or adat tribunals. Lazarev finds a sharp increase in the use of state courts by women in Chechnya.[28]

In response, however, Kadyrov subverted the formal legal system and downplayed Russian state courts, while also advocating for an increased role for sharia and adat laws in Chechen society. He praised honor killings and polygamy, which are frequently seen as part of Chechen customs or its local form of sharia even as these practices occasionally draw the ire of authorities in Moscow. Journalist Joshua Yaffa notes that Kadyrov has gone so far as to give his "approval to vigilantes who drove around Grozny firing paintballs at women deemed to be dressed immodestly, and displayed an ambivalent attitude toward so-called honor killings—the murder of family members believed to have brought dishonor on their clan."[29] Lazarev traces this move in favor of sharia and adat laws to Kadyrov's efforts to win the backing of village elders and former rebels who are an important base of support and bastions of Chechen patriarchy.[30]

Autocratic legalism is no less morally objectionable than more visible acts of repression. In some ways, it is more insidious because it is less likely to provoke a response from the public and international community. By justifying repression using legalistic or economic pretenses, these tactics require much greater effort and attention from the public, and rarely gain traction outside the activist community. Moreover, they undermine public trust in the very institutions, like the courts, police, and tax collectors, that should be providing legitimate services that society needs such as delivering justice, catching criminals, and collecting revenue.

These tactics are designed to induce fear, but also a sense of resignation, impotence, and a belief that the deck is so stacked, there is little to gain from engaging in politics. And they have worked so far. The Kremlin has avoided a Tiananmen Square–style crackdown on protesters, and mass jailing of opposition figures as in Maduro's Venezuela or Erdoğan's Turkey. It has avoided an outright coup attempt too by its fractious security agencies. This is no small feat given that coups and popular revolts are the two main threats to nondemocratic rulers.

The most effective types of state coercion are those that work merely by threat. When journalists bury stories out of fear of the repercussions, businesspeople sell their firms under threat of seizure by corrupt state officials, and citizens ignore calls to protest policies that they oppose, repression has already done its work.

For example, three political scientists wanted to learn the extent to which private advertising firms in Russia engaged in self-censorship out of political fear. They contacted more than 950 advertising companies in Russia and probed their willingness to post materials on the internet with six different types of political content on behalf of a fictitious NGO, known as Our Alliance. The emails sent to the advertising companies were identical except for the nature of the message that they wanted the company to post on the internet. The least provocative version called for a web advertisement that encouraged viewers to "Learn More about the Preservation of Historic Buildings in Russia" against a background photo of a decrepit yet formerly grand building, while the most provocative asked the companies to post an advertisement calling for viewers "To Join Us in Fighting for Free Speech in Russia" against a background photo of the Kremlin and a pair of handcuffs.[31]

The researchers found that 29 percent of the respondents were willing to publish the least provocative advertisement that encouraged viewers to "To Learn More about the Preservation of Historical Buildings," but this figure fell by 10 percentage points when it was framed as a request to "Join Us in Fighting for the Preservation of Historic Buildings." Advertising firms were sensitive to this small change in wording.

Moreover, the most provocative advertisements that called for a rally against free speech produced an 18 percentage-point drop in the willingness of firms to publish relative to the least provocative version. Just 11 percent of firms were willing to post the most provocative advertisement. There was nothing illegal about these advertisements. In this case, the expectation of punishment—even for a legal activity that would benefit the firm—served as an effective deterrent from taking steps that even marginally run against the interests of the government.[32]

By any measure, the rollback of civil liberties in Russia has accelerated since Putin returned to the presidency in 2012. The government further limited the scope of official protests and restricted political competition.[33] It strengthened the law on "foreign agents," which requires NGOs that receive foreign funds to register with the state; expanded the powers of the security services to block access to websites without a court order; and broadened the definitions of slander, extremism, and incitement to separatism as a way to intimidate journalists and others working with foreign organizations.

NGOs that engage in activities that are even remotely political have found their space for action restricted. Human Rights Watch reported, "In the first six months of 2017 alone, the number of people administratively punished by Russian authorities for supposedly violating the country's regulations on public gatherings was two-and-a-half times higher than throughout 2016."[34] With all these changes since 2012, each time I have gone through passport control at the Russian border in the last few years, my pulse beats a little quicker than during the previous trip.

Repression involves risks and rewards. Too much or badly deployed repression can provoke a backlash while also making the opposition appear sympathetic to the broader public. In Ukraine, Yanukovych's misguided attempts to put down a popular revolt on Maidan Square in 2014 only emboldened protesters and led to his embarrassing exit to Russia. Too little repression, however, risks allowing opposition forces to gather strength and ultimately pose a larger threat. Putin has been ruthless in taking on political opponents, but the means are often subtler than many realize.

Rebooting Repression after Protests

The Kremlin's response to the large protests of 2011–12 provides a good example of its multipronged approach to political opposition. In addition to promoting the counterrallies recounted in chapter 5, the regime co-opted some elements of the opposition. Alexis Lerner of the University of Toronto explored this process in an unusual medium: graffiti. Street art is important in autocratic regimes because it can evade censorship and subvert pro-state narratives. For researchers, it can shed light on state-society relations in ways that are hard to capture in standard surveys, focus groups, or interviews, and can be tracked and coded.

In painstaking fashion, Lerner examined the evolution of political graffiti in Moscow between 2012 and 2018. In the wake of the protests of 2011–12, political graffiti was subversive. One campaign mocked restrictions on liberty with stencils declaring "I LOVE A FREE PRESS" or "I LOVE AN INDEPENDENT JUDICIARY" throughout the city. Another was more direct and called for an "end to the lying and stealing" in block letters against a black and white depiction of Putin. Strategically placed throughout Moscow, this graffiti campaign sent a message to the public that was unfiltered by the authorities.

Rather than just painting over the murals and arresting the artists, the Russian authorities took a different tack. Beginning in 2013, state agencies, including the Moscow city government and Interior Ministry, held graffiti festivals. In addition to generous prize money, the winners received coveted spaces in central Moscow for their own projects with assurances that their works would not be erased. Winning projects were sympathetic to the powers that be. Lerner documents how the city government pushed opposition-oriented graffiti artists to the literal margins of Moscow while also giving graffiti artists willing to do the regime's bidding access to highly trafficked and visible public spaces. Some of the same artists painting anti-Putin murals in downtown Moscow in 2012 were depicting a Russian phoenix rising from the ashes, honoring World War II veterans, and celebrating Soviet-era cultural icons like ballerina Maya Plisetskaya in 2018.[35]

The Kremlin also turned up the heat on protesters without banning demonstrations outright. Three days after Putin became president, on May 6, 2012, police arrested hundreds of protesters and charged more than two dozen with assaulting the police—a serious accusation that carried the possibility of a long prison sentence. Past roundups of demonstrators targeted organizers rather than participants, and led to short sentences of fifteen days or less.[36] In the May 2012 protest, however, most of those charged had no prior experience as protesters and received significant jail terms of two to three years. The European Court of Human Rights issued numerous statements that these arrests violated the European Convention on Human Rights, and Amnesty International declared the jailed protesters "prisoners of conscience." Even the Human Rights ombudsman for the Russian Federation, Vladimir Lukin, objected to the charges.[37] Yet the Russian government was not swayed. That the Kremlin sent young and unknown demonstrators to jail on dubious charges of resisting arrest signaled to all that protest of any scale would come with great personal costs even for those without a history of political activity.

Furthermore, the government passed new legal barriers to protest. In June 2012, Putin signed legislation that increased fines for individuals involved in illegal protests from 100 rubles (US$3) to 10,000 rubles (US$300), but those breaching "the established rules of conduct" faced fines of up to 20,000 rubles. Previously, the maximum fines had been just 1,000 rubles. More important, organizers of illegal demonstrations had their maximum penalty increased from 50,000 to 600,000 rubles (upper equivalent: US$2,000). Beyond increased fines, the legislation barred anyone with a criminal record from organizing a protest—a substantial consideration given that criminal charges are an easy way to try to discredit political opponents. It also increased jail times for organizing illegal demonstrations to five years for repeat offenders. These formal penalties aside, security officials turned more often to violence to put down protests. The arrest (and occasionally beating) of randomly selected protesters to send the message that anyone attending an unsanctioned rally is vulnerable has become much more common.

These legal measures have had a chilling effect, but have not solved the problem. Political protests continued in 2018 in the run up to the presidential election even though they were much smaller and less effective than past demonstrations. A new wave of protests oriented around local issues marked 2019. Protesters blocked the creation of a new garbage dump in Archangelsk and the building of a Russian Orthodox Church in Ekaterinburg. In summer 2019, protests returned to Moscow when city officials barred opposition figures from running for seats on the Moscow city council. In 2020, despite a ban on protest due to COVID-19 restrictions, mass protests erupted in the far eastern city of Khabarovsk following the arrest of the relatively popular governor Sergei Furgal and continued every day for three months.

How Do You Solve a Problem Like Navalny?

The Kremlin's response to Alexei Navalny's political challenge also shows a recognition of the costs and benefits of coercion.[38] Navalny is a lawyer who launched his career by buying small amounts of shares in state-owned companies and asking embarrassing questions at shareholder meetings that were covered in the press. With the help of volunteer experts and a small paid staff, he publishes well-documented exposés of the ill-gotten wealth of the elites—even using drones to take videos of yachts and palaces. In addition, he organizes political rallies against the Kremlin—one of which spanned across ninety cities in 2017. He is one of Putin's most persistent critics and skilled in attracting attention. A Navalny video of the wealth of Prime Minister Medvedev has been viewed more than twenty-seven million times, while another exposé provoked a public challenge to a duel by Viktor Zolotov, the head of Russia's National Guard. Zolotov promised to turn Navalny "into a nice, juicy schnitzel within minutes."[39]

Navalny's anticorruption videos and blog posts are more than just entertainment for opposition-minded Russians. They can have real economic consequences. One academic study of Navalny's blog posts between 2008 and 2011 found that "the stock returns of the companies mentioned in Navalny's posts go down by .33 percentage points with more focused posts having an effect of 1.26 percentage points."[40] The researchers also found that companies mentioned in a Navalny blog post were more likely to have leadership turnover induced by the revelations of corruption in the post.

Rather than locking Navalny in jail, the Russian authorities for many years used various techniques of autocratic legalism to inhibit his operations. Navalny was allowed to run for one of the most powerful positions in Russia, the mayor of Moscow, in September 2013, but faced many obstacles. The mayor has the status of a governor, and directs vast sources of patronage and government spending given Moscow's outsize importance in Russian political as well as economic life. Local officials worried that heavy-handed fraud might rekindle protests and hoped that Mayor Sergei Sobyanin could win an election outright.

Six candidates made their way onto the ballot, but Navalny was the main challenger. By this time, Navalny had become an increasing problem for the Kremlin, and in April 2013, state officials accused him of embezzlement from a timber company while he was working as an adviser to the governor of the Kirov region in 2009—a charge that many saw as politically motivated. The case had been dismissed due to lack of evidence, but Navalny was sentenced to five years in jail in July 2013. In a rare move, the prosecution asked to delay Navalny's jail time until a higher court heard the case on appeal.[41] With a legal cloud over his head, Navalny was then allowed to run for mayor—a candidacy that needed the blessing of the Kremlin, which it appears wanted to give the race an air of legitimacy following the debacles of fraud in the 2011–12 electoral cycle.[42]

Navalny faced the usual administrative barriers during the race. He was not permitted on television, was denied access to large gathering spaces, was prevented from holding large rallies, and was running with a suspended sentence, which made it unclear whether he could take office. But he appeared on the ballot, campaigned across the city, and used crowdsourcing to fund his efforts. Navalny's get-out-the-vote campaign was unprecedented for a Russian election. He recruited more than twenty thousand volunteers to help turn out the vote, and held "meet and greet" events with voters throughout the city.

Navalny began the campaign polling in the single digits, but won a surprising 27 percent of the vote and almost forced a second round of voting as Sobyanin received just 51.3 percent of the total votes. After Navalny's strong showing in the mayoral campaign, the Kremlin upped the pressure on him by charging his bother Oleg with embezzlement in December 2014. Oleg was sentenced to 3.5 years in prison—a ruling that the European Court on Human Rights ruled violated his rights to a fair trial. He served his full sentence and went free in summer 2018.

In 2017, Navalny himself received a five-year suspended sentence based on the decision in the 2013 case. This ruling kept him out of jail, but also prevented him from engaging in political activities including running for political office—a move that forced him off the ballot in the 2018 presidential elections. Nonetheless, Navalny organized rallies across Russia and was arrested repeatedly for his efforts in 2017. After each arrest, he was let go following a short stay in jail.[43]

In summer 2019 during the campaign for the city of Moscow's Parliament, Navalny's Anticorruption Foundation released searing depictions of corruption among prominent city officials. In September, the Investigative Committee charged the foundation with money laundering and searched forty regional offices, removing computers and other equipment. In October, the Anticorruption Foundation was declared a "foreign agent" after purportedly receiving an unsolicited contribution from a mysterious donor from Spain who many believed worked on the orders of the Russian security services.[44] The foundation denied the allegation, appealed in the courts, and refused to register as a foreign agent. In March 2020, the Anticorruption Foundation found its bank accounts frozen following a lawsuit by Oleg Deripaska, one of Russia's longest-standing oligarchs.

But the worst was yet to come. On August 20, 2020, Navalny boarded a plane from the Siberian city of Tomsk after advising opposition groups about the regional elections scheduled for September. During the flight he became violently ill, and the pilot made an emergency landing in Omsk. Ambulance drivers delivered a dose of atropine, a common antidote to poison, on the way to the hospital and likely saved his life. Doctors in Omsk downplayed the likelihood of poisoning to the press and attributed Navalny's condition to "low blood sugar"—a diagnosis that convinced few. After three difficult days in Omsk, the authorities allowed Navalny to fly to Germany, where doctors ruled "without a doubt" that he had been poisoned with a form of *novichok*, a type of a nerve agent closely related to the poison used against the Skripal family in the United Kingdom in 2018.[45] Scientists in France and Sweden who tested the material also found traces of the poison as did researchers for the Organization for the Prohibition of Chemical Weapons.[46] Novichok is too dangerous, powerful, and rare to be used by anyone but highly trained professionals, and is almost impossible for civilians to obtain. All eyes turned to the Kremlin, with some arguing that the use of novichok was meant to signal that forces in the Russian state were behind the attack. Leaders across Europe and the United States condemned the poisoning, called on Moscow to investigate, and threatened Russia with renewed sanctions.

The Russian government offered a flurry of explanations. The Foreign Ministry accused Western powers of "organizing a massive disinformation campaign."[47] One Russian creator of novichok, Leonid Rink, accused Navalny of poisoning himself, and the head of the Russian Parliament, Vyacheslav Volodin, called the poisoning a "planned action against Russia designed to impose new sanctions."[48] President Putin reportedly told French president Emmanuel Macron that Navalny may have poisoned himself.[49] And as Navalny lay in a coma, Yevgeny Prigozhin, a longtime friend of Putin who oversees the Internet Research Agency that interfered in US elections, announced that he had bought the legal debts charged to Navalny's Anticorruption Foundation and planned to bankrupt him should he survive the poisoning.[50]

Putin's role in the affair is unclear. Some argue that such a high-level attack on the most prominent opposition activist in the country must have been sanctioned by the president, while others note that it may have been done by those who thought the FSB was not doing enough to deal with threats amid Russia's growing political uncertainty.[51] Whatever the level of Putin's involvement, it is clear that he has built a political system in which high-level officials have become able to target regime critics and opposition figures with little chance of being punished. This affair marks a serious and dangerous escalation of repressive tactics in Russian politics.

Overstating Repression

Political activists in Russia face harassment and constant risk of jail or physical violence, but Putin prefers the exit visa to the gulag. Many prominent journalists, academics, and opposition politicians have left the country to avoid persecution. For many ordinary Russians who do not openly oppose the regime, the risk of repression is low. It is small comfort, but Russia is not the Soviet Union. Gone are the days of Communist Party cells in every organization and blanket bans on foreign travel or communication. Repression is palpable in modern autocratic regimes like Russia, but it does not reach into every corner of daily life. Such a strategy would tax the weak Russian state and raise the risks of a public backlash. Preventing the politically disengaged from allying with opposition activists is a key task for all autocracies.

My US graduate students miss the "exotic" Moscow of the 1980s and 1990s, and sometimes complain that Moscow, with its burgeoning array of craft brew pubs and burger bars, might as well be Brooklyn. That is a stretch, but for those who are not engaged in politics or big business, Moscow is in many respects a more pleasant place to live and work than it was even ten years ago. Moscow has built more than a hundred miles of track and opened eighty-one subway stations since 2011.[52] City parks have undergone a makeover and now attract large crowds of families on weekends. And the Aeroexpress train provides reliable transport to Moscow's airports—a feat that I often contemplate while stuck in traffic on the way to Kennedy airport. Outside Moscow, progress has been slower yet still tangible.

Protests are part of the Russian landscape even as they frequently take place against a threat of repression.[53] Large political protests against the central government capture the most attention, but in her study of thousands of protests from 2009 to 2016, Tomila Lankina finds that most focus on local social and economic issues rather than national politics.[54] The Kremlin delegates the decision to approve protests to local governments, which allows it to shift blame should the local government mismanage the situation. In 2017–2018, one out of every three rallies was not approved by the local government, but went ahead anyway.[55]

Allowing some forms of protest is important as the Russian public overwhelmingly supports the right to engage in legal protest. Three researchers found that almost two-thirds of those who attended pro-Putin rallies in 2012 not only supported the right to protest but also had taken part in protests prior to December 2012.[56] Even pro-Putin Russians back the right to protest in public.

Under some conditions, the Kremlin can even benefit from allowing protests. Ekaterina Borisova and I surveyed sixteen hundred Muscovites in December 2011 around the time of the protests against electoral fraud and found that despite the protests being directed against the government, trust in the government increased after the protest as opposition-oriented voters were surprised that the government allowed them to demonstrate unmolested.[57] In this case, the respondents took their cue from the government's unexpected willingness to allow the protest rather than from the anti-government rhetoric of the protest. Unfortunately, the increase in trust was short lived as the government soon turned the screws on the protesters.

Small victories can occur. In October 2018, the crusading online outlet New Times run by the legendary activist and journalist Evgeniya Albats received a record fine of $330,000 on the pretext of failing to inform the Russian government of foreign funding. New Times turned to online crowd funding, and thanks to donations from more than twenty thousand Russians, paid off the fine in four days.[58]

Kirill Serebrennikov, the noted theater director who often works on controversial topics in Russia, was placed under house arrest in October 2017 on charges of embezzling more than $2 million.[59] During his confinement, he used Skype video calling to direct a ballet at the Bolshoi Theater, release a film at Cannes, produce plays at his theater in Moscow, and direct Così fan tutte for the Zurich Opera. Serebrennikov gave guided tours of his neighborhood during his one hour of free time on the street each day.[60] He was released from house arrest in April 2019. Small compensation to be sure, but a good example of creative resistance to state power.

Protests and a coordinated campaign by the media helped to free Ivan Golunov, a young anticorruption reporter arrested after a clumsy attempt by the police to frame him on drug charges. Immediately after the arrest, two high-profile journalists began negotiating with Moscow police to place Golunov under house arrest rather than in jail, while individual picketers took turns protesting in front of the Moscow police building to comply with legal restrictions on public demonstrations. Three newspapers ran identical headlines declaring "We Are Ivan Golunov," and several public figures announced their support. The timing of the arrest was problematic for the Kremlin as it occurred during the "Russian Davos" known as the Saint Petersburg International Economic Forum. During the forum, Golunov's name appeared more frequently on Russian social media than did Putin's.[61] That the arrest took place during the economic forum indicates a lack of coordination between the Kremlin and Interior Ministry. In the end, not only were the charges dropped, but Putin dismissed two high-ranking police officials and five lower-ranking officials overseeing the case in an embarrassing defeat for the Kremlin.[62] My colleagues Andrei Yakovlev and Anton Kazun identified seven high-profile cases between 2017 and 2019, when the authorities backtracked after protests in support of a human rights victim.[63]

These small victories, though, are rare exceptions to the rule.[64] Few Russians arrested for their political activities can count on the kinds of public outcry generated by these high-profile cases, and of course, a potential public outcry did not protect Anna Politkovskaya, or most prominently, Boris Nemtsov or Alexei Navalny.

The chill in Russian politics has not gone unnoticed at the research center that I codirect in Moscow. We are fortunate to be located at the HSE, which is one of Russia's most well–regarded universities. Created in 1996, the HSE is a state institution, but because it was opened after the fall of the USSR, it has a much less Soviet feel than other Russian universities. With campuses in four cities and more than thirty-five thousand students, the HSE is well funded by the state, but also earns much of its revenue from student tuition. It has attracted some of Russia's most respected scholars across a range of disciplines and has a reputation for independent thought that serves it well in academic circles. In 2013, the rector of the university even debated Alexei Navalny about corruption in higher education.

But this reputation also makes it a target for those who oppose a more outward-looking Russia. In recent years, the HSE has lost more than a few top-shelf academics, some of whom had public political profiles, while it has also struggled to define its role as a state academic institution that strives to stay "outside of politics."[65] The administration at the HSE walks a narrow line between defending academic integrity and making all the compromises of being a state institution in contemporary Russia.[66]

As researchers, we keep an eye on the political winds and recognize that conducting academic work on many topics has become more challenging in the last few years. Our early efforts at the center included attempts to study reforms of the Moscow police and state property registries—two hot issues at the time—but topics that we would now avoid.

Our center is focused on academic research rather than public politics, but we nonetheless exercise some caution in the topics that we choose to research and recognize this as a limitation. We are less interested in exposing individual examples of corruption (we leave this task to investigative journalists) than in trying to understand why corruption may vary across regions and over time in Russia. We are less interested in specific cases of corporate raiding than in understanding why some firms become victims of hostile takeovers and others do not. We are less interested in uncovering the ill-gotten gains of any particular oligarch than in understanding the political and economic roots of economic inequality in Russia. Within these restrictions, we are still able to produce research that with any luck, lands in a good academic journal—an outcome that benefits the HSE as well as our Russian and Western scholars. But the task is becoming more difficult.

My most direct experience with the security services in Russia occurred more than thirty years ago and was more comic than tragic.

While working for the US Information Agency in Tashkent, two of my fellow guides said that our Soviet guests had asked them to a private dinner, but they were suspicious about their motives. Our official counterpart was the USSR Chamber of Commerce, but this was a deeply Soviet organization with all the requisite ties to the security services, and my colleagues invited me to accompany them to help keep them out of trouble. We carried diplomatic passports, but lacked diplomatic immunity and had no interest in creating a public scandal that could get us thrown out of the country.

That night, the Soviet side provided a feast like we had never seen— rare Armenian cognac, piles of red and black caviar, mountains of lamb kebobs, and other delicacies. The Soviet second in command frequently interrupted his nominal boss from the Chamber of Commerce during the many toasts to peace and friendship, giving us all a good indication about who was really running the show. As we moved on to dessert, our all-male dinner party was joined by three youngish women who just happened to be in the neighborhood and took a special interest in us. We Americans looked at each other in amazement. This was supposed to be a new era with a more sophisticated KGB, but here we were in the middle of a transparent and crudely deployed honey trap that we all recognized. After a bit of dancing at a disco, the night ended with an Uzbek colleague whispering in my ear that they had an apartment where I could go with one of the women if I wanted. With visions of the blackmail that would surely follow dancing in my head, I demurred.

————

Putin's formula for governing Russia has long relied on two components: personal popularity reflected in high approval ratings and resounding victories in quasi-legitimate elections, and a loyal security apparatus able to keep political opponents at bay. Yet the mix of these two components has varied over time. Russian political scientist Vladimir Gel'man characterized Putin's first dozen or so years as a "vegetarian" form of autocracy during which the Kremlin turned massive economic growth into vast support for the president and managed to avoid heavy-handed repression even as it targeted specific political opponents.

Following the mass protests against the government in 2011–12, however, Gel'man argues that the Kremlin turned to the "politics of fear" with a reliance on overt intimidation of the public and selective persecution of regime critics.[67] The Kremlin depicted Russia as a besieged fortress surrounded by enemies abroad and fifth columns at home to justify increasing restrictions on political rights, while also using the hugely popular annexation of Crimea to boost popular support at least for a few years.

A decade of economic stagnation and recent missteps, however, have seen Putin's personal popularity and the ability of the Kremlin to produce "honest majorities" in national elections decline dramatically. Research from a 2020 survey finds that a combination of the Russian government's handling of the COVID-19 crisis, economic hardship, and Putin's decision to change the Russian Constitution and possibly rule until 2036 have shaved off roughly one-fifth of Putin's support among the mass public.[68] As both popular and elite backing for the Kremlin have declined, repression and coercion have come to play a much bigger role in Russian politics.

The danger for the Kremlin is that repression takes on a self-defeating momentum. One important study by political scientist Christian Davenport finds that the best predictor of state repression against the public is the past use of repression against the public. He argues that authoritarian regimes that turn to repression typically come to rely on it more heavily, in part because repression makes it more difficult to solve the underlying problems like slow growth and corruption, that generate opposition in the first place.[69] It also increases the leverage of the security services over other organizations.

While the skillful management of repression has helped to keep Putin in power and pushed the political oppositions to the margins, it has done little to resolve the fundamental problems that confront Russia. It has not promoted economic growth, strengthened property rights, or reduced corruption. It has only made these problems worse by empowering the security services and corrupt government officials who benefit most from them, and encouraging the flight of human and economic capital, which are essential to economic growth and good governance.

Rather than being a sign of strength, an outgrowth of Putin's worldview, or a result of Russia's autocratic past, the Kremlin's increased reliance on repression since 2012 is merely a sign that other tools for keeping Putin in power are failing. Emblematic of this problem is that in 2018, Russia spent more on prisons yet less on prisoners than any other country in Europe.[70]

8

Mysterious Ways

MEDIA MANIPULATION AT HOME

Vladimir Putin is a master manipulator.

—US CONGRESSMAN RYAN FITZPATRICK, 2018

Russians are not fools.

—POLITICAL SCIENTIST SCOTT GEHLBACH, 2010

PROPAGANDA WORKS in mysterious ways. In April 1986, I was a member of a three-person team of college-age Americans invited to debate Soviet students on the topic "US-Soviet Cooperation in Space as an Alternative to the Arms Race." The Soviet side chose the theme to emphasize Gorbachev's proposal to end nuclear testing and ban President Reagan's beloved strategic missile defense. The debates offered Russians a rare opportunity to hear directly from young Americans, and the Soviets made a one-hour documentary of our tour and widely broadcast a heavily edited version of it on national television.

In Kharkhiv, Baku, Leningrad, and Moscow, we argued the ins and outs of missile defense and nuclear test bans as well as why US-Soviet relations were so fraught. In my not-yet-fluent Russian, I drew a parallel between the US invasion of Vietnam and Soviet invasion of Afghanistan, and was labeled an "ardent anti-Soviet" by none other than popular television commentator Vladimir Posner. Given the small number of Americans in the Soviet Union in those days, my appearance in this documentary gave me a certain celebrity status in the country for the next few years as I was occasionally recognized on the street when I began speaking. Our last debate was in Moscow on April 29, and our tight schedules caused us to miss evening news reports of a technical problem at a nuclear reactor in Chernobyl. We flew out on April 30 and drank champagne to mark Pan American's first flight from Moscow since 1979.[1] We were somewhat relieved when the pilot joked that we had not seen any brown clouds over Minsk and Geiger counters run over our bodies at Frankfurt Airport found no evidence of contamination.

During the debates, I was struck by the intensity of the attacks by our Soviet counterparts. We knew that they were activists from the Communist Youth Organization (Komsomol) looking to make careers and that the debates gave them a platform to impress the higher-ups, but we were still somewhat caught off guard as our competitors railed against all the real and imagined ills of the heartless capitalism and faux democracy in the United States.

And yet as is often the case with propaganda, not all was as it seemed. In Baku, one of the Soviet debaters took me aside after dinner and told me that he wanted to go to the United States, and if he ever got there he was staying. Two years later while working as an exhibit guide in Leningrad, one of my former debate competitors sought me out. Over drinks he explained that he had been expelled from the Komsomol because he had pushed reform too fast. (*Ya slishkom bystro perestroilsya*). His conversion to reform and criticism of the Soviet system was surprising as he had been one of its most effective and energetic defenders during our debates just two years prior.

In the last few years, the battle of ideas between Russia and the United States has returned, and the Kremlin has gained a well-deserved reputation for "weaponizing" information at home and abroad. The conventional wisdom often depicts the Kremlin as a master manipulator of information with Putin leading Russia (and the rest of us) to a post-truth future. Perhaps the most prominent statement is Peter Pomerantsev's *Nothing Is True and Everything Is Possible*, which lays out how the Kremlin tries to manipulate information, muddy the waters with multiple explanations, and deny the existence of objective facts with increasingly sophisticated strategies. Pomerantsev notes, "At the core of this strategy is the idea that there is no such thing as objective truth. This notion allows the Kremlin to replace facts with disinformation."[2]

There is little doubt that information manipulation at home and abroad is key to Putin's Russia, but we know a lot more about the Kremlin's strategies and techniques of misinformation than we do about how Russians react to these efforts. We know that Russia is trying to shape narratives about election interference, the war in Ukraine, and Putin's omnipotence, yet are Russians buying it?

Academic research indicates that the answer is more limited than the conventional wisdom suggests, and depends on the importance and visibility of the issue. On many issues, autocrats struggle to sway public opinion in their favor. Before discussing this research, I look at the trade-offs confronting rulers who seek to manipulate the media and present the Russian media landscape.

Information Autocracy

Rather than treating Putin's penchant for manipulation to his KGB past or czarist-era Potemkin villages and Soviet disinformation efforts, much recent research focuses on how autocrats use information to secure their rule. Russia is a good example of what Sergei Guriev and Daniel Treisman call an informational autocracy. In their words, "Informational autocrats recognize that violent repression in modern societies is costly and often counterproductive. Rather than killing or imprisoning thousands to inspire fear, they attempt to convince citizens that they are competent and not violent. Such dictators win the sincere support of many of their compatriots, but this support is based in part on the manipulation and distortion of information."[3]

They argue that if rulers can demonstrate a degree of competence to the public, perhaps by overseeing an increased standard of living, defeating an insurgency at home, or gaining a victory in foreign policy, then there is less need to rely on coercion. But it is usually difficult for citizens to observe the competence of leaders directly. Was the ruler responsible for economic growth or did they just get lucky? This gives leaders an incentive to manipulate the media to convince citizens of their competence rather than block any bad news. It also gives them an incentive to allow at least a modicum of free media. If the public comes to distrust all media sources as overly biased, it becomes harder for rulers to demonstrate their competence via the media because people will not believe what is broadcast.

This approach helps us understand why personalist autocrats seek to control the media, but give some space for free media too. For instance, by one estimate, in Hungary about 90 percent of the media is now directly or indirectly controlled by those with personal connections to Orban's party.[4] Orban's strategy of strangling opposition media with red tape and obscure legal maneuvers rarely puts journalists in danger, but is often fatal for their newspapers.[5] In Turkey, the Erdoğan government slapped a $2.5 billion fine on an opposition media group in 2009 and now by one estimate "the government controls more than 85 percent of mainstream media."[6] A handful of independent media remain, but face frequent harassment from the state.[7] In Venezuela, Chávez long battled private newspapers that openly opposed him, eventually gaining control over major media outlets, radio stations, and newspapers.[8] Chávez's successor has only further restricted media freedom.[9]

Putin's informational autocracy too is built on the state control of all major forms of media, beginning with the takeover of television in the early 2000s, followed by newspapers in the early 2010s, and finally, major internet providers a few years later. As the economy has turned south in recent years and the charm of foreign policy successes has waned, the Kremlin has relied on cruder forms of censorship while continuing to manipulate the news that does get reported. Recognizing its limited ability to convince viewers that the government is uncorrupt, elections are free and fair, and local bureaucrats are looking out for the public interest, Russian television subtly argues that all governments are corrupt, all elections are rigged, and all citizens are powerless before the state.

Television is by far the most important source of information as well as the most tightly controlled. One of Putin's top officials meets weekly with editors of the main television channels to keep broadcasters in line. In close cooperation with the Kremlin, Russian television ignores or smears political opponents as needed, keeps political protests off the air, and shapes the master narrative about Russian politics in which Putin is treated as an indispensable figure. Kremlin control over television is critical as 80 percent of Russians get their news from the three main national channels.

The Kremlin's media strategy on television has evolved. Early in the 2000s, the Putin administration began by taking over two lively, if partisan, private television channels that had been the most critical of the government. The state companies that headed the takeover squeezed out much of the critical content in favor of feel-good movies that played on nostalgia and talk shows devoid of politics. News on the main channels offered a placid picture of the regime's success and suggested the redundancy of political activism, assuming that the public was tired of the political upheavals of the 1990s. Following the protests against election fraud in 2011–12 and Putin's return to power in 2012, Kremlin strategy shifted from the "infotainment" of the preceding years to what Vera Tolz and Yuri Tepper call "agitainment," combining the agitation and propaganda of ideological messages with viewer-friendly formats like talk shows and celebrity variety shows.[10]

Russian state television depicts a binary world. Outside Russia, there is protest, conflict, and instability, but inside Russia, the government is strong and life is stable. State television reports on Europe and the United States are not pure inventions—there is protest, conflict, and a degree of instability in every country—but the presentation is highly partial. A German colleague at the HSE who spends a lot of time in Russia remarked that even while he knows that Russian television is exaggerating reports of unrest in Germany, he is nonetheless still surprised to learn that all is calm on arriving in Frankfurt.

Exhibit A for the Kremlin's media management campaign is the popular Sunday night news broadcast hosted by Dmitry Kiselyov, a pro-Kremlin firebrand who rails against homosexuality, the West, and liberal values. At the height of the Ukraine crisis, standing before a backdrop of a nuclear mushroom cloud, he reminded viewers that "Russia is the only country in the world that is realistically capable of turning the United States into radioactive ash."[11] A master of the theatrical hand gesture, sly insinuation, and crude broadsides against political opponents, Kiselyov is one of Russia's best-known media personalities. After watching Russian state television for a week straight, novelist Gary Shteyngart observed that the news anchors are "a clan of attractive and dead eyed men and women" who "speak in the same unshakeable 'out of my mouth comes unimpeachable manly truth' that Putin uses in his public addresses sometimes mixing in a dollop of chilly sarcasm."[12]

The state, typically through Kremlin-friendly owners, dramatically increased control over major national newspapers following a host of takeovers, including *Kommersant* in 2011, *Gazeta.Ru* in 2013, *Lenta.Ru* and *Grani.Ru* in 2014, and the highly respected Russian version of *Forbes* in 2016.[13] To cement local control over the media, Russia forbids foreigners from owning more than 20 percent of media outlets.

These takeovers have consequences. A media researcher at Cambridge University, Rolf Fredheim, studied more than a million articles published from 2010 to 2015 on Russian news websites and found that following the takeover by Kremlin-friendly owners, *Lenta.Ru* and *Gazeta.Ru* pivoted toward lifestyle and human-interest stories. More precisely, he saw "a 50% reduction in coverage of controversial legal proceedings, together with the business dealings of Russian elites," after the takeover.[14] There were fewer reports on corruption and more puff pieces on pop culture.

The Kremlin pursued a similar strategy in the takeover of the successful Russian version of Facebook known as V Kontakte (In Contact) and the Russian version of Google known as Yandex. These takeovers hit hard the Russian information technology community as these two private companies were homegrown success stories not backed by the Russian state and had bested their far more famous US-based rivals. Russia is one of the few large countries in which Facebook is not the most popular social media site and Google is not the most popular search engine. But following the takeover, each platform has become more likely to toe the Kremlin line.[15] The popular online news *RBC* suffered a similar fate in 2018, and the well-respected newspaper *Vedomosti*, which changed owners in 2020, has gone down the same road.[16]

Sometimes media ownership is not enough. Intimidation and violence against journalists has long been a feature of contemporary Russia. According to the Committee to Protect Journalists, at least thirty-eight journalists have been murdered in Russia since 2000, with reporting from Chechnya being a particularly risky assignment.[17] Reports of local journalists receiving threats or beatings are all too common, particularly outside major cities. One example is Oleg Kashin, an opposition-minded Russian journalist who had reported on topics including corruption in the pro-Kremlin youth movement Nashi, environmental protests around the Khimki forests in Moscow, and the abuse of power by the regional government in Pskov. In November 2010, a beating by unknown assailants with a steel pipe left Kashin with a broken jaw, fractured skull, broken leg, and partially amputated finger. Many prominent public intellectuals, reporters, and newscasters who have been critical of the government have departed the country.[18] One of the best news sites reporting on Russia in Russian is *Meduza*, but it is now based in neighboring Latvia.

State control over information on the internet came later. As late as 2010, a report of the Internet in Russian Society program at the Berkman Klein Center for Internet and Society at Harvard University noted that "the political blogosphere appears to remain a free and open space for Russians of all political stripes to discuss politics, criticize or support government, fight corrupt practices and officials, and to mobilize others around political and social causes."[19] At the time, President Medvedev maintained an active online presence, pushed a range of proposals putting government services online, and famously hobnobbed with high-tech companies in Silicon Valley.

While Medvedev gained a reputation as the country's "Blogger in Chief," Putin bragged that he does not use email, claimed that the CIA created the internet, and railed against foreign influence on the web.[20] After Putin returned to the presidency in 2012, the Kremlin switched gears and persuaded loyal allies to buy news sites as well as introduced much stricter regulation of the internet. New laws, some of which were strongly opposed by the business community, limited internet freedom. One required Russian bloggers with more than three thousand viewers to register with state authorities, while another compelled Russian information technology companies to preserve all communications on their platforms for three years and provide their encryption keys to the state so that the security services can monitor conversations. In summer 2017, the Kremlin banned VPNs that allow users to mask their geographic location when accessing the internet.

The tactics used against the private cable news outlet TV Rain offer a good example of how the Kremlin controls information. With its mix of investigative reporting, lively political discussions, and hipster vibe, TV Rain targeted younger, better-educated Russians on television and the internet. It gained new prominence in 2011–12 when some of its broadcast personalities took part in protests in Moscow against electoral fraud. In January 2014, Russia's major cable TV providers dropped TV Rain from their packages—a move widely seen as prompted by government pressure. This forced TV Rain to rely on the internet to get out its message. Later that year, the state Duma passed a law banning advertising on subscription-based Russian cable and satellite TV stations, which further cut into TV Rain's revenue. To add to the insult, TV Rain was forced to leave its studios in the trendy "Strelka" district in central Moscow to broadcast from a private apartment. Viewership fell from several million in early 2014 to less than a hundred thousand by the end of the year. TV Rain continues its aggressive reporting and political commentary to an audience of about seventy thousand paid subscribers on the internet.[21] Because its stories are picked up by other outlets and its reports are discussed in the activist community, it is more important than its small subscription base indicates, but the Kremlin has clearly limited its influence.

Looking beyond TV Rain, the Kremlin has been much more active in policing content on the internet in recent years. A study by the Russian Human Rights organization Agora found that in 2017, the Kremlin blocked far more websites than in previous years.[22] Russian officials have also taken to singling out individual bloggers for political posts in a low-cost strategy to deter dissent on the internet.

In addition, the Kremlin hires an army of internet trolls—commentators paid to leave posts on chat boards on the internet—who seek to influence and disrupt online conversations in ways that help the Kremlin. A good illustration is the infamous troll factory known as the Internet Research Agency. Housed in a nondescript building in Saint Petersburg, the Internet Research Agency employs about a thousand trolls hired at the relatively good starting salary of $1,000 to leave posts online.[23] It is funded by Yevgeny Prigozhin, a restaurateur from Saint Petersburg who is favored by Putin, and coincidentally, won more than $8 billion worth of state contracts between 2011 and 2017. According to some detailed reports by former employees at the Internet Research Agency, trolls use Facebook, YouTube, and Twitter to create fake identities, and receive strict orders about which topics to cover and how. During the 2016 US presidential campaign, they created fake videos demeaning Hillary Clinton, organized sparsely attended rallies against immigration, and promoted Trump and Bernie Sanders. For their efforts, thirteen employees from the Internet Research Agency were indicted by Special Counsel Robert Mueller in summer 2018 for their activities during the 2016 US presidential election.

Moscow's recent efforts to control the internet are more modest than North Korea's strategy of sending citizens daily text messages to support the regime or China's "great firewall" approach to blocking access to sensitive information, but they do represent a significant tightening of control over social media and the internet.[24] Researchers from the Social Media and Political Participation Lab at New York University sum up the Kremlin's current strategy toward the internet: "Rather than trying to engage in a dialog or persuade, the government simply attempts to hammer down the official message, artificially increase the indicators of its take-up (propelling politicians into lists of top bloggers and their messages into lists of top posts), while simultaneously cluttering communication channels used by the opposition."[25]

Limits of State Control and Censorship

At the same time, if you devote some effort, you can learn a lot by following the Russian media—and not just in the Soviet-era sense of reading between the lines. News shows on the three national channels are friendly to the Kremlin, but political talk shows are often worth watching, and frequently discuss Kremlin intrigues and scandals without pointing fingers directly at the president himself. [26] Nonpolitical reporting in much of the mainstream Russian media is usually conducted without egregious bias.

Reporting in newspapers and on news websites is more diverse than on television, as owners want to sell papers and advertising space, and Russia's talented journalists want to tell stories. In 2012, *Vedomosti* published emails from WikiLeaks revealing that the deputy chief of staff of the Russian presidential administration proposed "a systematic manipulation of public opinion via social media." On the day after the 2018 presidential election, this same paper reported that Russian voting rolls had contracted by 1.5 million voters overnight so that Putin could claim to have been elected by a majority of registered voters. [27] The small though feisty newspaper *Novaya Gazeta* has faced incredible harassment from the state, but continues to publish exposés on human rights abuses and other politically sensitive topics.

Russian journalists broke the story of the Internet Research Agency troll farm in Saint Petersburg, and the best book on the internet in Russia, *The Red Web: The Kremlin's War on the Internet*, is by two Russian journalists, Andrei Soldatov and Irina Borogan. Newspapers face many constraints, but still manage to present a range of views even if some topics are off-limits such as Putin's private life, the sources of wealth of his closest associates, and direct criticism of the leader of Chechnya, Kadyrov, among others. This is in part because newspapers have less influence than television.

To gain some sense of the diversity of views on what could be seen as a sensitive issue, consider these reactions to the spring 2018 arrest of the Magomedov brothers, two wealthy and well-connected businessmen. Abbas Gallyamov argued that the arrest was payback from a business community unhappy with the brothers' tactics.[28] Nikolai Mironov of the Center for Economic and Political Reforms maintained that the arrests were the beginning of a "selective de-oligarchization" as part of the government's efforts to acquire additional funds to fulfill its electoral promises.[29] Political observer Mikhail Vinogradov viewed the arrest as an attack on Prime Minister Medvedev given his ties to the Magomedov brothers.[30] Others linked the arrest to local politics as the Magomedovs had political ambitions in the southern Russian region of Dagestan.[31]

Or consider this analysis of Putin's annual press conference in 2018 in one leading Russian newspaper: "[It is] a stage production with Putin as the lead actor, writer, director, and producer. But every year there are fewer and fewer reasons to watch the play."[32] Reporting on protests against the building of a church in Ekaterinburg in summer 2019, *Nezavisimaya Gazeta* noted that the "principal contradiction of Russian democracy in recent years" is that the "the middle classes demand the right to adjust the authorities' policies . . . while Russian officials believe they have carte blanche to take any action and that citizens must accept it."[33]

Not just elite newspapers, but tabloid papers can be critical too, as in this *Moskovsky Komsommolets'* article from February 2019 that reports on a poll showing that more Russians believe that the country is headed in the wrong than the right direction. The headline mocks: "We have Putin, but not happiness." Or this article from the same paper from May 2020 that ridicules Putin's claim that 70 percent of Russians are middle class using United Nations' criteria. The writer notes that Russians are paying about 40 to 50 percent of their income on food, adding, "Those lucky enough to have a job are working to eat. So what kind of middle class are we talking about?"[34]

In winter 2020, I spoke with the longtime editor of an independent newspaper in Russia about how he navigates the media landscape. He said that he felt free to criticize the government, but the reporting had to be good and it was essential not to insult anyone on a personal level. He noted that after a recent critique of top Kremlin officials in his newspaper, he received phone calls from several officials disputing his account, but nothing more. After our conversation, I noticed that he had three cell phones at the ready and commented that three phones seemed like a lot. He answered, "Yes, three is a lot, but I need them, and I change the numbers every few weeks to make it harder to eavesdrop on my conversations."

State control over the internet has increased in recent years, but it is far from complete. Laws requiring bloggers to register with the authorities if they have more than three thousand viewers are rarely enforced. Navalny has been ingenious in publishing his exposés on YouTube and social media to wide audiences.

Yuri Dud', a former sports journalist, has created a hard-hitting interview program on YouTube that has eight million subscribers.[35] Typically dressed in a T-shirt, torn jeans, and sneakers, Dud' interviews rappers, media celebrities, and political figures from Navalny and Khodorkovsky to the Communist Party candidate for the presidency in 2018, Pavel Grudinin. Dud' presses his guests on the hot-button issues of the day and has also produced pathbreaking reporting on topics that state media avoids: the HIV crisis in Russia, the horrific terrorist attack on a school in Beslan in 2004, and the legacy of the gulag (prison camp) in Kolyma in the Russian far east.[36]

Indeed, his reporting on HIV in Russia caused a sensation.[37] Released on February 11, 2020, the film attracted fourteen million views in its first week, caused a 5,000 percent increase in internet searches for HIV testing in Russia, and caught the attention of high-ranking government officials like Alexi Kudrin and Deputy Health Minister Oleg Sagai, who pledged to work on the issue.[38] Even more impressive, Dud"s interview with Navalny shortly after the activist was poisoned drew more than ten million views on the day it was released.[39]

With effort, one can learn a good deal about Russian politics from the media even with all the constraints imposed by the state. Most Russians, however, exhibit what political scientists call "rational ignorance." It is not worth the time and energy to become informed about politics because it is hard to put this knowledge to good use. Many Russians appear to recognize that the political deck is stacked against them, yet even if they were armed with better information, their ability to influence policy would be limited. So they tune out rather than tune in. To the extent that average Russians hold this view, the Kremlin's information campaign has been successful.

Effectiveness of Media Manipulation

The extensiveness of the Kremlin's efforts to manipulate media is beyond dispute. One study found that Russian bots (automated accounts that relay Kremlin propaganda, among other things) make up around half of the Twitter posts about Russian politics among the most politically active accounts.[40] Yet we should not equate effort with effectiveness. While most laypeople and many commentators believe that people are easy to manipulate, a large body of research suggests it is quite hard. Cognitive scientist Hugo Mercier sums up this view: "Political scientists know how ineffectual political campaigns are. Advertising researchers know that most ads have tiny effects. Historians know that authoritarian propaganda is reviled and mocked by the population (if they can get away with it). Psychologists have catalogued the cues people (as young as preschoolers) take into account when evaluating what they're told—the plausibility of the content, the quality of the argument, the competence and honesty of the source." He adds that "most mass persuasion attempts—from propaganda to advertising— nearly always fall on deaf ears."[41]

Moreover, just being exposed to information doesn't mean that we are affected by it. Because we select what type of information we consume, it is often difficult to measure the impact of exposure to any particular piece of information. If a politically conservative viewer elects to watch Fox News and then supports Trump, it is hard to know whether their vote for Trump is due to watching Fox News, or because the person holds conservative views and would have voted for Trump even without watching Fox News. More generally, it is not easy to disentangle whether conservatives elect to watch Fox News or people become more conservative because they watch it. The same problem holds for liberals watching MSNBC or Russians watching state television. This "selection" problem is well known to media researchers.

In addition, because we are exposed to so many different types of news, isolating the impact of any bit of news on political behavior is challenging. Voters receive information about politics from friends and family, new and old media, and various partisan groups. It is not easy to know which, if any, of these sources are important. I lived in the hotly contested state of Ohio during the presidential election in 2004 and was contacted twenty-five times by various political organizations in the week before the election even though I had long before chosen my candidate.

We can learn a lot about Moscow's intentions by studying Kremlin efforts to manipulate information, and these efforts should keep policy makers interested in protecting democracy and national interests awake at night, but this is a different task than identifying whether these attempts are effective. If hours of exposure to state-sponsored media determined citizen loyalty, then the USSR likely would not have collapsed. At the same time, it is hard to imagine that Kremlin efforts to control information do not have significant consequences. Why would the Kremlin be so obsessed with controlling information if it provided so few benefits?

To give some idea of how successful the suppression of free media can be, consider the following study by two Russian and two foreign researchers who gave free access to the independent TV Rain to randomly selected viewers in the run-up to the 2016 parliamentary election. Because access to TV Rain was randomly assigned, the groups of viewers that did and did not receive access were identical in all other respects except for their access to TV Rain.[42] The researchers found that the introduction of free media had a polarizing effect: reducing votes for United Russia in areas where past support for United Russia was low by about 4 percentage points and increasing it in cities where past support for United Russia was high by about 13 percentage points.[43] These are large effects for studies like this and indicate that private media may be especially important in a tightly controlled media environment like Russia. They also hint at how suppressing just one private channel may have altered the political landscape.

The paradigmatic case of Russian media success is the campaign to support the annexation of Crimea. In fall 2013, even prior to the annexation, state media barraged Russian viewers with unrelenting critical coverage of the popular protests against the Ukrainian government. When Ukrainian president Yanukovych fled to Russia in February 2014 and was replaced by a much less Moscow-friendly successor, state television regularly referred to the new government as a "fascist junta"—a loaded term given the Soviet experience in World War II and decades of antifascist propaganda in the USSR. Each demonstration by Ukraine's politically marginal yet visible and vocal extreme right movements received massive coverage on Russian television. Most egregiously, Russia's Channel One reported that Ukrainian soldiers had crucified a Russian-speaking child from eastern Ukraine. TV Rain, *Novaya Gazeta*, and other outlets quickly debunked the story, but Putin mentioned it sometime later. To Russian viewers, state media depicted the reunification of Crimea as a reassertion of Russian power, a noble effort to defend Russian speakers, and a victory over a fascist government.

The astute Russian journalist Maria Lipman and her coauthors observed that on the hot-button issue of Crimea, the Kremlin managed to combine great distortions in reporting without reducing the credibility of the message. They asserted that "contrary to the claim that inaccurate 'news' drives viewers away, the raw and aggressive propaganda on pro-Kremlin TV attracted larger audiences than before . . . not by selling accurate information but emotional gratification. They offer versions of reality that—although not infrequently untrue—made Russians feel good about themselves and their country."[44] This strategy paid great dividends on Crimea—an issue where there is a deep emotional resonance.

And yet despite a massive campaign in the Russian media, public support for more active measures to defend Russian speakers in eastern Ukraine who are fighting the government in Kyiv is muted. Surveys from the Levada Center indicate that rather than parroting unwavering support for Kremlin policies, the Russian public takes into account the costs and benefits of various courses of action. The annexation of Crimea, a bloodless and largely costless victory for the Russian troops, has received support across almost all sectors of the Russian public. In every month since March 2014, approval of the decision to annex Crimea has never fallen below 80 percent.[45]

But costlier policies in Ukraine occasion much less support. In May 2014, when fighting in eastern Ukraine was hot, only 31 percent of respondents supported, or more or less supported, "sending direct military assistance, such as the introduction of troops." By August 2015, this figure fell to just 20 percent.[46]

In a July 2015 poll, the Levada Center asked, "If you found out that among the ranks of the insurgents, regular Russian army troops were fighting, how would you respond?" Only 33 percent responded either positively (9 percent) or more or less positively (24 percent). These figures were down from 45 percent in November 2014, thereby indicating a decline in support for the introduction of regular Russian army troops into the conflict in eastern Ukraine. This may help explain why the Russian government has been so reluctant to recognize the presence of Russian soldiers in eastern Ukraine and characterizes those who are fighting there as "volunteers." By September 2017, just 41 percent of Russians thought that Moscow should help the breakaway regions of Donetsk and Luhansk in eastern Ukraine in any way.[47]

The Kremlin has also been keen to cover up the deaths of Russian "volunteers" in eastern Ukraine. Journalists in Pskov who uncovered fresh graves presumably for Russian soldiers killed in Ukraine were beaten when they tried to investigate the story.[48] The fear of reaction to Russian involvement on a larger scale gives some sense of the limits of the Kremlin's efforts to manipulate public sentiment even on this hot-button issue. It is just much more difficult to shape opinion on policies that can impose high costs on the public.

More generally, information campaigns that work at home also bring costs abroad. Kremlin denials of the presence of Russian troops in eastern Ukraine play well with viewers in Russia, but they provoke deep skepticism abroad, thus undermining Russia's credibility. Even more damaging was the Kremlin's response to the downing of an airliner traveling from Holland to Malaysia that was shot down over eastern Ukraine in 2014, killing 298 passengers, most of whom were Dutch. Following an extensive investigation, Dutch prosecutors in March 2020 charged four Russian citizens who were senior officials in the self-proclaimed Donetsk People's Republic with organizing the killings.[49]

The Kremlin's disavowal of responsibility with increasingly less plausible theories worked well at home, where only 2 percent of Russians pointed the finger at the Russian government for the downing of the plane.[50] But in Europe, it only served to harden public opinion against Moscow.[51] While many experts predicted that European sanctions on Russia would not last a year when they were imposed in 2014, lifting the sanctions unilaterally became politically untenable in Europe following the MH-17 downing, and the sanctions remain in place six years on.

The Television versus the Refrigerator

Foreign policy is a low priority for most citizens, and this makes it easier for politicians to manipulate citizens' views about the outside world. In contrast, economic issues are central for most citizens, and people can benchmark their experience against government reports. This makes manipulation much harder on economic issues. Political scientists Arturas Rozenas and Denis Stukal studied more than thirteen thousand news reports from 1999 to 2016 related to the economy on Channel One, the main television channel in Russia. Since nondemocratic regimes are more likely to fall during bad economic times, information about the state of the economy is a sensitive topic. To their surprise, Rozenas and Stukal found that the coverage of positive and negative economic news was highly symmetrical. Falls in the Russian stock market, sharp depreciations of the Russian ruble, and slow economic growth were just as likely to be reported as good economic news, such as a bumper harvest or increase in oil prices. Direct censorship of bad economic news did not seem to be at play.

The factors credited with creating good and bad news, however, were quite different. The researchers noted that "bad news is not censored, but it is systematically blamed on external forces. In contrast, good news is systematically attributed to domestic politicians."[52] A few examples highlight this strategy. In late 2000, the Russian stock market experienced a severe crash that stopped trading. That evening Channel One reported,

Today, due to the sharp decline in market quotes, trading in the Russian trading system was stopped. In the US, George Bush and Al Gore continue the battle in the courts. Democrats believe that the process will continue until December 18, when the electoral college will meet. . . . The uncertainty about the outcome of the U.S. presidential election, after all, was reflected in the stock markets. Indeed, not so much in the American markets, as in the Russian ones.[53]

Rather than attribute the poor performance of the Russian stock market to domestic causes, Channel One linked it to uncertainty caused by politics in the United States.

Alternatively, consider this discussion of pensions that paints the Kremlin much more favorably:

Cabinet ministers responsible for socio-economic issues gathered in Vladimir Putin's office in the Kremlin. . . . On the previous day, the president . . . heard many complaints that working retirees receive low pensions. The president promised to sort out the situation. And now we have a result. Working pensioners will receive higher payments. In the coming month, the president will issue a decree to raise pensions for working retirees.[54]

Or more subtly, consider how Channel One links Putin to a decline in inflation in Russia: "In 2009, inflation will be 13 percent lower than the previous estimate. The news was announced by the head of the Central Bank Sergei Ignat'ev in a meeting with the prime-minister Vladimir Putin."[55]

This approach of reporting bad news while attributing it to sources outside the Kremlin's control and giving the Kremlin credit for good economic news makes some sense, especially in a well-educated country like Russia and on issues that citizens can easily observe. Censoring or biasing such information risks undermining the credibility of state news sources. If the Soviet Union could (and did) hide airplane crashes from the public, this is much harder to imagine in today's Russia. At the same time, shifting blame from the state is a time-honored strategy for stories that reflect badly on the government.[56]

Yet the Kremlin's ability to hoodwink voters on economic issues is more limited than many suggest. Bryn Rosenfeld, a political scientist at Cornell University, explored how the economic effects of the financial crisis of 2008–9 influenced support for the government. Despite the Kremlin's efforts to deflect responsibility, she found that Russian voters in the parliamentary election of 2011 used local economic conditions to evaluate the government. Where local economic conditions were objectively worse, citizens gave lower evaluations to the government and voted less often for United Russia. Moreover, voters who were wary of government propaganda gave greater weight to local economic conditions in their assessment of the ruling party. Rosenfeld concludes that her results "suggest limits on incumbents' use of official media to distort economic reality in their favor."[57]

More recently, the Kremlin has tried to blame Russia's economic slowdown on sanctions imposed by the United States and European Union. To examine the impact of this campaign, I surveyed Russians in 2016 and found that simply reminding the respondents of Russia's bad economic performance yielded a 6 percent drop in support for the government. Moreover, both Putin supporters and skeptics sharply reduced their backing of the Russian government on being reminded of this bad economic performance. Despite the efforts to shift blame, most Russians—Putin supporters and opponents alike—fault the Russian government for the decline in the economy.[58]

This distinction in the state's ability to manipulate information about economics and politics is even apparent in online discussions. Anton Sobolev, a recent PhD graduate in political science from the University of California at Los Angeles, studied how seven hundred Russian trolls influenced conversations about politically sensitive topics in 2014–15 on social media.[59] He found that trolls were more successful in diverting online discussions from politically charged topics than in promoting a pro-government agenda. In addition, trolls were not able to shift discussions to other topics if the users were talking about economic problems like growth or unemployment. Even on the internet, it is easier to manipulate information about politics than economics.

Russians have long experience extracting useful information from biased sources. In the Soviet period, many Russians read between the lines of the media, and this continues today. Duke University political scientist and longtime expert on Russian media Ellen Mickiewicz contended that Russian "viewers expect commercial and government involvement in shaping the news. They believe it is a viewer's responsibility to extract significance and correct for the bias."[60] Indeed, the Levada Center reported in May 2020 that while 57 percent of Russians believe that state television reported accurately on foreign news, just 47 percent believe its reporting on the economy.[61]

When manipulating information, the Kremlin faces a familiar trade-off. Except for issues where emotions run high and information runs low, if people believe that they are being manipulated, then they will lose confidence in the source.[62] Public opinion polls show that as television became more highly politicized, Russian viewers' trust in television fell from 79 percent in 2009 to just 48 percent in 2018.[63] Similarly, the share of Russians who cited television as a source for their news dropped from 94 to 69 percent between 2009 and 2020.[64]

The Kremlin's control over the media is an essential feature of Putin's Russia. Blocking independent sources of information has undercut political opponents of the Kremlin and reinforced support for the regime. But we also need to keep the Kremlin's capacity to manipulate information in perspective. While conventional wisdom treats Putin as able to manipulate public opinion at will, he faces a well-educated public with a long history of exposure to bias in the state media. Looking more broadly, Putin confronts the general constraint that it is hard to persuade people, particularly on issues where they have a lot at stake or some personal experience. There is even a danger in overstating the case of Putin as a master manipulator. Attributing near magical powers of persuasion to Moscow's information warriors only reinforces Putin's image as an omnipotent ruler both at home and abroad—an image that the Kremlin works hard to create and is at the core of Putin's strategy to stay in power.

9

Great Power Posing

RUSSIAN FOREIGN POLICY

Ah, but a man's reach should exceed his grasp / Or what's a heaven for?
—ROBERT BROWNING, "ANDREA DEL SARTO"

PAST CHAPTERS have shown that the lens of comparative autocracy is helpful for understanding many aspects of Russia's domestic politics, but with its military power, nuclear weapons, large population, natural resource wealth, great geographic reach, and seat on the UN Security Council, Russia is an unusual autocracy in its foreign policy. Given this, how should we try to understand Russian foreign policy?

Some people focus on the background and worldview of its most important decision maker: Putin. Others discount Putin's personal role, and point to Russia's unique geography, culture, and history that generate values and interests largely at odds with Western liberalism. Russian foreign policy is a continuation of its past policies. Or as former National Security Council Russia expert Thomas Graham puts it, "The West has a Russia problem, not a Putin problem."[1]

These two conventional approaches have much to offer, but also come up short in three respects that reflect the themes of previous chapters. First, popular narratives take Russia's relative power in global politics as a historical given beyond the Kremlin's capacity to change.[2] Observers frequently note that Putin is "playing a weak hand well" or Russia is "punching above its weight" on the international stage.[3] But Putin's hand in global politics is weak in large part due to the constraints identified in previous chapters. As in its domestic politics, the Kremlin faces hard choices in foreign policy that reflect the power and interest of different groups. Like all leaders pursuing greater influence in global politics, Putin would like to spend more on guns and butter, but can't do both. Russia's more assertive foreign policy empowers those groups least supportive of economic reforms needed to spur economic growth and ultimately undercut Russia's global power. Power in international politics is not dealt at random from a deck of cards but instead is a function of state policy. Having been in power for the last twenty years, Putin's weak hand is largely his own doing.[4]

Second, the Kremlin's tools for managing foreign policy are often as blunt as they are in domestic politics. The Kremlin has exploited the annexation of Crimea to boost popular support, but has had much less success in convincing the broader public to support great power status over economic development. Moreover, Russia's military might is impressive, but it is hardly an all-purpose tool, and Russia's stagnant economy and poor governance hinder the use of economic aid as a means to gain influence.

Third, while the conventional wisdom traces Russia's anti-Westernism and assertive foreign policy to Putin's worldview or Russia's status as a great power, other personalist autocracies have used similar tactics to bolster legitimacy at home. While we need to recognize that Russia is an unusual autocracy in its foreign policy, the logic of autocratic politics can nonetheless help us understand why Russia's reach often exceeds its grasp on the international stage.[5] This chapter begins by describing Russia's current status in global politics, and then critiques two conventional wisdoms before tracing Putin's weak hand to the difficult trade-offs and blunt tools that are common to personalist autocracies.

A Great Power, but a Diminished One

For all the disagreement in popular debates on Russian foreign policy, all agree that Russia has expanded its international presence in the last decade. In its backyard, Russia unleashed a cyberattack on Estonia in 2007 and fought a shooting war with Georgia in 2008. Six years later, it annexed the Ukrainian territory of Crimea—the first example of a European country taking the territory of a neighbor since the end of World War II.[6] To boot, it sent troops and weapons to eastern Ukraine to battle the Ukrainian army.[7]

To counterbalance the European Union, Russia helped to form the Eurasian Economic Union, an organization including Belarus, Kazakhstan, Kyrgyzstan, and Armenia. This is hardly an effort to re-create the Soviet Union, but is an attempt to reassert influence in the region by developing stronger trade ties.[8]

Beyond its immediate neighbors, the Kremlin has stepped up its use of social media and funding for political groups to gain influence and increase social division in Europe. In Syria, it has provided considerable military support to keep al-Assad in power.[9] In Venezuela, it sent financial aid and military advisers to prop up President Maduro. From the Arctic, where Russia seeks to exploit untapped sources of energy by making claims on new territory, to Africa, where Russian firms provide security, capital, and technological advice to a handful of countries, Russia's global footprint is much larger than a decade ago.[10]

Russia has strengthened its military and trade ties with China, particularly in the wake of the global financial crisis of 2008, and then the imposition of sanctions by the United States and European Union in 2014.[11] Relations are complicated by geopolitical competition, but Russian and Chinese trade doubled in 2017, and three thousand Chinese soldiers took part in a massive military exercise in Russia's far east in September 2018. Personal relations between President Putin and General Secretary Xi Jinping are good. Putin celebrated his birthday with Xi over vodka and sausages—the only time he has done so with a foreign leader—while Xi referred to Putin as "his best, most intimate friend."[12]

The Kremlin has challenged the United States in ways that would have seemed hard to fathom a decade ago. Beyond trying to influence US presidential elections via social media and computer hacking, Russia backed the Maduro government in Venezuela and intervened in Syria in part to counter US influence in regions of central importance to Washington.[13] In its competition with the United States, the Kremlin has sought to modernize its nuclear arsenal and develop new weapons, including nuclear cruise missiles, although experts are divided about their effectiveness.[14]

Some aspects of Russian power never went away. With more than 6,800 nuclear warheads, Russia boasts the largest nuclear arsenal in the world. By comparison, the United States has 6,550, France, China, and Britain have between 200 and 300, while Pakistan, India, and Israel have lesser amounts.[15] According to the Stockholm Institute of Peace Research, Russia has about the fifth- or sixth-largest defense budget in the world, behind the United States, China, and Saudi Arabia, and just about the same as India and France.[16] It has more tanks than any other country, and can mobilize them quickly—a thought that keeps NATO war planners trying to protect the Baltic countries up at night.[17]

And Russia has used this might to good effect in Georgia, Ukraine, and Syria. In regions where the United States and Europe are unlikely to respond with force, Russia's military is a powerful persuader. Countries vary in their abilities to translate military power into foreign policy success, but by just about any measure Russia is a military force to be reckoned with.

With the second-largest gas and third-largest oil production in the world, Russia is an outsize force in global energy. Russian oil production has not fallen in the wake of sanctions. Even as shale gas production surged in the United States and global energy markets have liberalized, Russia continues to provide about one-third of Europe's energy and is likely to remain the low-cost provider of energy to the continent. Russia has also played an increasing role in forming global energy prices in recent years. With Saudi Arabia, Moscow helped prop up energy prices before causing a collapse in the price in 2020 to drive out competition. With its large financial reserves and low-cost production, Russia hoped to seize market share from US shale producers, who struggle to be profitable at these low prices. Few countries influence global energy markets on this scale.

Russia's great size, which includes borders with the United States, China, and even EU countries like Poland via its enclave in Kaliningrad, also gives it global reach. Finally, Russia holds a seat on the UN Security Council. Due to its geography, military power, natural resources, and participation (for better and worse) in some of the most intractable problems on the planet, such as the Syrian Civil War, conflict in eastern Ukraine, global warming, nuclear proliferation, and the struggle against Islamist extremism, Russia has become an increasingly important global player in recent years.

To be sure, Russia's resurgence should be kept in perspective. Russia is vastly outspent by its rivals. In 2017, NATO countries spent $900 billion on defense, while Russia spent $67 billion. For all the current problems between the Trump administration and its European allies, NATO spends about fifteen times what Russia does on defense. Even without US contributions, NATO defense spending is about four times larger than Russia's. The United States and China spend about nine and four times, respectively, what Russia does on defense. Russia's defense increased from 2010 to 2015, but has trended downward since.[18]

Russia's economy, which is roughly five times smaller than the economies of the United States, China, or the European Union at purchasing power parity, constrains Russia's ability to project power. Czarist and Soviet governments were brought down by economies that could not keep pace with the Kremlin's great power ambitions. While Putin's Russia is far from this fate, slow economic growth has already curtailed its ambitious plans to build military power laid out in 2012.[19] And Russia's ability to use the economic lever as a foreign policy tool is also limited. As political scientist Peter Rutland notes, "Twenty years of subsidized energy prices for Belarus, for example, has not produced a loyal and subservient ally for Russia, a striking example of how hard it is for Moscow to turn energy sales into political leverage."[20]

Moreover, Russia's ability to use soft power to persuade and cajole countries is limited.[21] With its autocratic government and vast corruption, Russia is an unappealing model. Russia has found some purchase as a champion of antiliberal sentiments in countries where these feelings run deep, but public opinion polls suggest that Russia is not trusted even in these places.[22] The Kremlin's opposition to gay rights, support for traditional families, and promotion of Orthodoxy is a rearguard action in response to developments in the West. To the extent that Russia's soft power has been effective in recent years, it is due more to the declining attractiveness of Western-style democracy and capitalism than to the inherent successes of Putin's own model.

One way to measure Russia's best friends is to explore support for a 2014 UN resolution declaring that the Russian annexation of Crimea was illegal. One hundred countries voted in favor of the resolution, fifty-eight abstained, and just ten voted against the declaration, specifically Armenia, Belarus, Bolivia, Cuba, Nicaragua, North Korea, Sudan, Syria, Venezuela, and Zimbabwe—a gallery of rogues to be sure, but apart from North Korea, not much of a challenge to the United States or its allies.

Russia's unconventional tactics in international affairs often speak to its weakness rather than its strength. Moscow's botched poisoning of the Skripal family in Salisbury, England, in 2018, reliance on cyberwarfare (explored in the next chapter), support for fringe movements that seek to undermine democracy in Europe, and attempts to compromise foreign policy elites in rival countries are better seen as weapons of a relatively weaker party than as an indication of newly powerful Kremlin.

Indeed, for all its muscle flexing in its immediate neighborhood, Russia has defied predictions that it would expand the war with Ukraine beyond Luhansk and Donetsk to re-create the czarist-era unit of New Russia. It has also not intervened with military force in the Baltics despite some forecasts.[23] And every few years since the mid-1990s, observers have predicted that Russia is planning to merge with Belarus. This may yet happen, but history suggests caution. Indeed, recent calls to tighten relations have largely come from Belarus' beleaguered autocrat, Alyaksandr Lukashenka, rather than from the Kremlin.

Russia is a great power, albeit a diminished one. Yeltsin would look on Russia's global position with delight, but Brezhnev would view it with panic.

The Role of Putin in Russian Foreign Policy

How can we account for Russia's more assertive foreign policy? Most observers trace Russian foreign policy to the attitudes and values of Putin. As noted in chapter 2, it is easy to find facile arguments linking Putin's background and experiences to specific policy choices, but subtler treatments can be made as well. In one of the best works in this vein, political scientist Brian Taylor focuses on the values, habits, and emotions not just of Putin but of those around him too. Taylor argues that Putin and his closest advisers are united by a set of core values rooted in statism, anti-Westernism, and conservatism that guide their policy choices. For Taylor, Putinism is not an ideology but instead more akin to Thatcherism and Reaganism in that it generates a way of seeing the world that leads to a clear set of policies, such as a dominant state role in the economy and the pursuit of great-power status on the global stage.[24]

One can distill the disparate views of Putin and his confidants into broad categories, but it is hard to go much further and link these views to specific policies. In addition, these views and policies have changed over time. Indeed, it is difficult to demonstrate the independent impact of elite attitudes on policy because these attitudes do not exist in a vacuum but rather are shaped by events and interactions with other countries. As Robert Legvold remarks, relations between Russia and the United States have deteriorated to the point that many on both sides exhibit what political psychologists call "the fundamental attribution bias"—the tendency to explain one's own behavior as a response to the situation and the other side's behavior by its innate characteristics.[25] In other words, each side thinks, "I had no choice to escalate given what the other side was doing, but the other side escalated because that is just who it is." And the other side follows the same self-defeating logic. In these situations, it is hard to determine if elite values are the causes or effects of policy choices. To the extent that Putin's attitudes are responses to the behavior of other countries, it is difficult to say that his core values are driving his policy.

One core value that does seem broadly held among Putin's inner circle is skepticism toward the United States—a view that has increased as relations have soured. William Zimmerman, a professor emeritus at the University of Michigan, and some collaborators organized eight rich waves of surveys between 1993 and 2020 that probed the views of Russian foreign policy elites. One analysis of these data by Danielle Lussier showed that while Russian foreign policy elites have rather diverse views on domestic politics and other foreign policy issues, they have increasingly similar views of the United States as a threat rather than a partner.[26] Using the same data Sharon Rivera and James D. Bryan found that "whereas 50.6% of elites agreed that the United States constituted a threat to Russia in 1995, fully 79.8% of respondents expressed that view in 2016."[27] In 2020, this figure fell to 57 percent, but foreign policy elites were also more supportive of sending Russian troops abroad than at any point in the study.[28] If in the past Putin's inner circle of policy makers was balanced between economic liberals and national security hard-liners, the latter have come to rule the roost as Putin's domestic political coalition shifted after he returned to the presidency in 2012.

The Continuity Thesis

Other observers downplay the importance of Putin's worldview and trace the more assertive Russian foreign policy in recent years to historical factors specific to Russia. A key component of this continuity thesis is Russia's topography. Russia is largely a flat plain with few natural borders or barriers—a condition that makes it vulnerable to invasion, but also makes territorial expansion easier. Having invaded or been invaded by just about all its neighbors at one point, czars in Imperial Russia, general secretaries in the Soviet era, and presidents in modern Russia have all seen military dominance in Russia's neighborhood as critical to the national interest.

Russia's historic role on the global stage reinforces the importance of great-power status. In the nineteenth century, Russia was a great power that fought with and against the empires of Europe and Asia in wars in Crimea, the Balkans, and Japan. It was a key member of the Concert of Europe with the United Kingdom, Austria, France, and Prussia that balanced the ambitions of European powers in the century leading up to World War I. During the Cold War, Moscow oversaw an external empire in Eastern Europe, an internal empire in the former Soviet Union, and a far-flung set of ties with regimes from Cuba to Angola to Vietnam as one of two global superpowers. In 1972, Soviet foreign minister Andrei Gromyko boasted correctly that "no international problem of significance anywhere can be resolved without Soviet participation."[29]

As in other great powers throughout history, elites in the Kremlin see Russia as an exceptional country with a mission to spread its values. Whether in the guise of Orthodoxy and monarchy in Imperial Russia, Marxism in the Soviet era, or national sovereignty and a multipolar world order in the Putin era, many Russian foreign policy elites do not see their homeland as just another important country but instead as one with an outsize role to play in global politics. Regardless of who occupies the Kremlin, great-power status, or what Russians call *derzhavnost'*, is thought to be central to Russian foreign policy.

Political scientist Seva Gunitsky sees two components in Russia's great-power status: "In Russia's immediate neighborhood, this means an unquestioned sphere of influence, similar to America's Monroe Doctrine. In dealing with other powerful states like the U.S., it implies respect, prestige, and peer recognition rolled into one—in other words, a seat at the table of managing global affairs."[30] Former NSC Russia expert Thomas Graham and political scientist Rajan Menon note that "at the core of Russian identity is the deeply held belief that Russia must be a great power and that it must be recognized as such."[31] British policy analyst Keir Giles writes, "The notion of greater-power status and superiority among nations is a key component of Russian national identity, and one that at present appears impossible to relinquish."[32] To make the case, these scholars point to the surge in national pride following the annexation of Crimea, increasing trust in the military among the Russian public, and Russia's acerbic reactions to perceived slights in international affairs, such as President Obama referring to Russia as "a regional power," being kicked out of the G-8 group of advanced industrialized economies, or being subject to economic sanctions. Russia's long-serving foreign minister Sergei Lavrov put it bluntly: "I am convinced that Russia simply cannot exist as a subordinate country of a world leader."[33]

One anecdote reveals how perceptions of Russia's great-power status sometimes emerge in subtle ways. I was in Moscow on September 11, 2001, to attend an academic conference. That night, on a television at a Russian bar called Uncle Sam's, I saw the Twin Towers collapse, flames rise from the US Pentagon, and mayhem engulf New York and Washington. In response to the horror of the attack, Russians created an enormous makeshift shrine in front of the US embassy of flowers, candles, condolence cards, and deeply felt testimonials, many of which were wrapped in cellophane to protect them from the rain. Some tributes referenced Russia's loss of life from recent acts of terrorism. Others mentioned Russia's staggering losses in World War II. Walking among the remembrances on the day after the attack, I cried.

Several days later I interviewed a high-level official at the Russian Central Bank. He had started working at the Central Bank in the Soviet period and was now in his mid-forties. He was not a Western-oriented liberal and was often critical of Yeltsin, but also appreciated that Russia needed to modernize its banking system and build ties with other market economies. I had interviewed him a few times about bank policy, and we shared a good rapport. He began by offering sympathies for the attack and enormous loss of life, and then turned to a long discourse on why the United States and Russia needed to ally against terrorism. After a heavy pause, though, he concluded by saying, "Well, you wanted to be the only superpower."

Good evidence for viewing Russian foreign policy as a continuation of great-power competition comes from the struggle to create security arrangements in Europe. Russia's relations with Europe have long been a tangle of attempts at integration and cooperation, followed by periods of tension and competition.[34] Russia is part of Europe, yet also apart from it. In the post–Cold War era, Russian and Western policy makers have clashed over how to accommodate Russia's interests and military power in the region, while also preserving the core principles of the Western alliance that have helped to keep the peace in Europe since 1945. One key issue has been Russia's relations with NATO. At various times, policy makers in Moscow and Europe floated the idea of Russia joining NATO, but it never got much traction.[35] To manage relations short of Russian membership, Brussels and Moscow formed several different bodies over the years, without much success, and NATO ended these efforts following the annexation of Crimea in 2014.

The issue took on new importance with NATO expansion—a policy that came to be bitterly opposed by Moscow.[36] With memories of Soviet dominance during the Cold War still fresh, Eastern European countries sought membership in NATO in the mid-1990s. After initial reluctance from the Western alliance, Poland, Hungary, and the Czech Republic joined NATO in 1999, followed in 2004 by seven more Eastern European countries, including three that share a border with Russia: Latvia, Lithuania, and Estonia.

In 2008, the Bush administration led efforts to bring Ukraine and Georgia into NATO. The stakes were high given Ukraine's size, complicated history with Moscow, and strategic significance. The United States faced criticism not only from Moscow but also from NATO allies such as Germany and France, and even some generally pro-Western Russians. After much internal debate, NATO pledged that Ukraine and Georgia "will become NATO members," but did not offer a Membership Action Plan with any details or start date. The open-ended commitment was the worst of all worlds. It encouraged Moscow's suspicions that NATO wanted to surround Russia, disappointed governments in Ukraine and Georgia that wanted NATO to move more quickly, and caused resentment among alliance members that were divided on the issue.[37]

Some argue that the threat of NATO expansion ultimately led Russia to annex Crimea and intervene in eastern Ukraine in response.[38] The most prominent proponent of this view sits in the Kremlin. In 2007, at an annual meeting of defense experts known as the Munich Security Conference, Putin stung Western observers with an acerbic speech that contended "it is obvious that NATO expansion does not have any relation with the modernization of the Alliance itself or with ensuring security in Europe. On the contrary, it represents a serious provocation that reduces the level of mutual trust. And we have the right to ask:

against whom is this expansion intended?"[39] After the annexation of Crimea in 2014, he remarked that Western nations are "constantly trying to sweep us into a corner because we have an independent position. . . . But there is a limit to everything. And with Ukraine our Western partners have crossed the line, playing the bear and acting irresponsibly and unprofessionally."[40]

Defenders of NATO expansion dismiss this view, and argue that countries in eastern Europe have the right to choose alliances as they please and that NATO helped keep the peace in much of this part of Europe for the last sixty years—no mean feat given the experience of two world wars in this region in the twentieth century.

Stephen Sestanovich, ex–Ambassador at Large for the former Soviet Union and now a professor at Columbia, views the Kremlin's attempt to link NATO expansion to Russian moves in Ukraine as an ex post facto rationalization of policies undertaken for domestic political reasons. He argues that NATO membership for Ukraine had been a dead issue since 2009 due to opposition in Europe and the Obama White House as well as lukewarm support in Ukraine itself. Sestanovich downplays the NATO threat to Russia by noting that the number of US troops in Europe in 2014 was about one-sixth as large as in 1990, the number of aircraft in Europe was down 75 percent, and the United States had removed all of its tank divisions from the continent.[41] In his view, Putin chose to annex Crimea to avoid being seen as the leader who "lost Ukraine." Michael McFaul observes that in his five years as a key Obama policy adviser and US ambassador to Russia, he "cannot remember a single serious conversation about NATO expansion between Obama and a Russian official."[42]

The clash over security policy in Europe has been an enduring feature of US-Russian relations, and reflects an underlying conflict of interests more than the worldview of any particular world leader, the ups and downs of the economy, or political events in Europe, Russia, or the United States. Historian Stephen Kotkin maintains, "What precluded post-Soviet Russia from joining Europe as just another country forming an (inevitably) unequal partnership with the US was the country's abiding great power pride and sense of special mission."[43]

The exceptional Russia approach to foreign policy too is not without criticism. History and a great-power legacy are important, but they are also not straitjackets. In his study of Russia's complicated ties with the countries of the greater Balkans, Dimitar Bechev takes issue with canned histories that emphasize Russia's "traditional influence in the region." He reminds us that "the past is not a monolith. Rather it is a repository of multifaceted, often dissonant and conflicting experiences, events, and memories. As such, what we call 'history' is susceptible to political distortion to the point of outright manipulation."[44]

Bechev's analysis of Russia's foreign policy in southeastern Europe provides a good test of the continuity thesis. Russia has long-standing cultural and religious ties with Bulgaria, Greece, Montenegro, and Serbia, but not with Croatia, Romania, and Slovenia. Looking across a range of issues, he finds that while Russian rhetoric emphasizes cultural ties, Russian policy reflects this cultural division only dimly. Across both sets of countries, Russia asserts its influence in the region by building economic relations and supporting local groups friendly to Moscow, but this is not due to a grand plan, deep cultural ties, or historical legacies. Instead he points to the Kremlin's desire to establish alternative routes for gas exports and develop Russian economic interests. Bechev notes that "hard-nosed pragmatism and the absence of ideological scruples differentiate Russia from both the Soviet Union and the Tsarist Empire."[45]

Similarly, great-power status, or *derzhavnost'*, is not codified in stone but is rather a flexible concept. Seva Gunitsky and Andrei Tsygankov argue that

> Russia's constant attempts to engage the United States in cooperation, including those following the 9/11 attack and over Iran and Syria, demonstrate the principal importance to the Kremlin of being recognized as a major power, or *derzhava*, in relations with the world outside Eurasia. Despite its internal institutional differences from Western nations, Russia sees itself as an indispensable part of the West and will continue to reach out to Western leaders in order to demonstrate Russia's great-power relevance.

In their view, Russia's great-power status does not necessarily mean an aggressive foreign policy; rather, Western powers should recognize Moscow as a member of the great-power club.[46]

Derzhavnost' implies a sphere of influence in Eurasia and recognition of status, but other policies that flow from it are not clear. Does it mean building a Eurasian economic union to counter the European Union or integrating more deeply into European markets? Does it mean abrogating (or cheating on) arms control treaties to show independence or concluding arms control treaties with the United States to demonstrate parity? It is also helpful to remember that Russia is not the first former great power to struggle with its diminished status, as evidenced most clearly by Britain and France.

Autocratic Politics and Foreign Policy

Russia is an unusual autocracy to be sure, but some insights from previous chapters can help us understand some aspects of its foreign policy. As in their domestic politics, autocratic rulers face difficult trade-offs in foreign policy. Even autocrats as unchallenged as Putin have to manage the interests of competing groups. Policies needed to generate economic dynamism in Russia—opening the economy to foreign trade, reducing corruption, strengthening the rule of law, increasing competition, and attracting foreign direct investment—are difficult to square with an assertive foreign policy that benefits precisely those groups opposed to these reforms, such as hard-liners in the security agencies, managers of state-owned companies, and firms in import-competing sectors.[47] The Kremlin's more assertive foreign policy toward the West has brought Moscow back as a global force and secured Putin's place in Russian history, but has also undercut much-needed economic and political reforms that would strengthen Russia's position abroad over the longer term as well as satisfy domestic constituents who want increased living standards. This trade-off is central not only in domestic politics but in foreign policy too.

One good example of this trade-off is Russian policy toward Ukraine. The annexation of Crimea brought a four-year surge in support for the

Kremlin in Russia, but also removed the largest and most pro-Russian voting bloc—the roughly 1.5 million Russians in Crimea—from Ukrainian politics. In past elections, parties openly sympathetic to Moscow regularly received around 40 percent of the vote, but advocating for close relations with Russia is a tougher sell with the Ukrainian electorate after the annexation of Crimea. The landslide victory of the thirty-eight-year-old Volodymyr Zelensky, a Russian speaker from eastern Ukraine, in the presidential elections in Ukraine in April 2019 suggests that the polarization between eastern and western Ukraine that served Russia so well is less important today than prior to 2014. Moreover, Ukraine's largest trading partner by far is the European Union ($40 billion per year) rather than Russia ($11 billion), and China is soon to replace Russia as its second-biggest trading partner.[48]

Moscow's policies toward Ukraine have bolstered NATO. By the end of 2020, NATO members are expected to have increased spending on defense by $100 billion.[49] NATO has moved roughly four thousand advanced troops to the Baltic states and a smaller number to Poland as a token force to deter Russia. Given the centripetal forces at work in Europe today, weakening of the European Union, and election of a NATO skeptic as US president, one would have expected NATO to be in grave danger, but it has held up better than anticipated. And that is largely due to Russia's moves in Crimea, eastern Ukraine, and elsewhere.

Moscow's annexation of Crimea and intervention in eastern Ukraine also led to economic sanctions that have further slowed the Russian economy.[50] Key features of the economic sanctions included prohibitions on access to finance, travel bans, asset freezes on sanctioned individuals and firms, and a total embargo on transactions and economic cooperation with Russian-occupied Crimea. The European Union, Switzerland, Canada, Norway, Australia, and other countries have followed suit too. Despite many predictions in 2014, both the United States and European Union have kept economic sanctions in place for more than six years to the surprise of just about everyone.[51]

Corruption and low oil prices have been a much bigger drag on the Russian economy, but the economic sanctions have had effects as well.[52] They have scared off foreign investors, and reduced Russian access to foreign technology and financing. That Kremlin elites frequently call for them to be removed gives some evidence of their impact. Sanctions have inflicted considerable, if intermittent, pain on specific oligarchs. In April 2018, the US government levied sanctions on companies held by Oleg Deripaska, a metals and energy magnate, for their role in the Kremlin's "malign activity around the globe," immediately leading to stock market losses of more than $3 billion for his main company. In 2019, Deripaska sued the US government, claiming losses of more than $7 billion.[53] Or consider the response of another wealthy Russian businessmen, Viktor Vekselberg, after being banned from doing business with or traveling to the United States in 2018: "For me this is a total crisis of my life. This is not about money, not about business. This is my personal situation. . . . For me, the whole world was about opportunity. Now, what can I do?"[54]

Some sectors in Russia, like agriculture, have benefited from Russian sanctions on agricultural products from Europe and the United States, but even Prime Minister Medvedev acknowledged in 2015 that "it is hard to name countries that have made continuing, steady progress by prolonged self-limitation in trade."[55] According to the OECD, Russian economic productivity per worker is at less than 40 percent of US levels, and an assertive foreign policy will do little to help improve this ratio.[56] Even before the collapse of oil prices and pandemic-induced recession of 2020, the World Bank estimated that Russia will hit its target growth rate of 3 percent no sooner than 2028, and only if it implements structural reforms and boosts the size of the workforce via immigration. These are two big ifs.[57]

The trade-offs of a more assertive foreign policy and slow economic growth are well known in the Kremlin. Alexei Kudrin, who for many years advised Putin on economic policy and now heads the Russian Audit Chamber, has argued that the success of Russia's economic policy depends on reducing tensions with the West—a comment that brought a quick rebuke from the Russian Ministry of Foreign Affairs.[58] Pursuing more accommodating policies abroad could boost the economy by attracting foreign investment and technology, and increasing economic competition, but also risks alienating interest groups within Russian that gain from a more forceful foreign policy and an economic status quo that delivers slow growth, yet generous benefits to incumbents in key sectors. Agricultural groups benefiting from protection against Western goods, defense-sector firms that rely on state contracts, nationalist groups that place a high priority on Russia's great-power status, and state-owned firms wary of privatization by foreign owners all oppose attempts to liberalize the economy, even if these efforts would benefit the country as a whole. Just as in domestic politics, decision makers often have to choose between competing visions in foreign policy as well.

Beyond having to navigate between rival interest groups, Putin faces a second limitation in foreign policy. Previous chapters have highlighted that public opinion does not always follow the Kremlin's lead, and this is true in foreign policy too. Thomas Sherlock's exhaustive review finds that most Russians welcome their country's return to global prominence, but are wary of a more assertive foreign policy and uninterested in great-power status.[59] Every year since 2003, the Levada Center has asked Russians whether they would like to see their country as "a great power which other countries respect and fear," or a "country with a high standard of living, albeit not one of the strongest countries in the world." Only in 2014 at the height of the Crimea crisis did Russians prefer seeing their country as a great power over one with a high standard of living (48 versus 47 percent). In every other year, more Russians preferred to see their country as one with a high standard of living than as a great power—and often by considerable margins.[60] In 2017, 56 percent of Russians favored a Russia with a high standard of living, and 42 percent favored a Russia as a great power.

In a 2014 national survey, the Russian Academy of Sciences asked respondents to "identify the values on which the future of Russia should be based" and gave eight options. Even as Russians were basking in the successful annexation of Crimea, just 32 percent said "Russia should become a great power"—a figure that was unchanged when the survey was repeated in 2018. During the post-Crimea honeymoon, public support for Russia's role as a superpower did not increase. Nor did support for seeing the introduction of a "strong hand," which was backed only by 26 percent of the respondents in both rounds of the survey. By far the most popular response in both surveys was that Russia should be built on the idea of "social justice."[61]

Surveys by Kremlin-friendly pollster FOM show that Russians are now much more likely to say that the Kremlin spends too much time on foreign policy (32 percent in 2019 versus 17 percent in 2015), and just 45 percent think that Russian policy has experienced more successes than failures in recent years.[62] When asked in fall 2018 whether Russia's top priority should be "superpower status" or the "welfare of its own citizens," 51 percent of Russians chose the second, up from 33 percent in 2014.[63]

Public support for the Syrian intervention has been modest. In August 2017, just 30 percent of Russians thought that the Kremlin should continue its military operations in Syria, and 49 percent thought the Kremlin should end them. And as noted previously, Russian attitudes toward intervention in eastern Ukraine have been sensitive to the costs in terms of Russian lives. Russians supported the Crimean annexation in large numbers in part because the military option itself involved so few costs.

President Putin may note that "Ukraine is not a country," and "Russians and Ukrainians are one people that cannot live without each other," but a January 2020 poll by the Levada Center found that 82 percent of Russians believe that Ukraine should be an independent state, and just 15 percent believe that "Russia and Ukraine must unite into one country."[64] Moreover, the lack of support for unification with Ukraine has changed little in annual surveys in Russia since 2008.[65] And in summer 2020, only one in four Russians supported unification with Belarus.[66]

Since 2011, President Putin and Russian state media have sharply increased their criticism of the United States for everything from stoking anti-government protests in Russia to renewing the arms race. But Russians don't seem to be following the script. Throughout 2012 and 2013, roughly 60 percent of Russians had a positive view of the United States, despite the Kremlin's harsher public stance toward Washington.[67] This figure fell to 18 percent after the imposition of US sanctions, as one might expect, but has rebounded steadily and reached 47 percent in December 2019. This increase has occurred even as a majority of Russians believe that the United States has had an "unfriendly/hostile" position toward Moscow since 2014.[68] Indeed, a January 2020 poll found that 67 percent of Russians feel that the Kremlin should view the West as a "partner," 11 percent as a "friend," and just 16 percent as a "rival."[69] One pollster at the Levada Center noted that these data "once again underline the mass exhaustion from foreign policy confrontation. . . . The conception of a "besieged fortress is weakening as the share of Russians who consider that Russia has nothing to fear from the countries entering NATO is higher than it has been in 20 years."[70] With official anti-Americanism at a high pitch, Russian mass attitudes toward the United States and the West have generally been on the mend. Russian foreign policy elites may share a deep-seated desire for great-power status and strong anti-American views, but the Russian public is much more ambivalent.[71]

The point is not that Russian public opinion tightly constrains the Kremlin, but for those who argue that Russian foreign policy is driven by deeply held historical and cultural patterns in support of great-power status, it is important to recognize that these patterns are political creations rather than objective facts. As political creations, they are shaped by political elites for strategic reasons, and these political creations may or may not find acceptance among the broader public.

Third, as in previous chapters, we do find some common patterns among personalist autocracies. Anti-Westernism and the use of bellicose rhetoric is hardly confined to Russia. Other personalist autocracies with far different types of leaders and historical legacies have also tried to legitimize their rule by seeking greater influence abroad. In Venezuela, Chávez used oil sales to create an Alliance of Tolerance and silence potential critics of his human rights policies among Latin American governments. He also embarked on an aggressive foreign aid program to buy support in the region, donated to Chavista-like parties across Latin America, and dramatically increased propaganda via television to foreign countries.[72] These tools are familiar to observers of Russian foreign policy.

In Turkey, Erdoğan has sought a greater role for Turkey in the Middle East that is more independent of the United States. More important, he has grown closer to Russia than any of his predecessors, including purchasing a sophisticated missile defense system from Moscow in a move that was widely opposed in NATO.[73] Turkey has also backed Azerbaijan's side in its renewed confrontation with Armenia over the contested territory of Nagorno-Karabakh.

In Hungary, Orban openly advocates on behalf of Hungarian minorities abroad and seeks to position himself as the nationalist alternative to the liberal, globalist vision embodied in the European Union.[74] As Orban noted on the hundred-year anniversary of the Treaty of Trianon, which defines Hungary's border, "The West raped the thousand-year-old borders and history of Central Europe. They forced us between indefensible borders, deprived us of our national treasures, separated us from our resources, and made a death row out of our country. Central Europe was redrawn without moral concerns. We will never forget that they did this."[75] This type of "besieged fortress" language is reminiscent of Russian foreign policy after the annexation of Crimea. Anti-Western sentiment and an assertive foreign policy stance seem to be as much a function of modern personalist autocracies as a feature specific to Putin's Russia.

Indeed, some observers see Russian foreign policy as driven less by the core principles of Kremlin elites or historical patterns, and more by opportunities and interests—the same factors that propel foreign policy in most countries.[76] In this view, Russia's resurgence is due more to disorder in the West than to an expansion of Russian power per se. Yes, the Russian economy has recovered from shocks of the 1990s, and military spending and living standards have rebounded, but in international affairs power is relative, and the financial collapse of 2008, discord within the European Union, the rise of illiberal regimes in Europe, and the current political chaos of the United States have hamstrung the Western powers in global affairs. In contrast to his predecessors, Trump harbors a deep aversion to NATO and the European Union, and his willingness to air doubts about commitments to NATO have undermined the US assurances to the alliance. In addition, the Trump administration's spats with allies from Canada to Australia to Germany have further weakened the broader alliance of democracies.[77]

No better example of Russia's opportunism exists than its enlarged footprint in the Middle East.[78] The Trump administration's recognition of Jerusalem as the capital of Israel and abrogation of the Iran nuclear deal signed in 2015 distressed allies in the Middle East and Europe, and the Kremlin has exploited this division. Moscow has maintained good relations with a diverse set of countries and interests in the region.[79] It is on good terms with both Israel and the Palestinians. It has worked with the longtime rivals Iran and Saudi Arabia. Russia maintains trade and military ties with Iran, while also cooperating with Saudi Arabia to manage international energy prices. Moscow's good relations with Saudi Arabia are notable as the two countries have long been on opposite sides of divisive issues in the Middle East and compete in global energy markets. Russia and NATO member Turkey have had a volatile yet on balance more productive relationship in recent years than in the past. In the Syrian conflict, Russia has worked with Turkey, Iran, Israel, and Iraq to try to broker a peace in the region without direct US involvement—a thought hard to imagine just a few years ago. In the Middle East, the Kremlin is not locked into relations with historical partners or driven by the core values of decision makers. One prominent Russian foreign policy analyst noted, "Virtually anyone can be a partner and practically anyone can be an opponent."[80]

By taking advantage of the United States and Europe's reluctance to intervene in Syria on a large scale, Russia established itself as a power-broker on the cheap, while also keeping President al-Assad in power, and protecting that country's naval and air bases. Russia has been effective in Syria with a small outlay of forces; around fifty thousand Russian troops have rotated through Syria since 2015, with most serving in the navy and air force rather than on the ground in order to limit casualties.

Continuing in this vein, Robert Legvold observes that events on the ground can generate openings for cooperation when they align the interests of the United States and Russia.[81] Even during a period of increasing rivalry, the Kremlin helped the United States provide troops and matériel to NATO soldiers fighting in Afghanistan via the Northern Distribution

Network, a commercial supply route stretching from the Baltic and Caspian Seas through Russia and Central Asia.[82] Designed to be less expensive than air transport and more reliable than moving goods through Pakistan, the Northern Distribution Network opened in 2009 and soon became an important route to transport troops and goods to Afghanistan.[83] Supporting the network made sense for Russia. Fearing the chaos that might ensue following a Taliban victory in Afghanistan, Putin supported the creation of NATO bases in Afghanistan in 2012, stating, "We have a strong interest in our southern borders being calm," and adding, "We need to help them [US and coalition forces]. Let them fight.... This is in Russia's national interests."[84] In an irony of history, Putin offered NATO the use of a transit base in Ulyanovsk, the birthplace of Lenin and home to the world's largest museum dedicated to the former Soviet leader. With the steep withdrawal of US forces in Afghanistan, this cooperation ended, but it still serves as a good example of tactical collaboration driven by an alignment of interests.

Moscow and Washington cooperated on the New START Treaty that sharply reduced nuclear weapons in 2011. The first verifiable arms control agreement between the countries since START 1 in 1994, this treaty capped nuclear warheads at 1,550, a 30 percent reduction from past agreements, and limited nuclear-capable launchers to 800, down from 1,600.[85] More important, it created new monitoring regimes and ways to exchange data that were designed to increase trust in the agreement.[86]

Finally, the two countries collaborated to slow Tehran's progress toward creating nuclear weapons.[87] The Joint Comprehensive Plan of Action of 2015 was backed by a number of countries, but Russian and US support for the agreement was critical.[88] Neither the United States nor Russia favor nuclear proliferation in the Middle East. Moscow also sought to build its economic ties with Tehran beyond weapons and energy infrastructure. President Obama noted,

> Russia was a help on this.... I'll be honest with you. I was not sure given the strong differences we are having with Russia right now around Ukraine, whether this would sustain itself. Putin and the Russian government compartmentalized on this in a way that surprised

me, and we would have not achieved this agreement had it not been for Russia's willingness to stick with us and the other P5-plus members in insisting on a strong deal.[89]

Cooperation between countries is always difficult, particularly in the case of Russia and the United States—two countries that trade little and have few common enemies. Moreover, it is hard to imagine cooperation on this level today given domestic politics in both places. But sometimes events can align interests and shift policies. Russian foreign policy is in many respects driven by reactions to events and the strategies of other countries.

———

In its domestic politics, Russia shares many commonalities with other personalist autocracies, but in its foreign policy Russia is unusual. As a great power, Russia faces a different landscape than do many autocracies. These differences make simple comparisons with other autocracies difficult, and insights from the rich cross-national research on the foreign policies of autocratic states should be applied to Russia with these caveats in mind.[90]

Nonetheless, a close evaluation of Russian foreign policy reveals some themes found in prior chapters. Putin faces some of the same constraints that he grapples with in domestic politics. He holds rather blunt tools for achieving policy goals and confronts a public that doesn't always echo the Kremlin line. More important, he must deal with the difficult trade-off that a more assertive foreign policy strengthens groups in Russia most opposed to the kinds of economic reform that would generate power over the long haul. Putin has to decide whether to continue playing his weak hand well in the short run and abet further long-term decline, or try to strengthen his hand with all the inherent political risks of altering the status quo at home.

10

Why Russia Hacks

DIGITAL PERSUASION AND
COERCION ABROAD

If you wrote out a list of the most important factors in the 2016 election, I'm not sure that Russian social media memes would be among the top 100. The scale was quite small and there is not much evidence that they were effective.

—ELECTIONS EXPERT NATE SILVER,
DECEMBER 17, 2018

U.S. intelligence missed it when Russian intelligence stole the presidency of the United States.

—RUSSIAN POLITICIAN VYACHESLAV NIKONOV,
SEPTEMBER 12, 2017

IN 2007, the Tallinn city government voted to move a statue of a Soviet soldier rescuing a child during World War II from the center of the capital to a military cemetery in the suburbs. The city government argued that by moving the statue to a less prominent place, it could reduce tensions between Estonians and Russians who occasionally scuffled around the monument. The Russian government took offense and warned of the consequences should Tallinn follow through on its plan.

The roots of the debate stretch back in time, with Russia claiming that it saved Estonia from Nazi Germany during World War II and the Estonians none too happy about the incorporation of their country into the Soviet Union in 1940. After the statue was moved, Estonia suffered a massive denial-of-service attack that shut down government offices, bank accounts, and access to vital web services. Estonia, the birthplace of Skype, was then and remains now one of the most digitally advanced countries in the world, thereby making it especially vulnerable. The attacks lasted twenty-two days, but hit a crescendo on May 9, also known in Russia as Victory Day, on which Russians mark the end of World War II. Immediately thereafter, the attacks stopped, and the statue remains on the outskirts of Tallinn. Jason Healey, a former White House adviser on cybersecurity and now a professor at Columbia University, observed that Russia's attack on Estonia "put everyone on notice that it was willing to behave badly in cyberspace."[1]

Few topics have gotten more attention and been less well understood than Russia's use of the internet to pursue foreign policy goals. And with good reason. Russian digital warriors and their pursuers in other countries operate in a setting where evidence is often ambiguous, identities are hard to prove, and the level of technological expertise needed to judge claims about who did what and why makes it difficult to separate fact from fiction and analysis from self-promotion.

One point of agreement is that Russia is a major player in the dark arts of digital warfare. *New York Times* cybersecurity expert David Sanger noted that "experts often list Russian hackers as the best in the world," while former US director of national intelligence James Clapper said that on cybersecurity issues, he worried "a lot more about the Russians than the Chinese."[2]

There is, however, less agreement about its effectiveness. For example, some argue that Russian trolls pulled off one of the greatest espionage victories in history by exacerbating discord in the United States and helping elect Trump. Others are more skeptical, viewing Russian digital threats as manageable and relatively minor. Disagreement over the effectiveness of digital activity is understandable. It is much easier to measure effort than efficacy. We know that Facebook posts generated by Russian trolls were shared 126 million times in the run-up to the 2016 US presidential election, but it is much harder to know whether these posts had any effect at the ballot box, particularly since they were a tiny fraction of all posts related to the election.

This chapter focuses on the scope and effectiveness of two broad categories of Russian foreign policy activity on the internet: *digital persuasion* via social media, state television, and radio to shape public opinion and voting behavior abroad; and *digital coercion* via hacking servers at state agencies, private firms, and public infrastructure, and disrupting the delivery of goods and services to achieve larger political goals.[3]

It finds that while many observers in the popular press are quick to credit Russian hackers with swaying public opinion and tipping elections abroad, academic experts are for the most part more circumspect. For example, there is much evidence that Russian social media efforts were too small and inept to have had much of an impact on the US election in 2016. Indeed, vastly more disinformation about US elections emanates from domestic than from foreign sources.[4] More generally, it is just difficult to divert attention, change minds, or mobilize voters in a world of information overload and deeply held partisan beliefs. At the same time, digital coercion in the form of "hack and dump" operations that leak sensitive information and cyberattacks on critical infrastructure are far more threatening propositions.

The Scope of Digital Persuasion

Countries have long used the media to try to influence mass politics abroad. In 1929, Radio Moscow was the first sustained state-funded effort to broadcast to foreign audiences, with the British Broadcasting Company emerging in 1932, and Voice of America following shortly thereafter.[5] Today, state-backed international broadcasting on radio, social media, YouTube, and television have become the norm, as national media companies enjoying varying levels of finance and degrees of independence from the state operate in many countries.

In summer 1990, I worked in Munich at Radio Free Europe / Radio Liberty (RFE/RL), funded by the US government. RFE/RL broadcast via radio into the USSR, housed a major archive on dissident writing from the Soviet Union, and published analyses about contemporary politics in the region. I wrote articles on Russian domestic politics for a weekly magazine that was widely read among Russia watchers and the policy community in the United States. The magazine was successful because the print content was less politicized than the radio content broadcast into the USSR. Some of the analysts were Soviet émigrés who adopted a harsher tone toward Moscow, but most were longtime Russia hands who took a more balanced approach. We received no instructions about topics, and my articles on political reform were edited for style, but not for content. The biggest complaint was not about pressure to push a political line but instead about the level of funding. Old-timers at RFE/RL told me that they relished the days before congressional oversight began in the 1970s when US government operatives would just bring suitcases of cash to cover any shortfalls.

Looking back, the format of our weekly magazine from RFE/RL seems quaint. Governments today spread information and disinformation to the far corners of the globe with a click. From television to social media, Russia exploits the internet across a range of platforms for digital persuasion. Most prominent is RT, formerly known as Russia Today, the flagship channel that broadcasts in Chinese, Arabic, Spanish, German, French, and English with an annual budget of roughly $200 million according to the US director of national intelligence. Putin was clear in laying out the goals behind the creation of RT: "When we designed this project back in 2005, we intended introducing another strong player on the international scene—a player that wouldn't just provide unbiased coverage of the events in Russia but also try, let me stress, I mean—try to break the Anglo-Saxon monopoly on global information streams."[6]

RT's motto is not "All the News That's Fit to Print" but rather "Question More." Much of RT's reporting tries to undermine Western institutions, especially the foreign media, to promote Kremlin-friendly versions of news events and flood the media landscape with alternative "truths" that disrupt established narratives. The emphasis on multiple truths is less to shed light than to sow confusion about the state of the world. RT struggles to find viewers on television, but is active on YouTube, where followers are treated to false stories of how the United Kingdom—not the Russians—poisoned Sergei Skripal in summer 2018, interviews with dubious experts that you've never heard of, and talk shows with well-paid foreigners like Larry King. It has a long track record of using actors (sometimes the same ones in different guises) as "eyewitnesses" to events.

In addition to television, the Kremlin uses social media. The trolls at the Internet Research Agency in Saint Petersburg not only seek to shape Russia's domestic politics but also its image abroad. Trolls with stronger foreign language skills are prized. According to one former Internet Research Agency employee, trolls receive quotas for the number of posts they must leave in the comments section of foreign media outlets each day.[7] They are active on Twitter and Facebook, spreading disinformation, amplifying negative stories about foreign rivals, and rebutting criticism of Russia. During the US presidential campaign of 2016, trolls from the Internet Research Agency warned of toxic fumes spreading from fictitious chemical plants in Louisiana, circulated rumors of Ebola outbreaks in the United States, and even tried to organize a political rally that brought together pro- and anti-Muslim groups in Texas and Florida.[8]

In the 2020 US presidential election, Moscow has continued these tactics, but also adopted some new strategies. For example, accounts linked to the Internet Research Agency created a fake website called Peace Data (a pun on a common Russian vulgarism) that recruited unwitting left-leaning journalists to write stories that according to the website, "shed light on the global issues and raise awareness about corruption, environmental crisis, abuse of power, armed conflicts, activism and human rights."[9] On September 1, 2020, Facebook and Twitter shut down the site for misrepresenting its true identity. In addition, Russian-backed trolls now prefer to amplify divisive content created by US sources than to create their own original content as in 2016.[10]

Attempts to persuade mass publics are important during elections. In the Ukrainian presidential election of 2014, Kremlin hackers fed false electoral results to Ukrainian media outlets.[11] The move was quickly corrected, but caused a panic in Kyiv. Prior to the French presidential election in 2017, Russian hackers dumped stolen emails that sought to embarrass the candidate most skeptical of the Russians, Emmanuel Macron.[12] In a brilliant countermove, Macron's team anticipated that Moscow might try a hack and dump operation and mixed false documents with true materials likely to be a target. Once the hackers leaked the material, Macron's team discredited the operation by pointing to the fraudulent documents it contained. And most prominently, Russia conducted a multipronged effort to influence the US presidential election in 2016.

In trying to influence elections by changing mass opinions abroad, isn't Russia just doing what the United States has done for decades? In discussing Russian electoral interference on Capitol Hill, Kentucky senator Rand Paul commented that everyone does it.[13] Certainly US support for Yeltsin in the run-up to the 1996 presidential election, including a large International Monetary Fund loan, had political motives. Political scientist Dov Levin found that between 1946 and 2000, the United States or the USSR intervened either overtly or covertly in 117 elections, or about every ninth election. The United States intervened far more frequently than did the USSR in democratic elections abroad (69 versus 31 percent), and covert interventions like the one attempted by the Kremlin in the United States in 2016 were largely ineffective.[14]

Tom Carothers of the Carnegie Endowment for International Peace offers a subtler evaluation. He argues that US interference in foreign elections was common during the Cold War, but these efforts have declined since 1989. Carothers adds that US democracy promotion does not seek to "undermine the technical integrity of elections" as do Russian efforts to subvert democracy, and that US democracy promotion attempts are also coordinated with democracies like Sweden, Denmark, and the Netherlands, which are not known for geopolitical interventionism. He notes that while "the domain of US democracy promotion is hardly free of flaws and serious past mistakes; it is not the dark twin of the illicit covert election meddling that Russia seems intent on making one if its defining signatures abroad."[15]

Kremlin efforts to mold public opinion extend beyond specific elections and campaigns. Researchers at Clemson University gathered almost 3 million tweets generated from 3,841 sources that Twitter identified as connected to the Internet Research Agency between 2016 and 2018. Consistent with the view that Russian hackers were trying to help Trump, they found that Russian troll activity was highest during moments of vulnerability for the Trump campaign. When President Trump was caught on tape bragging about "grabbing women by the pussy" and seducing married women, Twitter activity from the Internet Research Agency spiked to its highest level. They also found that Russian troll activity did not end on Election Day. One researcher observed, "There were more tweets in the year after the election than there were in the year before the election. I want to shout this from the rooftops. . . . It's a continuing intervention in the political conversation in America."[16]

Russian trolls remained active on Facebook as well. In summer 2018, Facebook reported that it had closed thirty-two fraudulent accounts that had been used to sow disinformation and exacerbate political polarization in the United States.[17] The accounts were created in spring 2017, and called on users to attend counterprotests against Far Right movements and fight against Trump's "fascist" regime. They encouraged Native Americans and African Americans to assert their rights against the white majority. Perhaps most alarming, the hackers' strategy had evolved to avoid the mistakes of previous efforts. Following the election, they used different sources of payment and a wider array of third-party pass-through accounts to mask their original source.

The Effectiveness of Digital Persuasion

For all the talk of Russia's propagandists, there is less attention paid to their effectiveness, and this is understandable as it is much easier to measure effort than efficacy. Some initial evidence suggests that Russia's ability to persuade others and improve its image abroad is overstated. The Pew Research Center conducts a global survey on attitudes toward other countries each year, and finds that Russia and Putin remain quite unpopular abroad. Despite all the resources devoted to projecting Russian soft power, a Pew international survey from thirty-seven countries in summer 2017 found that just one in four respondents had confidence in Putin to do the right thing on the international stage and only 34 percent of respondents had a favorable rating of Russia. In a similar survey in 2020, only 12 percent of Swedes, 18 percent of Americans, 26 percent of Britons, and one-third of Germans held a positive view of Putin.[18]

That Russian is losing its status as the lingua franca in the former Soviet space as English and local languages gain popularity is further testimony to the limits of Russian soft power. Only five former Soviet countries have Russian as one of their official state languages, and Russian language schools across the former Soviet Union are far fewer than in the past.[19]

A more directed study found that Russian propaganda had rather surprising effects. Political scientists Arturas Rozenas and Leonid Pesiakhin studied Russia's disinformation campaign in Ukraine in 2014. They take advantage of the spillover of Russian television into eastern Ukraine, where some villages, but not others, are able to receive the television signal to estimate the impact of having access to these programs on voting and political attitudes. Rozenas and Pesiakhin found that Russian efforts to discredit the Ukrainian government worked, but only on receptive ears. Pro-Russian Ukrainians who watched Russian television programs were more likely to vote for pro-Russian candidates in the 2014 presidential and parliamentary elections, as one might expect.

Still, they also identified a backlash among anti-Russian Ukrainians who became even more likely to vote for pro-Western politicians after watching the same programs. Individuals who had weaker political commitments were unmoved by the programing. By hardening views on both sides of the political spectrum in Ukraine, Russian propaganda had a polarizing effect.

On the positive side, Rozenas and Pesiakhin show that not all citizens were affected by Russian propaganda. Moderates were largely unfazed by the programs. In addition, the backlash effect suggests that there is a natural limit to the persuasive power of propaganda. Increases in pro-Russian votes were somewhat offset by votes for pro-Western politicians. At the same time, it indicates that the main effect of Russian propaganda in this case was to exacerbate social tensions—which seems to be one of the Kremlin's main goals.[20] Given the depth of political polarization across many Western democracies today, this is not a pleasant thought.

Others have focused on whether Russian efforts have swayed election outcomes abroad. Two scholars at the University of Toronto, Lucan Way and Adam Casey, conducted a preliminary study of twenty-seven examples of Russian interference in democratic elections between 1991 and 2017. They identified two waves of activity that differed in intensity and target. Prior to 2014, Russia focused on the states of the former Soviet Union where Moscow intervened not to undermine democracy per se but instead to help pro-Russian candidates or parties. Way and Casey found that in four of eleven cases, the election outcomes favored Russia, and in only one case—the presidential election in Ukraine in 1994—was the Kremlin able to have a significant impact on the outcome. In this instance, Russian-language television that spilled over into eastern Ukraine helped to elect a candidate more sympathetic to Moscow.

They also found that since 2014, Russia has been more active in and focused on elections in Western democracies. In the sixteen cases of Russian interference that occurred after 2014, including national elections in the United States, France, Britain, Norway, and Germany, they saw results favorable to Moscow in nine elections. Way and Casey note two cases where the results turned out as the Kremlin had hoped, Brexit and elections in the Czech Republic in 2017, and seven cases where the results partly reflected Russian interests, as in the strong showing yet ultimate defeat of Marie Le Pen by Emmanuel Macron in France. They state that "favorable outcomes in nine out of 16 elections may seem like a lot. But it's not at all clear that Russia's efforts made any difference," remarking that other factors like increased immigration, economic concerns, and the failure of parties to address voters' concerns were likely far more important. Way and Casey conclude that only three election results in their sample "can be plausibly attributed even partly to Russian efforts."[21]

Yet because the costs are low and upside of influencing elections is so high, the Kremlin continues these efforts, particularly given that Western countries have been unwilling to impose costs on Russia for doing so.

The big question about the effectiveness of Russian social media efforts concerns the 2016 presidential election in the United States.

Popular commentators are quick to make the case. Former Director of US National Intelligence Clapper pointed out, "When you consider that the election turned on 80,000 votes or less in three key states, it stretches credulity to conclude that Russian activity didn't swing voter decisions, and therefore swing the election."[22] Clint Watts, former FBI agent and author of *Messing with the Enemy*, observes, "Without the Russian influence effort, I believe Trump would not have even been within striking distance of Clinton on Election Day."[23]

Kathleen Hall Jamieson, a leading scholar in political communication, asserts that it was not so much the direct effect of Russian social media that helped candidate Trump but rather the US media's treatment of Russian meddling that was influential. She maintains that the press coverage of Russian/WikiLeaks release of incriminating material about Clinton hacked from the Democratic National Committee swung crucial votes to Trump.

Rather than treating the Russian/Wikileaks material as stolen information selectively released by a foreign power to damage a candidate, the US media viewed the material as largely legitimate and kept stories damaging to Clinton in the public eye. For several weeks in the run up to the election, news stories from the Wikileaks material repeatedly played up Clinton's perceived duplicity and dishonesty—key themes echoed by the Trump campaign. Jamieson argues that foreign interference brought Trump to power because the US media failed to put purloined information in its proper context, and remind readers of the dubious and illegal nature of the source material.

Jamieson admits that the 2016 election was unusual. It was very close, and Clinton may have been more susceptible to this kind of campaign given her failure to disclose her use of a private email server as secretary of state. There is no smoking gun evidence, but this seems like the strongest argument for how Russian interference in the election might have affected large numbers of voters in 2016. Whatever the impact of the Russia/Wikileaks hack and dump operation on the 2016 election, the media's uncritical reporting of hacked information is a great problem for US democracy.[24]

Other experts who study elections, however, are more skeptical that Russian efforts turned the tide in favor of Trump. Researchers at

Harvard's Berkman Klein Center for Internet and Society cast doubt on Jamieson's account by analyzing millions of election-related articles and web posts from 2015 to 2018.[25] Their data reveal that the Russian trolls tried to hijack the media narrative, but largely failed. They find that attempts to divert attention from the "Access Hollywood" tape in which Trump brags about sexually assaulting women by releasing damaging emails hacked from the Democratic National Committee were unsuccessful. While the hacked emails generated about 140 to 400 stories per day over the next week, the "Access Hollywood" tape generated 2,000 to 3,000 stories per day over this period. The researchers also note that just 7 percent of Trump supporters cited Facebook as a primary news source and "support for Trump is highest in demographic groups with the least exposure to the internet."[26]

Nate Silver adds that it is hard to determine whether Russian efforts helped Trump because the disinformation campaign occurred over a period of months and was so similar to that of other extreme groups. Moreover, Silver explains that while the Internet Research Agency was devoting around $1.25 million per month toward interference efforts in the election, the Clinton and Trump campaigns along with their supporting political action committees raised $1.2 billion and $617 million, respectively, during the campaign.[27] Similarly, while Twitter reported that Russian bots tweeted 2.1 million times before the election, this represented just .05 percent of the tweets viewed related to the election.[28] So while Russian efforts were nontrivial, they were a tiny fraction of the efforts devoted to political messaging by the candidates and their surrogates.

Political scientist Brendan Nyhan reports that there is much research in US politics that shows it is hard to change people's minds, especially among committed Democrats and Republicans. His own research bears this out. With his coauthors, he argues that fake news on social media during the 2016 campaign appears to have reinforced existing biases rather than changed minds. Based on a deep dive into visits to fake news websites, Nyhan and coauthors found that during the 2016 campaign, one in four Americans visited at least one pro-Clinton or pro-Trump fake news website, but 60 percent of all visits to fake news websites were concentrated in the 10 percent of Americans with the most conservative information diets.[29] Instead of influencing unsuspecting independents, it appears that the main effect of this propaganda was to reinforce the already pro-Trump views of his most ardent supporters. Indeed, many studies from political science find that political advertising on television in US elections has little to no effect on voting or outcomes, and it would be surprising if Russian trolls on social media had better success.[30]

Fake news also attracts less attention than do other sources of news. Researchers from New York and Stanford Universities used big data techniques and a survey to track social media consumption around the election of 2016, finding that "even the most widely circulated fake news stories were seen by only a small fraction of Americans" and thus demonstrating that fake news tends to be overwhelmingly used by a small number of dedicated viewers. They estimate that the average adult saw and remembered about one fake news story during the campaign.[31]

Of course, these results depend on how we define fake news. Academic studies tend to adopt restrictive approaches that include only obvious examples. Alex Jones's InfoWars is fake news, while Fox and MSNBC are not. These academic studies may capture the most egregious examples of fake news, but they miss the partisan bias in more mainstream media—a trend that is also worrying.

Beyond attempting to influence behavior at the ballot box, Russian-led efforts on social media encouraged Americans to join racially divisive protests in Florida, New York, and Texas in 2016. These efforts, though, found few takers. One oft-cited such attempt in Houston—America's fourth-largest city of more than 2.3 million residents—drew a grand total of sixty protesters.[32] The Internet Research Agency also attempted to send messages under the guise of fake local news outlets on Twitter, but these efforts were also quite clumsy and small scale.[33]

Proving or disproving claims that Russian efforts tipped the balance in the 2016 US presidential election is a challenge, and strong claims from either side should be met with skepticism. This does not mean that fake news of the kind generated by Russian trolls (and political trolls of all nationalities) is not a concern. It can harden the views of committed partisans, exacerbate polarization, and simply degrade the quality of political discussion. More generally, Russian disinformation efforts and cyberattacks extend well beyond voting, and just because it is hard to assess their impact on the 2016 presidential election does not mean that they should be dismissed.

Moreover, it is critical to recognize that foreign rivals are unlikely to succeed in changing election outcomes on their own. Dov Levin finds that over the last seventy years, successful foreign election interference is usually an "inside job" that involves cooperation from major players in the target country. In many countries over the decades, the United States and USSR have provided cash, aid, technical assistance, and dirty tricks in overt and covert attempts to influence election outcomes, but these attempts generally fail if resisted by the target country.

The US case fits Levin's argument. Moscow has a long history of trying to influence elections in the United States. Kremlin operatives reached out to Democratic presidential candidates in 1952, 1960, and 1968 with an offer to improve their election prospects in various ways, but were rebuffed by the campaigns of Adlai Stevenson, John Kennedy, and Hubert Humphrey.[34] In 1992, three top operatives in the Republican Party raised the possibility of asking Moscow for information on candidate Bill Clinton's activities during his visits to the Soviet Union as a student in an attempt to discredit him. White House chief of staff James Baker quickly shot down the proposal. Without a willing partner in the United States, the Kremlin's attempts to influence elections in the United States went nowhere. This is a far cry from US presidential elections in 2016 and 2020, when the Republican candidate courted foreign assistance from Russia with little criticism, and in many cases, active support from his party.[35]

Kremlin attempts to use social media to sway the 2016 election are just one effort to influence US politics. The Kremlin courted high-level Trump administration officials and found its overtures well received, if still falling short of the legal definition of conspiracy. That Trump's campaign manager, Paul Manafort, shared internal campaign data with a Russian partner connected with the intelligence services and met with other Russians who promised to share compromising material on Clinton are the best examples of coordination between Team Trump and the Russian government.[36] More broadly, the range of contacts between high-level Trump administration officials and Russians with varying links to the Kremlin is well documented and unlike anything we have seen in any other presidential administration in US history.[37] The breakdown of the norm against using foreign help in elections is another warning bell for democracy in the United States.

The Scope of Digital Coercion

Beyond digital persuasion, the Kremlin uses digital coercion to shape politics abroad by targeting government agencies and officials, hacking public infrastructure and large private companies, and spying on public officials. These efforts include stealing bank accounts and financial data as well as harassing foreign governments that oppose Russia. Borrowing a play from its suppression of opposition groups in Russia, the pro-Kremlin cyberwarriors are good at selectively releasing damaging information against foreign officials. To try to divide the European Union and United States on their strategy toward Ukraine after the fall of the Yanukovych government in 2014, groups linked to Russia released a phone conversation between US State Department representative Victoria Nuland and the US ambassador to Ukraine where they discuss who they would like to see in a new Ukrainian government. A transcript of the call has Nuland saying "Fuck the EU" for not wanting UN officials to become part of efforts to strike a political deal in Kyiv. While foreign governments regularly eavesdrop on the conversations of foreign officials as best they can, they rarely release them to the public.[38]

In an audacious use of the internet for digital coercion, hackers allied with Russia shut down the electric power grid in the Ukrainian region of Ivano-Frankivsk in December 2015.[39] Russian hackers took control of the power plant, shut down operations, and left 225,000 Ukrainians literally in the dark. The attack not only implanted software that wiped out hard drives but also disabled the company's call center so customers could not register their complaints. This move may have been in response to a physical attack on a power plant in Ukraine that supplied electricity to Crimea and knocked out power on the recently annexed territory. Ukrainian engineers managed to restart the plant in six hours and return electricity to their subscribers, but they were forced to spend months repairing the system.

Cyber incursions can also be used to signal foreign policy intentions. In October 2014, as the United States was discussing a new round of punitive sanctions against Russian firms and individuals involved in the annexation of Crimea, Russian hackers infiltrated the unclassified sections of the US White House and State Department. At the same time, the volume of recognized attempts from Russia to break into servers at large US companies and firms peaked. In this way, the Russians were using activity on the internet to remind the United States of its vulnerability in the cyber realm should the Obama administration go ahead with sanctions.[40] Undeterred, the Obama administration approved the sanctions.[41]

Russia has used digital attacks during international crises too. In addition to the Estonian example that starts this chapter, Russia leaned on digital techniques in its short war with Georgia in 2008. For two decades, a tenuous peace held in South Ossetia, a small region of Georgia that fought for independence in the early 1990s. Peacekeepers from Russia, Georgia, and Ossetia stationed in South Ossetia ended the violence, but Georgia chafed at the lost territory. Border skirmishes between Georgia and Russia in 2008 eventually led to Russian tanks, troops, and artillery crossing into Georgia. As the intervention unfolded, government websites, financial institutions, and media outlets in Georgia were taken off-line or defaced by hackers. These coordinated attacks from thousands of computers flooded Georgian websites with requests for information that overwhelmed their capacities. The hackers used a public forum to recruit ordinary Russians to add to the frenzy by signing up at the website www.StopGeorgia.ru. *Slate* magazine's technology writer Evgeny Morozov described how he became a digital warrior in the Georgian conflict in less than an hour by signing up at the website and using his computer to add to the attack.[42]

Beyond damaging infrastructure and supporting military moves, Russian-backed hackers engage in the usual hand-to-hand combat that takes place in cyberspace, such as gaining access to defense ministry accounts in Denmark in 2011, snooping on German parliamentarians in

2015, breaching unclassified email accounts at the US White House in 2015, and hacking the emails of Norwegian members of Parliament in 2020.[43]

Moscow uses computer specialists hired directly by the security services, but also employs a large number of freelancers who can give the government a degree of plausible deniability should they be identified.[44] One ex-hacker notes that the Russian Ministry of Defense and FSB have "diffuse networks for attracting and incentivizing criminal hackers and creating the conditions for their work, supplying them with the necessary information." For example, the intelligence agencies in the Russian Ministry of Defense and the FSB sometimes provide safe houses to hackers who are being pursued by the Russian police.[45]

But are Russian cyber strategies distinct? Two studies suggest yes. The Council on Foreign Relations created a cybertracker that includes all publicly known state-sponsored cyberattacks by nineteen nations since 2005 categorized across different types of attacks and targets.[46] Because it only includes digital assaults that are state sponsored and uses quite restrictive criteria about attribution, the council's estimate is conservative. Russia, with around forty-five cyberattacks, is the second most active country in the sample after China, with more than eighty attacks. Russia's assaults are especially frequent in the political realm, including an attack on the Dutch organization investigating the downing of the passenger airliner MH-17 over eastern Ukraine in 2015, attempts to compromise the World Anti-Doping Agency in 2016, and targeting the citizen-journalist website Bellingcat in 2017, among others.

Three scholars who have conducted a rare cross-national study of cyberwar agree. Brandon Valeriano, Benjamin Jensen, and Ryan Maness collected data on more than 192 cases of cyber coercion between 2000 and 2014. They find that the United States and Israel tend to target military and government systems, China favors stealing industrial and governmental secrets, and North Korea usually goes after specific companies, as in its hacking of Sony for publishing a parody of Kim Jong-un.[47]

In contrast, Russia is much more likely to work with criminal elements, and is "unique in how it has used a mix of cyber power and propaganda to shape electoral institutions and undermine faith in the democratic process."[48] Valeriano, Jensen, and Maness add that through its extensive disruption efforts in Georgia and Estonia, punishing attacks on Ukrainian infrastructure, and attempts to discredit elections in the United States, Germany, and France, "Russia has been one of the most aggressive and destructive actors in cyberspace."[49] Yet they also note that Russia has exercised caution in using cyber strategies during conflicts to avoid escalation and has tended to avoid military targets during peacetime.[50]

The Effectiveness of Digital Coercion

If judging the effectiveness of digital persuasion is difficult, so is assessing the impact of digital coercion. One can argue that cyberattacks have mostly been a nuisance to date. Despite suffering one of the most prolonged and intense cyberattacks in history, Estonian officials did not return the statue of the Soviet soldier to its former location. Ukraine weathered the shutdown of its regional power system in 2015 and was back online in less than a day. In their study of 192 cybersecurity attacks by national governments, Valeriano and his coauthors observe that "Russia fails more often than it succeeds" and even its victories can be counterproductive when they provoke countermeasures. A good example is Estonia. After it suffered a massive denial-of-service attack in 2007, Estonia hardened its defense and is now the centerpiece of NATO's cybersecurity strategy.[51]

This view suggests that escalation in cyberspace is constrained by a fear of retaliation. As in the nuclear realm, the concept of mutually assured destruction reigns even with the worrisome nuance that attribution for an attack is much more difficult in the digital world than in the physical world.

But this seems too rosy, especially for countries like the United States that rely so heavily on the internet and technology for everything from finance to national security. Digital security experts often underscore that there are two types of companies: those that have been hacked and those that don't know it yet. And the worlds of economic crime and security usually overlap. The Russian government frequently uses hackers from the private sector who specialize in economic crimes. In an embarrassing discovery, the United States arrested four Russians for breaking into five million Yahoo email accounts. Two of these hackers turned out to be FSB officers who were also the FBI's official points of contact on a joint US and Russian task force on cybercrime.[52]

Even the threat of digital coercion can be effective. Russia's ability to strike infrastructure targets in the United States weighed heavily on the Obama administration's response to Russian interference in the 2016 presidential election.

In the run up to the election, the Obama White House learned that hackers believed to be working for Russia scanned at least twenty-one state-level databases of election rolls and were well placed to disrupt the election by claiming to have altered the results.[53] This knowledge stymied the White House. Most observers believe that hackers did not alter vote tallies, perhaps out of concern of how the United States would respond to this significant escalation. But just by letting the White House know that they had scanned state voter rolls, these hackers tied the Obama administration in knots. Some advisers urged the president to take aggressive action against the Kremlin, perhaps by revealing damaging information about President Putin or conducting a cyberattack of his own against Moscow. Others feared that an escalatory move by the White House would only lead to a more aggressive response from the Kremlin and increase the risks of chaos on Election Day.[54]

Ultimately Obama warned Putin in person, and Russian influence efforts on social media subsided somewhat, but many in the Obama White House would have preferred a more forceful response in retrospect. That White House officials were so occupied with whether and how to respond to Moscow in the months before the election reveals the power of foreign electoral interference. In 2016, digital coercion in the form of the hack and dump operation against the Democratic National Committee and the threat of altering voting data was a far more effective tool than digital persuasion via social media.

Moreover, the impact of the threat of retaliation by the Kremlin did not end on Election Day. Following Trump's victory in November 2016 and the subsequent revelation of Russia's interference efforts during the campaign, the Obama White House considered a range of possibilities for punishing Moscow before leaving office, including retaliatory strikes on digital infrastructure in Russia and releasing incriminating personal information on Putin, but ultimately took much less damaging steps. The United States tossed out thirty-five Russian diplomats from the country, closed the Russian consulate in San Francisco, and shuttered Russian government properties in Long Island and Maryland—steps that were quickly matched by Moscow. One key consideration in the White House was the fear of escalating a cyberconflict with Russia given the far greater reliance of the United States on the internet.[55] In this case, the United States was "cyberdeterred" by fear of Russia's capabilities in digital coercion.

The prospect of a digital attack on critical infrastructure, including voting booths, election records, power grids, and government computers by a foreign threat, is easy to imagine. There is much evidence that hackers sympathetic to Russia have conducted similar attacks in Ukraine, Georgia, and possibly elsewhere. The Chinese hacked into the Obama and McCain campaigns in 2008. North Korean cyberwarriors caused significant damage to Sony for its movie parody of Kim Jong-un by leaking damaging private emails. These are more than just hypotheticals. For example, the US intelligence community believes that Russia sought to find the passwords of state-level election officials in the United States in 2016.[56] In 2020, US election bodies have experienced a high number of ransomware attacks that threaten to leak sensitive election data if payment is not made.[57] Should these efforts succeed in a future election, it could spark a major political crisis under the right conditions.

Perhaps the best evidence of the power of digital coercion comes not from Russia but rather from operation "Olympic Games," a US and Israeli effort to plant malicious Stuxnet software on computer systems running Iran's infant nuclear program around 2010. The highly sophisticated software caused the centrifuges that enrich uranium to speed up and slow down at odd intervals, thereby slowing the process. The plan worked for several years before being detected and arguably set back Iranian efforts to develop nuclear weapons by more than a year.[58]

More recently, in summer 2019, the United States let it be known that it had placed "potentially crippling malware on Russia's electrical grid."[59] This move was a "digital shot across the bow" for the Kremlin in hopes of deterring cyberattacks on US targets from Moscow. That officials at the US National Security Council did not criticize the *New York Times* for publishing the story suggests that hacking served as a public signal of US capabilities to other countries as well.

Clearly the United States and its Western allies need to educate citizens about foreign efforts to shape public opinion via social media and state broadcasts, particularly during elections. Moreover, foreign efforts to shut down electric grids, tamper with election results, and hack into private communications are far reaching and demand constant attention.

———

Russia's efforts in the digital world help us understand the Kremlin's intentions and capabilities. That the content pushed by Kremlin-backed trolls is crafted to sow discord in the West by disseminating disinformation and supporting extremist groups tells us a good deal about Moscow's objectives. A different approach would be to simply back candidates favorable to Russia and promote a more positive view of Moscow. Although the Kremlin does these things as well, it devotes more effort to discrediting Western political institutions than to advocating Russian interests. That Russian trolls and hackers are much more likely than other cyberpowers to target political institutions also gives a good indication of the Kremlin's goals.

More broadly, it is important to view Russia's use of cyber techniques as a weapon of a country that is at a disadvantage with major rivals. Valeriano and his team contend that Russia uses the "tactics of a weak and declining power that is fighting for influence. . . . Russia acts in cyberspace—and will continue to do—because it has few options. Harassing, undermining and challenging the United States in the shadows are the tactics of a state fighting for influence."[60] This overstates the case of Russian weakness, but digital coercion offers a relatively cheap alternative to other tools, and allows Russia to take advantage of its highly skilled computer programmers, weak rule of law, and nondemocratic political system. Russia is not on the verge of collapse, and the Putin regime is not on the brink of falling, but Russia faces deep problems that inhibit its ability to project power using conventional means. Viewing Russia's efforts at digital persuasion in this light helps puts the threat from Russian cyberhacking in perspective. Adam Segal of the Council on Foreign Relations notes, "Cyber is not a superweapon: it is one tool among many."[61]

In viewing Russia's cyber capabilities abroad, it is crucial to keep some perspective. Russia's activities in the digital world are worrying and tell us a lot about Russia's intentions toward the West, but they are only one tool in Russia's foreign policy arsenal. Just as the United States favors economic sanctions because of its central position in the global economy, Russia favors cyberattacks because it plays to the Kremlin's comparative advantage. Digital persuasion and coercion are especially attractive precisely because they are so cheap, and other tools in Moscow's foreign policy bag are so blunt.

11

Conclusion

THE DEATH OF EXPERTISE?

Today everyone knows everything; with a quick trip through
WebMD or Wikipedia, average citizens believe themselves to be
on an equal intellectual footing with doctors and diplomats.

—TOM NICHOLS, *THE DEATH OF EXPERTISE*

OVER THE PAST thirty years I have written about topics ranging from
petty corruption in Poland to voter mobilization in Venezuela, but I'm
always lured back to Russia. I sometimes joke that I'm like Michael Cor-
leone in the *Godfather*: "I want to get out, but they keep pulling me back
in." It is easy to see why. For anyone interested in the stuff of politics—
the bluffs and threats, use and abuse of power, and simple struggle to
hold onto office—Russia is the gift that keeps on giving. While Russian
politics are always interesting, now is a particularly important and challenging moment to dig deep into why the Kremlin does what it does.

One source of urgency lies close to home. We observe Russian politics not only by what happens in Moscow and Tomsk but also by what
happens in Washington and Dubuque. Current concerns over the state
of democracy and uncertainty of the role of the United States in global
politics cannot help but color our views about contemporary Russia.
For some on the Far Right, this means seeing the supposed advantages

of strongman rule and racial homogeneity in Russia.[1] For some on the Left, it too often means exaggerating Putin's ability to hoodwink voters and manipulate politics at home and abroad.[2] Looking across the US political spectrum, views of Russia in the United States have become much more partisan, with many Democrats and Republicans staking out different positions on the issue. Rather than viewing Russia by what it does, laypeople take their cue from the elites in the political party they support. To the extent that the popular narrative on Russia is shaped by domestic politics in the United States, we see Russia with less clarity.

The rise of the "post-truth" era further compels us to take a hard look at Russia. Lying and propaganda in politics are nothing new, but the ease with which governments and private groups can use technology to spread political falsehoods is unprecedented. Moreover, the traditional guardrails against political untruths, such as the free press, political parties, and the rule of law, have all grown weaker, thereby giving demagogues, opportunists, and activists of all sorts far greater rein to distort interpretations about how politics work in other countries. While it is easy to overstate the impact of the mainstream and social media on popular attitudes, academic research suggests that casual observers are more likely to be influenced by elite opinions on low-information issues like foreign policy than on high-information issues like the economy. This makes it even more crucial to ground our views on Russia in the best evidence available rather than on dated stereotypes, partisan biases, or simple ignorance.

Most important, the condition of domestic politics in Russia makes this an especially propitious moment to turn our attention to Russia. In his first decade in office, Putin reaped the gains of unprecedented economic growth, and in his second, he rode a wave of nationalist sentiment following the annexation of Crimea, but these narratives have gone stale. Few believe in Putin's promise of future economic prosperity, and Russia's foreign policy "victories" are far down the list of priorities for most Russians. Putin's twenty years in power and the prospect of many more on the horizon have led to a strong bout of Putin fatigue among the mass public.[3]

Tensions among the elite appear to be rising as well, although there is always a good bit of guesswork in divining relations among the Kremlin insiders. For the first time in modern Russian history, a sitting minister of economics was jailed on bribery charges. In December 2017, Alexei Ulyukayev, a long-standing Russian official, was sentenced to eight years in prison for accepting a $2 million bribe from Igor' Sechin, the head of Rosneft' and a close Putin confidante. That the bribe was so small by Russian standards, was given directly to Ulyukayev by the CEO of Rosneft' himself in a bag thought to contain sausages, and led to such a harsh prison sentence suggests the political nature of the case.

In recent years, we have seen Rauf Arashukov, a sitting Russian senator, taken into custody on murder charges on the floor of the upper house of Parliament, and the arrest of Mikhail Abyzov, a former minister and close confidant of Prime Minister Medvedev. Alexander Ishayev, a former influential governor from the far east, is now in custody as is Pavel Kon'kov, a former governor of the Ivanov region.[4] In 2019, a number of high-profile businesspeople, including Michael Calvey, an American with several decades of experience in Russia, David Yakobashvili, a food products magnate who began business in the 1990s, and Sergei Petrov, the head of Rolf, the largest auto dealer in Russia, have also found themselves behind bars or facing charges with long jail terms.[5] Conflicts (often involving criminal charges) among the security services have been more open than any time in recent memory as rival clans in the FSB, police, Procuracy, and Investigative Committee vie for influence.[6] These are the kinds of interelite disputes that Putin was able to resolve before they became public in his first two decades in office.

With the days of easy economic growth and low-cost foreign policy victories in the past, the Kremlin is struggling to find a new story to tell. Great-power nationalism is likely to be part of the narrative, but it is hard to pull this off at a 1 percent growth rate. As it gropes for a new formula to justify its claim to rule, the Putin administration has turned up the screws on the public. Recent years have seen stricter limits on free speech, more severe restrictions on political competition, and targeted repression against political opponents—policies that are unlikely to help Russia address its deeper economic and social problems. The ultimate content of the Kremlin's legitimation strategy will be well worth watching. No less important will be how the Russian public receives this message.

The constitutional amendments of 2020 have hardly resolved Putin's political dilemma. The problem of uncertainty around a possible presidential transfer of power is lower, but remains. Putin now has a clear constitutional path to run for office in 2024 and will not be seen as a lame duck for the next four years, but he also retains the option of stepping down. At a minimum, he has pushed off the succession question until 2024, and at a maximum, he may intend to rule until 2036, when he will be eighty-three. The expectation that Putin will stay on as president will likely reinforce the status quo of economic stagnation and heighten popular frustration over the Kremlin's inability to improve standards of living or raise the quality of governance. It will do little to lure back to Russia talented Russians who have left the country, discipline corrupt bureaucrats, or spark greatly needed economic innovation.

Another much-discussed possibility for Putin, stepping down as president, but continuing to exercise power by heading a revamped State Council, raises risks for Putin too. He would have to control a new president, who will want to expand their powers in ways big and small. The possibility that a new president will turn on their predecessor can never be discounted. While Putin managed this problem by serving as prime minister during Medvedev's presidency, it will be much harder for him to do so as a senior citizen.

This constitutional maneuver highlights the value of viewing Putin as a weak strongman. Russia's leader has been unrivaled in domestic politics, but this supremacy is the result of weakening state institutions, distorting the economy, and choosing unsound policies—three important elements of state power.

Whether Putin will step down as president as he did in 2008 is an open question, but the mere possibility of this creates an intriguing decision point for Russian elites who would like to succeed Putin.[7] Loyalty to the president will be rewarded, yet only as long as he stays in office. Choose the winning side and reap the benefits, but back a loser and prepare for punishment.

Battles over the possibility of succession are rarely smooth in personalist autocracies like Russia, and the jockeying for political and economic influence are underway. With Putin's sky-high ratings a thing of the past, a deep economic crisis, and a well-educated and urban population critical of the government, Russia's next few years will likely be rocky. It will be essential to have a clear-eyed view of Russian politics if a transfer of power takes place, and if it doesn't. In a word, the reassessment of Russian politics offered here comes at an important moment.

A Reassessment

This reexamination finds that Russian politics are not simply an extension of Putin's worldview, or a reflection of Russia's unique literature, history, or culture, but rather involve many of the same trade-offs that all authoritarian governments face. Cheat too much on elections and signal weakness, but cheat too little and risk losing office. Use anti-Westernism to rile the base, yet not so much that it provokes an actual conflict with the West. Use corruption to reward cronies, though not so much that it stunts economic growth. Manipulate the news, but not so much that people distrust the media. Repress political opponents, but not so much that there is a popular backlash. Keep the security services strong, yet not so strong that they can turn on you. While many depictions of Russia focus on Putin's seemingly unlimited power, this view recognizes that even autocrats as influential as Putin face significant constraints and difficult choices over policy because of the nature of autocratic rule.

This research also provides a more nuanced view of Russia's role on the global stage. In foreign policy, Russia is neither a Potemkin power that will collapse with just a little more economic pressure nor is it a great power committed to overturning the Western order at any cost; unfortunately, the Western powers seem to be doing a pretty good of job of that themselves with only marginal help from Moscow. Rather, Russia is a much more opportunistic power that uses its military and economic might to influence weaker countries in its neighborhood, while picking its spots against more powerful rivals like the European Union, United States, and China.

This reassessment has critical implications for Russia's future.[8] The current tendency to link Russia's various ills to Putin implies that once he leaves office, so will these pathologies. Remove the autocrat and the autocracy is weakened. Remove the aggressor and Russian foreign policy will be less aggressive. But this argument puts too much emphasis on the individual leader. It is more important to change the rules of the political game than to change the leader.

Deep-seated political change is not likely to occur with Putin in the Kremlin, but a Russia without Putin as president may disappoint those seeking a more open and friendly Russia. Research finds that when rulers leave office in a nondemocracy, the most likely government to follow is another nondemocracy. Based on data of all nondemocratic governments from 1946 until 2008, the University of Rochester's Hein Goemans found that the prospects for transition to democracy were far dimmer for personalist governments like Russia. Only 16 percent of personalist autocracies were replaced by democratic governments compared to 35 percent of military-led autocracies.[9] Personalist autocracies like Russia are especially likely to beget another nondemocratic regime. None of this is reassuring for global stability considering that the Putin regime is very much a personalist autocracy and looms large in world politics.

A post-Putin Russia may also not produce a radical shift in foreign policy. Whoever sits in the Kremlin will retain military predominance in Russia's neighborhood, a resource-rich economy, and a good deal of elite skepticism toward the West. It is hard to imagine that a post-Putin Russia would abandon cyberhacking given its comparative advantage in using this tool compared to other foreign policy instruments. Russia, with its overwhelming military and economic power relative to its immediate neighbors, will continue to use these tools to shape politics in the region, and given its relatively weaker position vis-à-vis the European Union, China, and the United States, Russia will likely continue to rely on low-cost opportunistic tactics to limit Western influence. These points of view underpin the "dismal consensus" that dominates most contemporary discussions of Russia.[10]

And yet another broad line of academic research offers a more optimistic perspective. Compared to other countries, Russia is too rich and well educated to be so nondemocratic, corrupt, and illiberal. Research suggests that a country's income and education levels are correlated with its type of government. By these measures, Russia's prospects are more promising. In 2017, Russia was wealthier than fifteen of the sixteen Latin American democracies on a per capita basis. Although measuring education levels is tricky, Russia scores high by most formal indicators, and mass education levels in Russia exceed those of all the Latin American democracies by a considerable margin. Also in Russia's favor are relatively high levels of urbanization as well as cultural and ethnic homogeneity. Russia is oil rich, but less so than many petrostates, and it has the potential to develop other economic sectors should a new leader pursue that path. Economic inequality is high in Russia, but lower than in many Latin American democracies. Generational change also points in the direction of reform. Younger Russians are more socially active, pro-Western, individualist, expect less from the state, and are less vulnerable to Kremlin messaging than are older cohorts.[11] To be sure, we don't have a good sense of how these deep social factors lead to political change and the transition from autocratic rule may produce great instability in the short run, but by these social and economic indicators Russia's future looks less dismal than many realize.

Russia's future will not unfold in a vacuum. While Russians will ultimately determine the fate of Russia, their efforts will be shaped by interactions with the outside world, for better and worse. At the moment, foreign relations provide little incentive for deep political change in Russia. The bleak condition of relations between Russia and the West has strengthened the groups in Russia most invested in the political status quo, such as the security services, state-sector firms, state workers, and agricultural lobby as well as groups dependent on the state for their livelihood. Moreover, skepticism in foreign capitals toward Russia's intentions in foreign policy—much of it warranted—is at high levels and will not recede easily.

In addition, the continued willingness of New York, London, and other financial centers to allow foreign elites to park their ill-gotten gains abroad only reinforces political stasis in Russia.[12] As long as foreign officials—and Russians are far from alone in this—can loot their own countries and stash their assets abroad with impunity, they will have little incentive to stop preying on their own people.[13] Greater scrutiny of financial transactions by Russian elites abroad will hardly cause a political revolution in Russia on its own, but by shaping the kinds of trade-offs highlighted above, it might push Russia toward better governance.

Most important, the failure of Western governments to put their own houses in order further reduces the likelihood of political change in Russia. The decline of democratic norms, rise of ugly forms of nativism, and deep political polarization in many Western countries has made democracy, openness, and liberalism less attractive than they were a decade ago, and undermined groups within Russia that oppose Russia's autocracy, protectionism, and statism. Any leverage that the United States and Europe may exercise to push for human rights in Russia is compromised by democratic erosion in the West. Few Russians want their government to be a facsimile of a Western democracy, but to the extent that the Russian government can convince its citizens that there is little difference between a Western-style democracy and Putin-style autocracy, hopes dim for a Russia that is a "better version of itself."[14] Whatever the near future brings for Russia, it will be important to keep our eyes open to the possibility of political change

How to Understand Russia

The findings from the preceding chapters not only inform our views of the substance of Russian politics but also have implications for how we should go about understanding Russia. The research suggests that shifting our gaze from Putin to broader forces at work in Russian politics is a far more profitable strategy than trying to put Putin on the couch or ascribe everything that happens in Russia to an extension of Russian history.

Moving beyond a focus on Putin's personal characteristics also has the advantage of giving us guidance for the post-Putin era. By viewing Russian domestic politics as having much in common with other nondemocratic regimes and analyzing Russian foreign policy as akin to that of other major powers, we can better identify patterns and possibilities regardless of the personal quirks and temperament of any particular leader. Barring a dramatic change in the political system, whoever rules Russia will face many of the same policy trade-offs that have occupied the Putin administration for the last twenty years, and understanding the costs and benefits of different policy choices should be at the center of our attention when we talk about Russian politics.

Above all, the research presented here indicates that we need to raise our standards in evaluating arguments about Russia. All too often commentators rely on a selective reading of the evidence, a quick reference to Putin's background, or some cherry-picked evidence from Russian history to support their case. This is unfortunate because the opportunities for gathering data and testing arguments are far better than in the past. When I began studying the USSR in the 1980s, we relied heavily on reading cryptic articles in the Soviet press, deciphering the Aesopian language of Soviet academic writings, and trying to make sense of official data that bore little resemblance to reality. Some Sovietologists did a lot with a little, and some did a little with a little, but all were severely constrained in how they could study the Soviet Union.

But times have changed. Previous chapters have shown how scholars have used traditional methods, like surveys, ethnography, and archival research combined with more cutting-edge techniques like web scraping, field experiments, and big data, to study topics from vote fraud to the legacy of Stalinist terror. New technologies have undoubtedly helped, but no less important has been collaboration with Russian academic colleagues. It is hard to study Russia, and some research questions remain out of bounds, but scholars have given us a much richer picture of Russian politics than we have of most nondemocratic regimes.

Of course, the academic research cited in prior chapters has its own shortcomings. Scholars have given more attention to Russian domestic politics than to foreign policy. Academic research is often laden with jargon and arcane statistical techniques. And don't get me started on the quality of most scholarly writing. At the same time, this body of work helps to address, however imperfectly, some of the weaknesses of popular discussions about Russia watching identified in chapter 1. Without ignoring the role of Putin's personality and background, academics studying Russia's authoritarian regime try to identify the general constraints and resources available to Putin. They seek to learn the ways in which Putin behaves like other autocratic leaders and when he leaves his personal stamp on policy.

Politicization is hard for all Russia watchers to avoid as we bring our own preconceptions to our research. At the same time, the peer review process that undergirds academic research helps to rub off the most blatant and obvious forms of bias. The successive drafts of academic articles, friendly and not so friendly comments of reviewers and discussants, and requirement in the words of your third grade math teacher "to show your work" by sharing your data all combine to constrain as well as reduce the inherent biases and unstated assumptions that we all bring to our work. Peer review has its problems, but it does work to reduce the politicization of arguments in the field. In our supposedly post-truth era, we should place an even greater premium on the transparency and richness of evidence provided in the best academic research.

To address parochialism, academic Russia watchers have joined with other experts to create impressive research projects on nondemocratic governments across countries and over time that allow us to put Russia in a comparative perspective. Databases that classify different types of nondemocracies, trace their different patterns of rule, and catalog the personal features of individual autocrats reveal patterns that were not available to previous generations of scholars. Moreover, the increased role of Russian scholars in debates on Russian politics provides a further check on foreign scholars being blinkered by parochialism.

To be sure, no two countries are alike, and Russia has its own specific features that make simple comparisons misleading in some areas. Most important, as a major player in international politics, Russia can stoke great-power nationalism among its citizens far more easily than can most countries. Russia is also an energy superpower with resources that only the United States and Saudi Arabia can match. All countries have their own unique features, and Russia is exceptional in the same sense that all countries are exceptional, but that does not mean that we cannot learn a great deal by comparing Russia to other countries.

And as for excessive confidence in our analyses, I have tried to distinguish between more speculative arguments where the evidence is equivocal and more well-founded arguments rooted in convincing data. Some questions are more difficult to research than others, and some insights here are based more on conjecture than hard evidence, so it is important to alert the reader to which arguments fall into which category. For all the difficulties of understanding Russian politics present and future, we are well advised to ground our views in the kinds of evidence-based arguments of the kind cited herein.

I have championed this work for a broader audience because, unfortunately, it has not had much impact on public debate. Commentary on Russia in the popular media today is dominated by journalists, politicians, think tankers, activists, and former policy makers. That the field of Russia watching has become much more diverse since the end of the Cold War is on balance a healthy development, even if the quality of commentary is highly uneven. But it has also meant that scholars conducting basic research on Russia are more marginal than they were during the Cold War, when relations between academic Russia watchers and policy makers were closer.[15]

The reasons for this are many. Partisan think tanks, consulting firms, and public relations firms supported by foreign governments and big business are playing an increasing role in shaping popular narratives on Russia, and academic research that questions conventional wisdom on Russia may be seen as threatening to these competitors for policy influence.

In addition, the experiences of academic Russia hands are not that much different from experts in other areas trying to influence policy in our era of political polarization, hyperpartisanship, and skepticism toward credentials. The popular narrative on Russia is another example of the "death of expertise" in political discourse more generally as expert voices are pushed to the margins of debate.[16]

Academia too deserves blame for its own marginalization from popular discussion on Russia. Universities do too little to reward public engagement on policy debates, particularly for younger scholars who have not yet obtained tenure.[17] These incentives are changing with the rise of social media and data-driven journalism, but still much more can be done to make social science research on Russia accessible and useful for policy makers and the general public. The stakes are too high to get Russia wrong.

This problem is not unique to the United States. I asked a Russian academic friend who had worked tirelessly over the past two decades to use academic research to inform policy debates in the far less hospitable environment of Putin's Russia. He cited a few of his successes and many of his failures over the years. When pressed about why he continued, he said what keeps him going is economist Albert Hirschman's guidance that when giving policy advice, one should always retain a "bias for hope" because although we can always point to many reasons why good policy advice will be blocked by vested interests, we can never be sure that our advice won't make a difference, so we should forge ahead.[18] This is good advice for us all.

When I was an exhibit guide for the US government in the late 1980s, I sometimes jolted our visitors by noting that I hoped that these exhibits, as successful as they were, would end. After some objections from our visitors, I noted that we didn't have such exchanges with France or Sweden, because if people wanted to learn more about these countries, they could read their press, watch their movies, or even travel there. I wanted Americans and Russians to see each other outside the artificial setting of a state-run cultural exchange program.

In many respects this has already happened. I'm about as likely to hear Russian as French on the streets of the Upper West Side of Manhattan where I live. I work with Russian colleagues at the HSE in Moscow. Hundreds of thousands of Russians come to the United States every year on nonimmigrant visas, and Russians are active in many parts of US life from the legions of software engineers in Silicon Valley to the many financial analysts on Wall Street to the thousands of students at US universities. We have learned a great deal about Russia based on increased contacts over the last quarter century, but more needs to be done to improve our understanding of Russia, and academic research on Russia should be a much larger part of the effort.

ACKNOWLEDGMENTS

THIS BOOK shares many personal experiences, but could not have been written without my friends. It is a pleasure to recognize all those who shared ideas or took the time to give me comments on the manuscript. Special thanks to Kay Achar, Jon Bassett, Kevin Bernard, Ekaterina Borisova, Deborah Boucoyannis, George Breslauer, Noah Buckley, Gail Buyske, Peter Clement, Jordan Gans-Morse, Scott Gehlbach, Elise Giuliano, Seva Gunitsky, Jason Healey, Ira Katznelson, Egor Lazarev, Robert Legvold, Rajan Menon, Ben Noble, Katharina Pistor, Tom Remington, Ora John Reuter, Brad Robins, Bryn Rosenfeld, Steve Sestanovich, Doug Smith, David Szakonyi, Katerina Tertytchnaya, Dan Treisman, Joshua Yaffa, and Andrei Yakovlev. I look forward to returning the favor of commenting on your work. I also thank my colleagues at the Harriman Institute, Columbia University, and the Higher School of Economics for supporting the work in ways both big and small.

Anastasia Gergel and Helen Simpson provided invaluable research assistance. A hat tip to Masha Lipman for encouraging me to get back to the book when I had almost abandoned the idea. The legendary Gloria Loomis of Loomis Watkins provided sage advice, brutal honesty, and warm encouragement. Without her help, the book would not have been possible.

The team at Princeton University Press deserves special thanks. I couldn't ask for a better editor than Bridget Flannery-McCoy, whose great enthusiasm for the project was only matched by her brilliant editing skills. Thank you for making the manuscript better. Cindy Milstein worked at light speed to copyedit the manuscript and did so with a deft touch. Nathan Carr ensured that production was smooth, while Kate Hensley provided great help with publicity. Three excellent reviewers provided feedback that gave the book much more coherence. Tobiah Waldron did a wonderful job compiling the index.

Closest to home, I thank Kira and Vanya for their love and patience. I also thank my mother, Betty Lou Frye, whose love and optimism picked me up on many hard days of writing. This book is dedicated to my father, Richard A. Frye (1933–2019), who would have loved to talk with me about it.

————

A Note on Transliteration

I generally adhere to the British Standard style to transliterate Russian words into English, but depart from the system for proper names that have become common usage, such as Dmitry, Alexei, Yevgeny, and Khodorkovsky, among others.

NOTES

Preface to the Paperback Edition

1. Alannah Francis, "Ukraine War: Kremlin Advisor Is Shocked by Putin's Actions," iNews, March 2, 2022, https://inews.co.uk/news/ukraine-war-russia-kremlin-adviser-putin-actions-invasions-1493128.

2. "Will There Be a War over Ukraine?" *Politico Magazine*, January 26, 2022, https://www.politico.com/news/magazine/2022/01/26/russia-ukraine-putin-experts-00000019; see also "What Does Putin Really Want?" *Politico Magazine*, February 25, 2022, https://www.politico.com/news/magazine/2022/02/25/putin-russia-ukraine-invasion-endgame-experts-00011652.

3. One source close to the Russian government noted, "Nobody was anticipating anything like this. We trained for some stressful scenarios, but nothing at this level. We were counting on relatively soft sanctions." Meduza, March 9, 2022, https://meduza.io/en/feature/2022/03/09/blindsided.

4. Frances Fukuyama, "Preparing for Defeat," American Purpose, March 9, 2022, https://www.americanpurpose.com/articles/preparing-for-defeat.

5. This framework should apply to any personalist leader in Russia and is not specific to Putin. A main theme of *Weak Strongman* is the need to look beyond Putin to understand Russian politics.

6. Anton Troianovsky and Ivan Nechepurenko, "Navalny Arrested On Return to Moscow in Battle of Wills with Putin," *New York Times*, January 17, 2021, https://www.nytimes.com/2021/01/17/world/europe/navalny-russia-return.html.

7. Shaun Walker, "New Russian Law Revives Sweeping KGB Powers," *Independent*, July 7, 2020, https://www.independent.co.uk/news/world/europe/new-russian-law-revives-sweeping-kgb-powers-2030371.html.

8. Yelena Rykovtseva and Robert Coalson, "Russian State Takes Ominous Steps to Bolster 'Foreign Agents' Law," Radio Free Europe/Radio Liberty, July 28, 2021, https://www.rferl.org/a/russian-foreign-agents-law/31382204.html. See also "There Is a Feeling That the Country Is Preparing for a Dictatorship," *Meduza*, July 27, 2020, https://meduza.io/feature/2020/07/27/takoe-oschuschenie-chto-v-strane-gotovyatsya-k-diktature.

9. Andrei Soldatov and Irina Borogan, "The Man behind Putin's Military," *Foreign Affairs*, February 26, 2022, https://www.foreignaffairs.com/articles/2022-02-26/man-behind-putins-military.

10. "Nadeemsya shto v Vashingtone vozobladaet zdraviiy smysl," Kommersant', July 4, 2021, https://www.kommersant.ru/doc/4762137; "Russian Security Chief Warns of US, Atlantic Allies Becoming More Erratic and Belligerent," TASS, September 2021, https://tass.com /defense/1340539.

11. Filip Kovacevic, "The Second Most Powerful Man in Russia," New/Lines Magazine, March 9, 2022, https://newlinesmag.com/reportage/the-second-most-powerful-man-in-russia.

12. Erica Frantz, Autocracy: What Everyone Needs to Know (Oxford: Oxford University Press, 2018), 54.

13. "War optimism" is not unique to personalist autocracies even if the problem is more severe in this setting. See Charles Vandepeer, "Self-Deception and the Conspiracy of Optimism," War on the Rocks, January 31, 2019, https://warontherocks.com/2019/01/self-deception -and-the-conspiracy-of-optimism.

14. "From Bad Intel to Worse," Meduza, March 11, 2022, https://meduza.io/en/feature /2022/03/11/from-bad-intel-to-worse.

15. "From Bad Intel to Worse."

16. Jessica Weeks, "Strongmen and Straw Men: Authoritarian Regimes and the Initiation of War," American Political Science Review 106, no. 2 (2012): 326–47.

17. Caitlin Talmadge, The Dictator's Army: Battlefield Effectiveness in Authoritarian Regimes (Ithaca, NY: Cornell University Press, 2015).

18. Vladimir Putin, "On the Historical Unity of Russians and Ukrainians," President of Russia, http://en.kremlin.ru/events/president/news/66181.

19. "Russian-Ukrainian Relations," Levada Center, February 13, 2020, https://www.levada .ru/2020/02/13/rossijsko-ukrainskie-otnosheniya-7.

20. "Putin References Neo-Nazis and Drug Addicts in Bizarre Speech to Russian Security Council," Guardian, February 25, 2022, https://www.theguardian.com/world/video/2022/feb /25/putin-references-neo-nazis-and-drug-addicts-in-bizarre-speech-to-russian-security -council-video.

21. "Two Top Russian Billionaires Speak Out against Invasion," Guardian, February 27, 2022, https://www.theguardian.com/world/2022/feb/27/two-top-russian-billionaires-speak-out -against-invasion-of-ukraine.

22. Address of the Russian Union of Rectors, https://www.rsr-online.ru/news/2022-god /obrashchenie-rossiyskogo-soyuza-rektorov1.

23. For a list of petitions against the war in Russian, see "'No to War': A List of All Open Letters against the Invasion of Ukraine," February 27, 2022, Holod Magazine, https://holod .media/2022/02/27/otkrytye-pisma.

Preface

1. Kyle Dropp, Joshua D. Kurtzer, and Thomas Zeitzoff, "The Less Americans Know about Ukraine's Location, the More They Want the US to Intervene," Washington Post, April 7, 2014, https://www.washingtonpost.com/news/monkey-cage/wp/2014/04/07/the-less -americans-know-about-ukraines-location-the-more-they-want-u-s-to-intervene/?arc404 =true.

Chapter 1. Information Warrior

1. The exhibits did not run from 1979 to 1985 in the wake of the Soviet invasion of Afghanistan.

2. For a history of the US Information Agency exhibits, see https://2009-2017.state.gov/p/eur/ci/rs/c26473.htm.

3. Timothy Frye, *The Perils of Polarization: Building States and Markets after Democracy* (New York: Cambridge University Press, 2010), 244.

4. For a similar scene, see Francis Spufford's brilliant novel, *Red Plenty* (Minnesota: Greywolf Press, 2012).

5. Why would the Russian government support us during this period of anti-Western sentiment? The Russian government wants the HSE to rise in the international rankings of higher educational institutions, and our work can help. Our main purpose is to publish, and we are evaluated by the number and quality of our publications in international peer-reviewed academic journals.

6. Timothy Frye, "Russian Studies Is Thriving, Not Dying," *National Interest*, October, 2017, https://nationalinterest.org/feature/russian-studies-thriving-not-dying-22547.

7. Articles using public opinion data from Russia have been published in the top journals in economics, political science, and sociology.

8. Cf. Barbara Geddes, *Paradigms and Sand Castles* (Ann Arbor: University of Michigan Press, 2003); Beatriz Magaloni, *Voting for Autocracy: Hegemonic Party Survival and Its Demise in Mexico* (New York: Cambridge University Press, 2006); Milan Svolik, *The Politics of Authoritarian Rule* (New York: Cambridge University Press, 2012).

9. It is perhaps no accident that a Russian studies expert, Tom Nichols, wrote the best-selling *The Death of Expertise: The Campaign against Established Knowledge and Why It Matters* (New York: Oxford University Press, 2017).

10. This line of argument predates the Trump presidency, but has gained steam in recent years.

11. Anne Applebaum, "The False Romance of Russia," *Atlantic*, December 12, 2019.

12. Rachel Maddow, *Blowout: Corrupted Democracy, Rogue State Russia, and the Most Destructive Industry on Earth* (New York: Crown Publishing, 2019).

13. A 2018 poll taken right after the Helsinki summit between Presidents Trump and Putin revealed that 40 percent of Republicans consider Russia an ally. "Trump Effect: Republican Support for Putin Has Doubled," *Hill*, July 18, 2018, http://thehill.com/opinion/white-house/397672-trump-effect-republican-support-for-russia-has-doubled.

14. "John McCain Says That Russia Is a Gas Station Masquerading as a Country," *Week*, March 16, 2014, http://theweek.com/speedreads/456437/john-mccain-russia-gas-station-masquerading-country; Paul Goble, "Piontkovsky Says Putin Has the Foreign Policy of Hitler and the Domestic Policy of Mussolini," *Window on Eurasia*, July 18, 2016, http://windowoneurasia2.blogspot.com/2016/07/putin-has-foreign-policy-of-hitler-and.html.

15. Tom Pepinsky, "Everyday Authoritarianism Is Mostly Boring and Tolerable," *Vox*, January 9, 2017, https://www.vox.com/the-big-idea/2017/1/9/14207302/authoritarian-states-boring-tolerable-fascism-trump.

16. In addition, Putin's personal relations with Khodorkovsky were far from harmonious. Not only had Khodorkovsky criticized Putin personally in a gathering of Russia's business elites, Khodorkovsky did not wear a tie when he met with Putin.

17. Andrew Nagorski, "Power First, Economics Later," *Newsweek*, November 16, 2003, https://www.newsweek.com/power-first-economics-later-133805.

18. Nina Boyarchenko, "Turning Off the Tap: Determinants of Expropriation in the Energy Sector," Federal Reserve Bank of New York, 2007, 1–14, https://papers.ssrn.com/sol3/papers.cfm?abstract_id=963779. See also Timothy Frye, "The Limits of Legacies," in *Historical Legacies of Communism in Russia and Eastern Europe*, ed. Mark Beissinger and Stephen Kotkin (New York: Cambridge University Press, 2014), 90–110.

19. Sergei Guriev, Anton Kotolin, and Konstantin Sonin, "Determinants of Nationalization in the Oil Sector: Evidence from Panel Data," *Journal of Law, Economics, and Organization* 27, no. 2 (2011): 301–23.

20. Journalists do an impressive job of covering Russia even as cutbacks in foreign reporting have left far fewer eyes on the ground to cover a country of eleven time zones where national policy is run by a tight-lipped group close to Putin. Longer-form journalism on Russia is strong. David Remnick at the *New Yorker* has nurtured an impressive stable of writers on Russia, including at various times Masha Gessen, Julia Ioffe, Joshua Yaffa, and Masha Lipman. This is all before mentioning Remnick's own insightful writing on Russia. Book-length journalistic accounts from Catherine Belton, Ben Judah, Arkady Ostrovsky, Steven Lee Myers, Andrew Meier, Anne Garrels, Shaun Walker, and others have provided rich descriptions of critical moments and important individuals in Russia over the last decade. Peter Pomerantsev's account of the absurdities of the Russian media world, *Everything Is Possible and Nothing Is True: A Journey into the Surreal Heart of Russia*, as well as Andrei Soldatov and Irina Borogan's *Red Web* highlight aspects of Russian life known to few, while William Browder's *Red Notice* reads like a real-life spy thriller. Novels by Gary Shteyngart, Viktor Pelevin, and A. J. Miller also merit notice. The list could easily go on. We also benefit from commentary by those who combine policy-making and academic experience, like Nicholas Burns, William Burns, Tom Graham, Fiona Hill, Michael McFaul, Stephen Sestanovich, and Angela Stent, but observers with this kind of experience are few.

21. Duncan J. Watts, *Everything Is Obvious*: Once You Know the Answer* (New York: Random House, 2011).

22. Watts, *Everything Is Obvious**, 157.

Chapter 2. Putinology and Exceptional Russia

1. "'No Putin. No Russia' Says Kremlin Chief of Staff," *Moscow Times*, October 23, 2014, https://themoscowtimes.com/articles/no-putin-no-russia-says-kremlin-deputy-chief-of-staff-40702.

2. Karen Dawisha, *Putin's Kleptocracy: Who Owns Russia?* (New York: Simon and Schuster, 2014), 63–64.

3. "What Role for Putin after 2024?," Levada Center, January 30, 2020, https://www.levada.ru/2020/01/30/rol-vladimira-putina-posle-2024/print/.

4. For a sampling of the large literature on Putin, see Anna Arutunyan, *The Putin Mystique: Inside Russia's Power Cult* (New York: Skyscraper Publications, 2011); Masha Gessen, *The Man without a Face: The Unlikely Rise of Vladimir Putin* (New York: Riverhead Books, 2013); Brian D. Taylor, *The Code of Putinism* (New York: Oxford University Press, 2018).

5. Daniel Treisman, "Why Putin Took Crimea: The Gambler in the Kremlin," *Foreign Affairs* 95, no. 3 (2016): 47–56.

6. Fiona Hill and Clifford G. Gaddy, *Mr. Putin: Operative in the Kremlin* (Washington, DC: Brookings Institution Press, 2011), 84. "Surviving in a hostile and competitive world means thinking about the worst thing or things that could happen, and having something to rely upon to ensure yourself, and the state, when external shocks come along. These ideas have governed Putin's policies as Russia's preeminent leader since 2000."

7. Timothy Snyder, *The Road to Unfreedom: Russia, Europe, America* (New York: Penguin Books, 2018).

8. Robert Legvold, *Return to Cold War* (Medford, MA: Polity Press, 2016).

9. Dawisha, *Putin's Kleptocracy*.

10. Snyder, *The Road to Unfreedom*.

11. Hill and Gaddy, *Mr. Putin*, 84.

12. Erik Berglof, Andrei Kunov, Julia Shvets, and Ksenia Yudaeva, *The New Political Economy of Russia* (Cambridge, MA: MIT Press, 2003).

13. Snyder, *The Road to Unfreedom*.

14. Sophie Pinkham, "Zombie History," *Nation*, May 20, 2018, https://www.thenation.com/article/timothy-snyder-zombie-history/.

15. Marlene Laurelle, "In Search of Putin's Philosopher," *Riddle*, April 19, 2018, https://www.ridl.io/en/in-search-of-putins-philosopher/.

16. Others point to Aleksandr Dugin, a contemporary Russian philosopher and activist, as a source of Putin's thought. Much of the evidence of Dugin's influence comes from interviews with Dugin himself. Searches for Dugin on the internet in Russia indicate that there is little public interest in him. See Kirill Kalinin, "Neo-Eurasianism and the Russian Elite: The Irrelevance of Aleksandr Dugin's Geopolitics," *Post-Soviet Affairs* 35, no. 5–6 (2019): 461–70.

17. Robert Caro, *The Years of Lyndon Johnson: Means of Ascent* (New York: Vintage Books, 1991). See also Gleb Pavlovsky, *Genialnaya Vlast'! Slovar' Abstraktsii Kremlya* (Moscow: Evropa, 2011).

18. Michael Kinsley, "Gaffes to the Rescue," *Time*, February 8, 2007, http://content.time.com/time/magazine/article/0,9171,1587283,00.html#ixzz1VhxakL73.

19. Ex-Putin insiders who fit this category include Sergei Pugachev, Alexander Lebedev, Mikhail Kasyanov, Vladimir Yakunin, and others.

20. Maggie Fox, "Why Does Putin Walk Like That?," *NBC News*, December 15, 2015, http://www.nbcnews.com/health/health-news/why-does-vladimir-putin-walk-n480611.

Doubling down, Brenda Connors, a former US Department of State official and researcher at the Naval War College, surmised that Putin likely suffered a stroke, perhaps as a child, and links his resoluteness in defending Russia to the hard work needed to overcome his disability. Paul Starobin, "The Accidental Autocrat," *Atlantic*, March 2005, https://www.theatlantic.com/magazine/archive/2005/03/the-accidental-autocrat/303725/.

21. "Putin's Jewish Embrace: Is it Love or Politics?," *Haaretz*, March 12, 2014, https://www.haaretz.com/jewish/putin-s-jewish-embrace-1.5332487.

22. Kelly McParland, "Putin Acts Like a Former Soviet KGB Agent: Why Are We Surprised?," *National Post*, March 5, 2014, http://nationalpost.com/opinion/kelly-mcparland-putin-acts-like-a-former-soviet-kgb-agent-why-are-we-surprised/wcm/39b9a6cc-17fa-4288-b888-5717950d0ae9; Marc Champion, "Putin Isn't Crazy, He's KGB," *Bloomberg*, March 5, 2014, https://www.bloomberg.com/view/articles/2014-03-05/putin-isn-t-crazy-he-s-kgb. Certainly Russia had contingency plans to seize Crimea, however that would still require a decision to put them in place. For more quotes about Putin by US politicians, see "From Honest to Killer, US Leaders Have Said Many Disparate Things about Putin," *Washington Post*, June 10, 2015, https://www.washingtonpost.com/news/the-fix/wp/2015/06/10/from-honest-to-killer-u-s-leaders-have-said-many-disparate-things-about-putin/?utm_term=.750ab69f99a0.

23. Marcus Warren, "Putin Lets NATO 'Recruit' in Baltic," *Independent*, June 25, 2002, as cited in Kimberly Marten, "Reconsidering NATO's Expansion: A Counterfactual Analysis," *European Journal of International Security* 3, no. 2 (2018): 136–61.

24. Valentin Yumashev claims to have played a key role in convincing Yeltsin to appoint Putin. Steve Rosenberg, "The Man Who Made Ex KGB Officer Vladimir Putin President," *BBC World*, December 17, 2019, https://www.bbc.com/news/world-europe-50807747. Catherine Belton provides rich detail on the elite politics behind this decision with special input from Yumashev and Sergei Pugachev. They disagree on some points. Catherine Belton, *Putin's People: How the KGB Took Back Russia and Then Took on the West* (New York: Farrar, Straus and Giroux, 2020), 136–51.

25. For the best interpretation, see Taylor, *The Code of Putinism*.

26. Dawisha, *Putin's Kleptocracy*.

27. Alex Cooley and John Heathershaw, *Dictators without Borders: Power and Money in Central Asia* (New Haven, CT: Yale University Press, 2017).

28. Peter Reddaway, "Will Putin Be Able to Consolidate Power?," *Post-Soviet Affairs* 17, no. 1 (2001): 23–44; Peter Reddaway, "Is Putin's Power More Formal Than Real?," *Post-Soviet Affairs* 18, no. 1 (2002): 31–40.

29. The only partial exception was Putin in 2008, when he stepped down to cede formal power to Dmitry Medvedev, but still exercised great influence as prime minister. Thanks to Anastasia Gergel for research assistance on this point.

30. William Taubman, *Khrushchev: The Man and His Era* (New York: W. W. Norton and Company, 2004), 598.

31. Daniel Treisman, introduction to *The New Autocracy: Information, Politics, and Policy in Putin's Russia*, ed. Daniel Treisman (Washington, DC: Brookings Institution Press, 2018), 19–20.

32. Andrei Soldatov and Irina Borogan, *Red Web: The Struggle between Russia's Digital Dictators and the New Online Revolutionaries* (New York: Public Affairs, 2018).

33. Michael Schwirtz, "Top Secret Russian Unit Seeks to Destabilize Europe, Security Officials Say," *New York Times*, October 8, 2019, https://www.nytimes.com/2019/10/08/world/europe/unit-29155-russia-gru.html.

34. Mark Galeotti, "Controlling Chaos: How Russian Manages Its Political War in Europe," European Council on Foreign Relations, September 1, 2017, https://www.ecfr.eu/publications /summary/controlling_chaos_how_russia_manages_its_political_war_in_europe.

35. "MH17: Russia 'Liable' for Downing Airliner over Ukraine," BBC News, May 25, 2018, https://www.bbc.com/news/world-europe-44252150.

36. "'Maiskie Ukazi' Vladimira Putina pyat' let spustya. Oni ispolnenii?," Meduza, May 16, 2017, https://meduza.io/feature/2017/05/16/mayskie-ukazy-vladimira-putina-pyat-let-spustya -oni-ispolneny.

37. In June 2020, President Putin found out about a massive oil spill two days after the event and only on social media. This is further evidence of the weakness of the bureaucratic chain of command. Isabelle Khurshudyan, "Arctic Oil Spill Prompts Russia's Putin to Declare Emergency and Slam Slow Response," Washington Post, June 4, 2020, https://www.washingtonpost.com /world/europe/russia-arctic-oil-spill-siberia/2020/06/04/a1d24ad8-a667-11ea-b619-3f9133bbb482 _story.html.

38. Alena V. Ledeneva, Can Russia Modernise? Sistema, Power Networks and Informal Governance (Cambridge: Cambridge University Press, 2013).

39. Sean L. Haney, "'Sistema': How Putin's Russia Is Governed," University College London, March 11, 2013, https://blogs.ucl.ac.uk/ssees/2013/03/11/sistema-how-putins-russia-is -governed/.

40. Duncan J. Watts, Everything Is Obvious*: Once You Know the Answer (New York: Random House, 2011).

41. For one of the best discussions on political leadership, see Archie Brown, The Myth of the Strong Leader: Political Leadership in the Modern Age (New York: Basic Books, 2014).

42. Martin Malia, Russia under Western Eyes, from the Bronze Horseman to the Lenin Mausoleum (Cambridge, MA: Harvard University Press, 2000); Seweryn Bialer, Soviet Paradox: External Expansion and Internal Decline (New York: Knopf, 1986).

43. To cite just a few, see Andrei Markevich and Ekaterina Zhuravskaya, "Economic Effects of the Abolition of Serfdom: Evidence from the Russian Empire," American Economic Review 108, no. 4–5 (2018): 1074–117; Stephen Kotkin, Stalin: Paradoxes of Power, 1928-1941, (New York: Penguin Press, 2014); Yuri Slezkine, The House of Government: A Saga of the Russian Revolution (Princeton, NJ: Princeton University Press, 2017); Alexei Yurchak, Everything Was Forever, Until It Was No More: The Last Soviet Generation (Princeton, NJ: Princeton University Press, 2005).

44. Mark R. Beissinger and Stephen Kotkin, "The Historical Legacies of Communism: An Empirical Agenda," in Historical Legacies of Communism in Russia and Eastern Europe, ed. Mark R. Beissinger and Stephen Kotkin (New York: Cambridge University Press, 2014), 3.

45. James Stavridis, "What Russian Literature Tells Us about Vladimir Putin's World," Foreign Policy, June 2, 2015, https://foreignpolicy.com/2015/06/02/what-russian-literature-tells-us -about-vladimir-putins-world/.

46. Charles King, "You Can't Understand How Russians Think by Reading Russian Literature," Washington Post, June 16, 2015, https://www.washingtonpost.com/news/monkey-cage /wp/2015/06/16/how-can-you-find-out-how-russians-really-think-spoiler-not-by-reading -gogol/?utm_term=.6578ef8d316b.

47. Richard Pipes, "Flight from Freedom: What Russians Think and Want," *Foreign Affairs* 83, no. 3 (2004), https://www.foreignaffairs.com/articles/russia-fsu/2004-05-01/flight-freedom-what-russians-think-and-want.

48. Peter Savodnik traces the "sources of Putin's evil" to Fyodor Dostoyevsky, and notes that Putin "is a mobster and he views his fellow countryman the way a mobster views the little people in his neighborhood with a mix of sympathy and disdain. But Putin is also Russian, and the same angers and longings that permeate the wider Russian psyche are presumably his, too." Peter Savodnik, "The Secret Source of Putin's Evil," *Vanity Fair*, January 2017, https://www.vanityfair.com/news/2017/01/the-secret-source-of-putins-evil.

49. "James Clapper Says Watergate Pales in Comparison with Trump and Russia Scandal," *Guardian*, June 7, 2017, https://www.theguardian.com/us-news/2017/jun/07/james-clapper-says-watergate-pales-in-comparison-with-trump-and-russia-scandal. Elsewhere Clapper noted that Russians are "almost genetically driven to co-opt, penetrate, gain favor." https://www.nbcnews.com/meet-the-press/meet-press-may-28-2017-n765626.

50. Misha Friedman, "For Russians, Corruption Is Just a Way of Life," *New York Times*, August 19, 2012, https://www.nytimes.com/2012/08/19/opinion/sunday/for-russians-corruption-is-just-a-way-of-life.html; Timothy Frye, "Russians Pay Bribes, But They Don't Like It," *Washington Post*, February 17, 2014, https://www.washingtonpost.com/news/monkey-cage/wp/2014/02/17/the-culture-of-corruption-russians-pay-but-they-dont-like-it-2/.

51. David Satter, "A Christmas Encounter with the 'Russian Soul,'" *Wall Street Journal*, December 22, 2017.

52. Franz Sedelmayer, "The Putin I Knew, the Putin I Know," *New York Times*, February 4, 2019, https://www.nytimes.com/2019/02/04/opinion/the-putin-i-knew-the-putin-i-know.html.

53. For the origins of the term, see Alexander Zinoviev, *Homo Sovieticus* (Boston: Atlantic Monthly Press,1985).

54. Lev Gudkov and Eva Hartog, "The Evolution of Homo Sovieticus to Putin's Man," *Moscow Times*, October 13, 2017.

55. Gudkov and Hartog, "The Evolution of Homo Sovieticus."

56. Masha Gessen, *The Future Is History: How Totalitarianism Reclaimed Russia* (New York: Riverhead Books, 2017), 3.

57. See also Sean Guillory, "Arrested Development: Masha Gessen Offers a Familiar Diagnosis of Her Home Country," *BookForum*, September–October 2017, https://www.bookforum.com/print/2403/masha-gessen-offers-a-familiar-diagnosis-of-her-home-country-18469.

58. Gulnaz Sharafutdinova, "Was There a 'Simple Soviet' Person: Debating the Politics and Sociology of 'Homo Soveticus,'" *Slavic Review* 78, no. 1 (2019): 173–95.

59. Robert J. Shiller, Vladimir Korobov, and Maxim Boykco, "Hunting for Homo Sovieticus: Situational versus Attitudinal Factors in Economic Behavior," *Brookings Papers on Economics Activity* 1 (1992): 127–93.

60. Ada Finifter and Ellen Mickiewicz, "Redefining the Political System: Mass Support for Political Change," *American Political Science Review* 86, no. 4 (1992): 857–87.

61. James Gibson, "Social Networks, Civil Society, and the Prospects for Consolidating Russia's Democratic Transition," *American Journal of Political Science* 45, no. 1 (2001): 62.

62. Alain Cohn, Michel Andre Marechal, David Tannenbaum, and Christian Lukas Ziin, "Civic Honesty around the Globe," *Science* 365 (2019): 70–73, https://science.sciencemag.org/content/365/6448/70/tab-pdf.

63. Anton Sobolev and Alexei Zakharov, "Civic and Political Activism in Russia," in *The New Autocracy: Information, Politics, and Policy in Putin's Russia*, ed. Daniel Treisman (Washington, DC: Brookings Institution Press, 2018), 249–76.

64. Ted Brader and Joshua A. Tucker, "The Emergence of Mass Partisanship in Russia, 1993–1996," *American Journal of Political Science* 45, no. 1 (2001): 75: "Overall, core partisans align themselves sensibly; there is no evidence that core voters identify with parties that are inconsistent with their interests and beliefs. To the contrary, most parties appear to have won adherents among precisely the groups of voters to whom their rhetoric and policies are designed to appeal." See also Timothy Frye, "Markets, Democracy, and New Private Business in Russia," *Post-Soviet Affairs* 19, no. 1 (2003): 24–45.

65. "Number of Protests in Russia Spikes in 2018, Researchers Say," *Moscow Times*, November 8, 2018, https://www.themoscowtimes.com/2018/11/08/number-protests-russia-spikes-in-2018-researchers-say-a63428.

66. Grigore Pop-Eleches and Joshua A. Tucker, *Communism's Shadow: Historical Legacies and Contemporary Political Attitudes* (Princeton, NJ: Princeton University Press, 2017).

67. Grigore Pop-Eleches and Joshua A. Tucker, "Communist Socialization and Post-Communist Economic and Political Attitudes," *Electoral Studies* 33 (2014): 77–89, especially 85.

68. For a good use of political psychology in the Russian context, see Samuel A. Greene and Graeme B. Robertson, "Agreeable Authoritarians: Personality and Politics in Contemporary Russia," *Comparative Political Studies* 50, no. 13 (2017): 1802–34.

69. Samuel P. Huntington, "Will More Countries Become Democratic?," *Political Science Quarterly* 99 (1984): 193–218; Alfred Stepan and Graeme B. Robertson, "An 'Arab' More Than 'Muslim' Democracy Gap," *Journal of Democracy* 14, no. 3 (2003): 30–44.

70. Joshua Yaffa, *Between Two Fires: Truth, Ambition, and Compromise in Putin's Russia* (New York: Penguin Random House, 2020).

71. Jason Horowitz and Emma Bubolo, "On Day 1 of Lockdown, Italian Officials Urge Citizens to Abide by Rules," *New York Times*, March 8, 2020, https://www.nytimes.com/2020/03/08/world/europe/italy-coronavirus-quarantine.html.

72. James C. Scott, *The Weapons of the Weak: Everyday Forms of Peasant Resistance* (New Haven, CT: Yale University Press, 1985), 33–34.

73. Gudkov and Hartog, "The Evolution of Homo Sovieticus."

74. Russian political scientist Vladimir Gel'man states that "ideology as such has probably been the least meaningful factor in Russian politics since the Soviet collapse." Vladimir Gel'man, *Authoritarian Russia: Analyzing Post-Soviet Regime Change* (Pittsburgh: University of Pittsburgh Press, 2015), 11.

75. Andrew Kuchins, "Vladimir the Lucky," Carnegie Endowment, July 25, 2006, https://carnegieendowment.org/2006/07/25/vladimir-lucky-pub-18571.

76. World Bank, https://data.worldbank.org/indicator/NY.GDP.PCAP.PP.CD?view=chart.

77. World Bank, https://data.worldbank.org/indicator/NY.GDP.PCAP.PP.CD.

78. "Tourism Review News, Russian Outbound Tourism," February 11, 2019, https://www.tourism-review.com/russian-outbound-tourism-industry-news10935.

79. Lorenz Kueng and Evgeny Yakovlev, "Long-Run Effects of Public Policies: Endogenous Alcohol Preferences and Life Expectancy in Russia," May 2016, https://ideas.repec.org/p/cfr/cefirw/w0219.html; Daniel Treisman, "Death and Prices: The Political Economy of Russia's Alcohol Crisis," *Economics of Transition* 18, no. 2 (April 2010): 281–331, https://onlinelibrary.wiley.com/doi/abs/10.1111/j.1468-0351.2009.00382.x.

80. "Russian Life Expectancy Hits Record High," *Moscow Times*, June 17, 2017, https://themoscowtimes.com/news/russian-life-expectancy-hits-record-high-58274.

81. "Number of Smartphone Users," Statista, https://www.statista.com/statistics/467166/forecast-of-smartphone-users-in-russia/.

82. "Media Landshaft," Levada Center, August 1, 2019, https://www.levada.ru/2019/08/01/rossijskij-media-landshaft-2019/.

83. Clifford Gaddy, "Room for Error: The Economic Legacy of Soviet Spatial Misallocation," in *Historical Legacies of Communism in Russia and Eastern Europe*, ed. Mark R. Beissinger and Stephen Kotkin (New York: Cambridge University Press, 2014), 52–68.

84. "Rosstat nazval dolyu Rossiyan bez dostupa k kanalizatsii," *RBC*, April 2, 2019, https://www.rbc.ru/economics/02/04/2019/5ca1d7949a79475d1c2f6e4a.

85. Paul Goble, "Windows on Eurasia," January 7, 2019, http://windowoneurasia2.blogspot.com/2019/01/one-russian-in-four-lacks-indoor-toilet.htm; Stephen Ennis, "US Radio Liberty Misrepresents Russian Outdoor Toilet Statistics," *BBC Monitoring*, January 8, 2019, https://monitoring.bbc.co.uk/product/c200j90d.

86. "Pochti polovini rossiiskikh semei khvatilo tol'ko deneg na edu i odezhdu," *RBC*, May 28, 2019, https://www.rbc.ru/economics/28/05/2019/5cebd9cf9a79474ebd28be0c?from=newsfeed.

Chapter 3. The Autocrat's Dilemmas

1. Christopher H. Achen and Larry D. Bartels, *Democracy for Realists: Why Elections Do Not Produce Responsible Government* (Princeton, NJ: Princeton University Press, 2017).

2. Some of the most prominent data sets used to study autocratic regimes are Polity IV and V-Dem. See also Barbara Geddes, Joseph Wright, and Erica Frantz, "The Autocratic Regime Data Set," *Perspectives on Politics* 12, no. 2 (2014): 213–331; Adam Przeworski, Michael E. Alvarez, Jose Antonio Cheibub, and Fernando Limongi, *Democracy and Development: Political Institutions and Well-Being in the World, 1950–2000* (New York: Cambridge University Press, 2000); Giacomo Chiozza and Hein Goemans, "Archigos: A Data Set of Political Leaders," *Journal of Peace Research* 46, no. 2 (2009): 269–83. Freedom House is often cited in the popular press, but has largely been replaced in academic studies by more rigorous treatments.

3. For a foundational work that popularized this three-part categorization of nondemocratic governments, see Barbara Geddes, *Paradigms and Sand Castles* (Ann Arbor: University of Michigan Press, 2003). For alternative ways of categorizing autocracies, see Milan Svolik, *The Politics of Authoritarian Rule* (New York: Cambridge University Press, 2012).

4. Erica Frantz, *Authoritarianism: What Everyone Needs to Know* (New York: Oxford University Press, 2018), 50–53.

5. Javier Corrales and Michael Penfold, *Dragon in the Tropics: Hugo Chávez and the Political Economy of Revolution in Venezuela* (Washington, DC: Brookings Institution Press, 2011).

6. The Organization for Security and Cooperation in Europe shared this determination.

7. For elaboration, see Barbara Geddes, Joseph Wright, and Erica Frantz, *How Dictatorships Work: Power, Personalization, and Collapse* (New York: Cambridge University Press, 2018).

8. Geddes, Wright, and Frantz, *How Dictatorships Work.*

9. For especially good books on relations between the ruler and elites in Russia, see Henry Hale, *Patronal Politics: Eurasian Regime Dynamics in Comparative Perspective* (New York: Cambridge University Press, 2014); Ora John Reuter, *The Origins of Dominant Parties: Building Authoritarian Institutions in Post-Soviet Russia* (New York: Cambridge University Press, 2017).

10. Ernest Hemingway, *The Sun Also Rises* (New York: Scribner, 1926).

11. Gleb Pavlovsky, interview with Tom Parfitt of the *Guardian*, January 2012, in *New Left Review*, July–August 2014, https://newleftreview.org/issues/II88/articles/gleb-pavlovsky-putin-s-world-outlook.

12. In Geddes's classic formulation, personalist regimes are those in which the "leader himself maintains a near monopoly over policy and personnel decisions. . . . Although they are often supported by militaries or parties, these organizations have not become sufficiently developed or autonomous to prevent the leader from taking personal control of policy decisions and the selection of regime personnel." Geddes, *Paradigms and Sand Castles*, 53.

13. H. E. Goemans, "Putin's Peers," in *The Policy World Meets Academia: Designing US Policy toward Russia*, ed. Timothy Colton, Timothy Frye, and Robert Legvold (Cambridge, MA: American Academy of Arts and Sciences, 2010), 79–92, https://www.amacad.org/sites/default/files/publication/downloads/policyTowardRussia.pdf.

14. Svolik, *The Politics of Authoritarian Rule.*

15. Joseph Wright, "Do Authoritarian Institutions Constrain?: How Legislatures Affect Economic Growth and Investment," *American Journal of Political Science* 52, no. 2 (2008): 322–43.

16. To be sure, democracies also face a risk of coups, but far less so than do most autocracies.

17. Svolik, *The Politics of Authoritarian Rule*, 41.

18. Alena V. Ledeneva, *Can Russia Modernise? Sistema, Power Networks and Informal Governance* (Cambridge: Cambridge University Press, 2013); Karen Dawisha, *Putin's Kleptocracy: Who Owns Russia?* (New York: Simon and Schuster, 2014).

19. Eric Chang and Miriam Golden, "Sources of Corruption in Authoritarian Regimes," *Social Science Quarterly* 91, no. 1 (2010): 1–20.

20. Beatriz Magaloni, *Voting for Autocracy: Hegemonic Party Survival and Its Demise in Mexico* (New York: Cambridge University Press, 2006), 19.

21. Joshua Yaffa, *Between Two Fires: Truth, Ambition, and Compromise in Putin's Russia* (New York: Penguin Random House, 2020).

22. "Kolichestvo ugolovnikh del protiv biznesa rezko vozroslo," *Vedomosti*, February 19, 2020.

23. Erica Frantz, Andrea Kendall-Taylor, Joseph Wright, and Xu Xu, "Personalization of Power and Repression in Dictatorships," *Journal of Politics* 82, no. 1 (2020): 372–77.

24. When choosing how to organize their agents of repression, rulers grapple with an additional trade-off. They can increase their chances of putting down a popular revolt by creating

a single powerful repressive agency, yet such an agency is well positioned to stage a coup. Conversely, rulers may reduce the chances of a successful coup by fragmenting the security services into different branches and limiting their budgets, but doing so leaves them more vulnerable to popular protests from below.

25. Svolik, *The Politics of Authoritarian Rule*; Sheena Greitens, *Dictators and Secret Police: Coercive Institutions and State Violence* (New York: Cambridge University Press, 2015).

26. Doug Macadam, *Political Process and the Development of Black Insurgency* (Chicago: University of Chicago Press, 1982).

27. Craig Whitney, David Binder, and Serge Schmemann, *"How the Wall Was Cracked—A Special Report; Party Coup Turned East German Tide,"* New York Times, November 19, 1989, http://www.nytimes.com/1989/11/19/world/wall-was-cracked-special-report-party-coup-turned-east-german-tide-clamor-east.html?pagewanted=all. This was quite uncharacteristic of Erich Mielke, who oversaw the Stasi and had few qualms about using violence to repress political protests.

28. One can argue that personal rule is merely a reflection of a deep Russian tradition going back to the czars and Stalin, but personalist traditions run deep in many other countries as well. Moreover, the last thirty-five years of the Soviet Union featured collective versus personalist rule.

Chapter 4. Better to Be Feared and Loved: President Putin's Popularity

1. Tatiana Stanovaya, "Dosrochnoe nastalo," Carnegie Center Moscow, December 23, 2019, https://carnegie.ru/commentary/80666.

2. "The Transfer of Powers Begins," *Meduza*, January 16, 2020, https://meduza.io/en/feature/2020/01/16/the-transfer-of-power-begins.

3. "What Changes Will Be in the Constitution of the Russian Federation?," State Duma, March 12, 2020, http://duma.gov.ru/en/news/48039/.

4. Tyler Gillett, "Russia's Constitutional Court Approves Amendment Allowing Putin to Serve Two Terms," *Jurist*, March 17, 2020, https://www.jurist.org/news/2020/03/russia-constitutional-court-approves-amendment-allowing-putin-to-serve-two-additional-terms/.

5. Ben Noble, "Coronavirus Derails Russia's Constitutional Reform Vote: What This Means for Vladimir Putin, *Conversation*, March 24, 2020, https://theconversation.com/coronavirus-derails-russias-constitutional-reform-vote-what-this-means-for-vladimir-putin-134418. See also "No Referendum Required to Amend Russia's Constitution—Rights Advocate," RAPSI, January 17, 2020, http://www.rapsinews.com/legislation_news/20200117/305335350.html.

6. Putin did not have to invoke a referendum or constituent assembly because the amendments did not address chapters 1, 2, or 9 as specified in the Constitution. To be sure, Putin was cagey on this point and referred to a "nationwide vote," which is not defined in the Russian Constitution, rather than a "referendum," which has a legal definition. Labeling the vote a referendum would have required a majority vote with 50 percent turnout. The "nationwide vote" Putin proposed differs from the referendum requirements in the Constitution.

7. "Putin predlozhil vnesti novye popravki k konstitutsii," January 15, 2020, *NTV Novosti*, https://www.ntv.ru/novosti/2278566/.

8. As political scientist Ben Noble noted, "A nation-wide vote was proposed, I suspect, for the veneer of legitimacy that the Kremlin thought it would provide. Of course, the Kremlin could engineer a vote result by using administrative resources. But right now, the Kremlin is doing its best to try and make this whole process seem legitimate and democratic." Interview with Ben Noble, 4FreeRussia.org, February 12, 2020, https://www.4freerussia.org/examining -russia-s-constitutional-reforms-an-interview-with-prof-ben-noble/.

9. "Data Scientist Claims Staggering Fraud at Russia's Constitutional Vote," *Moscow Times*, July 3, 2020, https://www.themoscowtimes.com/2020/07/03/data-scientist-claims-staggering -fraud-at-russias-constitution-vote-a70769.

10. Nicolo Machiavelli, *The Prince*, Project Gutenberg, 2006, https://www.gutenberg.org /files/1232/1232-h/1232-h.html.

11. Martin Dimitrov, "Popular Autocrats," *Journal of Democracy 20, no. 1 (2009): 78–81*, https://muse.jhu.edu/article/257586/pdf.

12. Kim Lane Scheppele, "Autocratic Legalism," *University of Chicago Law Review* (2018): 545–83, https://lawreview.uchicago.edu/publication/autocratic-legalism; Chris Kraul, "Despite Outcry, Chavez Plan Likely to Pass," *Los Angeles Times*, November 14, 2007, https://www .latimes.com/archives/la-xpm-2007-nov-15-fg-chavez15-story.html.

13. Anastasiya Kornya, "Levada Tsentr: kem zamenit' Vladimira Putina," *Vedomosti*, December 24, 2012, https://www.vedomosti.ru/politics/articles/2012/12/24/zamena_putinu.

14. Steven Lee Myers, *The New Tsar: The Rise and Reign of Vladimir Putin* (New York: Knopf, 2015), 374.

15. Perry Anderson, "Russia's Managed Democracy," *London Review of Books 29, no. 2 (2007)*, https://www.lrb.co.uk/v29/n02/perry-anderson/russias-managed-democracy.

16. Saeed Ahmed, "Vladimir Putin's Approval Rating Now at a Whopping 86 percent," CNN, February, 26, 2015, https://www.cnn.com/2015/02/26/europe/vladimir-putin-popularity /index.html.

17. Public opinion polls are far more frequently conducted online or in face-to-face interviews. I have never conducted a phone survey in Russia due to concerns about the quality of the responses. Barack Obama, "Remarks by the President at America for Hillary Event," September 13, 2016, https://obamawhitehouse.archives.gov/the-press-office/2016/09/13/remarks -president-hillary-america-event-philadelphia-pa.

18. "Pochemu ne stoit doveryat' mneniyu grazhdan," *Slon.Ru*, August 22, 2014, http://slon .ru/russia/pochemu_ne_stoit_doveryat_mneniyu_grazhdan-1146924.xhtml.

19. Xiaoxiao Shen and Rory Truex, "In Search of Self-Censorship," *British Journal of Politics*, March 16, 2020, https://www.cambridge.org/core/journals/british-journal-of-political-science /article/in-search-of-selfcensorship/BC47657718E97A0BBED98CC391F06F88. They also find that regimes where the ruler is selected in wholly noncompetitive races exhibit higher levels of self-censorship in surveys.

20. In August 2017, the Russian government offered funds to the Levada Center as part of its broader program to develop civil society in Russia; some saw this as a signal of acceptance by the Kremlin. But this truce did not last long as Levada's "foreign agent" status prevented it from publishing polls covering the Russian presidential election of 2018.

21. To be sure, even in democratic settings the use of surveys to gauge public opinion faces many challenges. Designing and interpreting questions is as much art as science. Response rates are often low, and reported behavior usually differs from actual behavior.

22. Timothy Frye, Scott Gehlbach, Kyle Marquardt, and Ora John Reuter, "Is Putin's Popularity Real?," *Post-Soviet Affairs* 33, no. 1 (2017): 1–15.

23. For a different view on this question, see Kirill Kalinin, "A Study of Social Desirability Bias in the Russian Presidential Elections, 2012," (unpublished manuscript, University of Michigan).

24. We also ran a battery of tests to ensure that the respondents understood the question and were not confused by its format.

25. Denis Volkov, "How Authentic Is Putin's Approval Rating?," May 27, 2015, https://carnegie.ru/commentary/60849.

26. Daniel Treisman, "Presidential Popularity in a Hybrid Regime," *American Journal of Political Science* 55, no. 3 (2011): 606; Daniel Treisman, "Putin's Popularity since 2010: Why Did Support Plunge, Then Stabilize?" *Post-Soviet Affairs* 30, no. 5 (2004): 370–88.

27. Samuel A. Greene and Graeme B. Robertson, "Agreeable Authoritarians: Personality and Politics in Contemporary Russia," *Comparative Political Studies* 50, no. 13 (2017): 1819.

28. Henry Hale, "How Crimea Pays: Media, Rallying 'Round the Flag and Authoritarian Support," *Comparative Politics* 50, no. 3 (2018): 369–91.

29. Samuel A. Greene and Graeme B. Robertson, *Putin v. the People: The Perilous Politics of a Divided Russia* (New Haven, CT: Yale University Press, 2019), 9.

30. Rajan Menon, "Russian Roulette: The West's Dangerous Sanctions Play," *National Interest*, August 14, 2014, https://nationalinterest.org/feature/game-russian-roulette-the-wests-dangerous-sanctions-play-11075.

31. "Trump's Advisor Says Sanctions against Russia Had the Opposite Effect," *Russia Behind the Headlines*, January 17, 2017, https://www.rbth.com/news/2017/01/17/trumps-advisor-says-us-sanctions-against-russia-had-opposite-effect_682543.

32. Timothy Frye, "Economic Sanctions and Public Opinion: Evidence from Russia," *Comparative Political Studies* 52, no. 7 (2018): 967–94.

33. Treisman, "Presidential Popularity in a Hybrid Regime"; Hale, "How Crimea Pays." Treisman finds that shorter-term and lower-profile events that evoke nationalist pride—like the brief war with Georgia, and subsequent creation of Russia-friendly statelets in Abkhazia and South Ossetia in 2008—had brief but fleeting effects on Putin's approval.

34. Other sanctioned countries, like Iran, Sudan, North Korea, and Cuba, range from very difficult to impossible places to conduct public opinion surveys. Russia is a rare sanctioned autocracy with relatively good public opinion polling.

35. "Levada Center Indicators, Relations with Other Countries," https://www.levada.ru/indikatory/otnoshenie-k-stranam/.

36. Andrei Tsygankov, "Vladimir Putin's Last Stand: The Sources of Russia's Ukraine Policy," *Post-Soviet Affairs* 31, no. 4 (2015): 279–303, http://dx.doi.org/10.1080/1060586X.2015.1005903; Daniel Treisman, ed., *The New Autocracy: Information, Politics, and Policy in Putin's Russia* (Washington, DC: Brookings Institution Press, 2018), 284–86.

37. Tsygankov, "Vladimir Putin's Last Stand," 17–18.

38. As told by Pavlovsky, and reported in Greene and Robertson, *Putin v. the People*, 114.

39. Less than 10 percent of respondents express rapturous adoration.

40. Samuel A. Greene, "From Boom to Bust: Hardship, Mobilization and Russia's Social Contract," *Dædalus* 146, no. 2 (Spring 2017): 113–27; Angelina Flood and Simon Saradzhyan, "Russians See Putin More as Champion of the Oligarchs," *Russia Matters*, April 15, 2020, https://www.russiamatters.org/blog/russians-see-putin-more-champion-oligarchs-polls-show.

41. "Doverie Politikam," VTsIOM, February 16, 2020, https://wciom.ru/news/ratings/doverie_politikam.

42. Henry Hale, *Patronal Politics: Eurasian Regime Dynamics in Comparative Perspective* (New York: Cambridge University Press, 2014), 283.

43. "Rossiyane schitayut armiyu i gozbezopastnost' samymi avtoritetnimi institutami," *Vedomosti*, February 5, 2020.

44. Greene, "From Boom to Bust," 113.

Chapter 5. The Surprising Importance of Russia's Manipulated Elections

1. "Amurskim izbiratelyam predlozhili otkrepitsya na stolye s shashlikami," *Kommersant'*, August 31, 2018.

2. Timothy Frye, Ora John Reuter, and David Szakonyi, "Hitting Them with Carrots: Voter Intimidation and Vote Buying in Russia," *British Journal of Political Science* 49, no. 3 (2019): 857–81.

3. Henry Hale, "The Myth of Mass Support for Autocracy: The Public Opinion Foundations of a Hybrid Regime," *Europe-Asia Studies* 63, no. 8 (2011): 1357–75. Hale and others find that including the word "democracy" in a survey question produces less support, perhaps because Russians associate it with the harsh 1990s, while asking about support for the core elements of democracy, such as elections, voting rights, and free speech, produces greater support.

4. Ora John Reuter and David Szakonyi, "Electoral Manipulation and Regime Support: Survey Evidence from Russia," (unpublished manuscript, 2018). See also Timothy Colton and Michael McFaul, "Are Russians Undemocratic?," Carnegie Working Papers, no. 20, June 2001.

5. Ellen Carnaghan, *Out of Order: Russian Political Values in an Imperfect World* (University Park: Pennsylvania State University Press, 2007).

6. Reuter and Szakonyi, "Electoral Manipulation and Regime Support."

7. Grigore Pop-Eleches and Graeme B. Robertson, "Information, Elections, and Political Change," *Comparative Politics* 47, no. 4 (2015): 459–95.

8. Javier Corrales and Michael Penfold, "Venezuela: Crowding out the Opposition," *Journal of Democracy* 18, no. 2 (2007): 101.

9. Elisabeth Zerofsky, "Viktor Orbán's Far-Right Vision for Europe," *New Yorker*, January 7, 2019, https://www.newyorker.com/magazine/2019/01/14/viktor-orbans-far-right-vision-for-europe.

10. Kim Lane Scheppele, "Autocratic Legalism," *University of Chicago Law Review* 85 (2018): 578.

11. Henry Hale, *Why Not Parties in Russia? Democracy, Federalism, and the State* (New York: Cambridge University Press, 2006).

12. Henry Hale and Timothy Colton, "Sources of Ruling Party Dominance in Non-Democratic Regimes: The Surprising Importance of Ideas and the Case of United Russia," (unpublished manuscript, 2018), 4.

13. Scheppele, "Autocratic Legalism," 578.

14. Valentin Baryshnikov and Robert Coalson, "12 Million Extra Votes for Putin's Party," *Atlantic*, September 21, 2016, https://www.theatlantic.com/international/archive/2016/09/russia-putin-election-fraud/500867/. See also Podmoskovnik, http://podmoskovnik.livejournal.com/; Dmitry Kobak, Sergey Shpilkin, and Maxim Pshenichnikov, "Integer Percentages as Electoral Falsification Fingerprints" (unpublished manuscript, Champalimaud Centre for the Unknown, Lisbon, Portugal, 2014); Dmitry Kobak, Sergey Shpilkin, and Maxim S. Pshenichnikov, "Statistical Anomalies in 2011–2012 Russian Elections Revealed by 2D Correlation Analysis," (unpublished manuscript, Imperial College London, 2012).

15. Ashlea Rundlett and Milan Svolik, "Deliver the Vote! Micromotives and Macrobehavior in Electoral Fraud," *American Political Science Review* 110, no. 1 (2016): 180–97.

16. Mebane and Kalinin cite another example. If you add up all the last digits in all the reported vote totals in all the electoral precincts in Russia, the result is exactly 4.5, which is precisely the number that one would expect to find in a completely honest election. Another common forensic analyses of vote totals produces an equally perfect result in this election.

17. Walter Mebane and Kirill Kalinin, "When the Russians Fake Their Election Results, They May Be Giving Us the Statistical Finger," *Washington Post*, January 11, 2017, https://www.washingtonpost.com/news/monkey-cage/wp/2017/01/11/when-the-russians-fake-their-election-results-they-may-be-giving-us-the-statistical-finger/?utm_term=.fa017731db65.

18. Ruben Enikolopov, Valery Korovkin, Maria Petrova, Konstantin Sonin, and Alexei Zakharov, "Field Experiment Estimate of Electoral Fraud in Russian Elections," *PNAS Early Edition*, 2013, https://www.pnas.org/content/pnas/early/2012/12/19/1206770110.full.pdf.

19. Enikolopov et al., "Field Experiment Estimate." Andrei Buzin, Kevin Brondum, and Graeme B. Robertson conducted a similar field experiment in twenty-one cities in Russia, and saw much smaller effects. One difference between the two studies is that Enikolopov and colleagues used teams of three or four observers rather than just one, as in the Buzin study. It may be that having multiple observers at a single precinct has a much larger effect than having a single observer. Andrei Buzin, Kevin Brondum, and Graeme B. Robertson, "Election Observer Effects: A Field Experiment in the Russian Duma Election of 2011," *Electoral Studies* 44 (2016): 184–91.

20. Timothy Frye, Ora John Reuter, and David Szakonyi, "Political Machines at Work: Electoral Subversion in the Workplace," *World Politics* 66, no. 2 (2014): 195–228.

21. Frye, Reuter, and Szakonyi, "Hitting Them with Carrots."

22. Susan C. Stokes, Thad Dunning, Marcelo Nazareno, and Valeria Brusco, *Brokers, Voters, and Clientelism: The Puzzle of Distributive Politics* (New York: Cambridge University Press, 2014).

23. Frye, Reuter, and Szakonyi, "Hitting Them with Carrots."

24. They fared poorly for a variety of reasons such as a booming economy that favored incumbents, their association with the economic policies of the 1990s, and weak coordination among opposition groups. They also struggled as the government ramped up the administrative barriers facing opposition parties.

25. Vladimir Kara-Murza, "If Putin Is So Popular, Why Is He So Afraid of Competition?," *Washington Post*, January 12, 2018, https://www.washingtonpost.com/news/democracy-post/wp/2018/01/12/if-putin-is-so-popular-why-is-he-so-afraid-of-competition/?utm_term=.dba952bd6db3.

26. For many observers, this election cycle was a turning point. As Navalny noted, "Up until today, Putin had some claim on legitimacy as a political leader, but now that he has run this fake election by mass fraud to become emperor, he has none." Quoted in Ellen Barry and Michael Schwirtz, "After Election, Putin Faces Challenge to Legitimacy," *New York Times*, March 5, 2012.

27. Adam Przeworski, *Democracy and the Market* (New York: Cambridge University Press, 1990).

28. Timothy Frye, *Building States and Markets after Communism: The Perils of Polarized Democracy* (Cambridge: Cambridge University Press, 2010), 180.

29. Mikhail Myagkov, Peter C. Ordeshook, and Dimitri Shakin, *The Forensics of Election Fraud: Russia and Ukraine* (New York: Cambridge University Press, 2009).

30. Richard Rose and William Mishler surveyed Russians following the 2007–8 election cycle, and found that 69 percent of them "felt that the elections corresponded to reality." Surveys by Stephen White and Ian McAllister reached similar conclusions. See Kenneth Wilson, "How Russians View Electoral Fairness," *Europe-Asia Studies* 64, no. 1 (2012): 145–68.

31. Henry Hale and Timothy J. Colton, "Who Defects: Unpacking a Defection Cascade from Russia's Dominant Party, 2008–12," *American Political Science Review* 111, no. 2 (2017): 322–37.

32. Alexander Bratersky, "Putin Bids for Kremlin amid Protests," *Moscow Times*, December 8, 2011.

33. Timothy Frye and Ekaterina Borisova, "Elections, Protest, and Trust in Government: A Natural Experiment from Russia," *Journal of Politics*, 81, no. 3 (2019): 820–32; Vladimir Gel'man, "Cracks in the Wall: Challenges to Electoral Authoritarianism in Russia," *Problems of Post-Communism* 60, no. 2 (2013): 3–10; Graeme B. Robertson, "Protesting Putinism: The Election Protests of 2011–2012 in Broader Perspective," *Problems of Post-Communism* 60, no. 2 (2013): 11–23.

34. Quoted in Aleksandr Tsubiks, "Abuses in Parliamentary Elections Predicted," *Infozine*, December 3, 2011, http://www.infozine.com/news/stories/op/storiesView/sid/49931/.

35. Yulia Latynina on *Echo of Moscow* radio show, December 10, 2011.

36. Gel'man, "Cracks in the Wall."

37. "Politsii blagodarili za poryadok," *Kommersant'*, December 12, 2011.

38. Tomila Lankina and Anna Voznaya, "New Data on Protest Trends in Russia's Regions," *Europe-Asia Studies* 67 (2015): 327–42; Katerina Tertychnaya, "Protests and Voter Defections in Electoral Autocracies, *Comparative Political Studies* 53, no. 2 (2019): 1926–56.

39. Regina Smyth, Anton Sobolev, and Irina Soboleva, "A Well-Organized Play," *Problems of Post-Communism* 60, no. 2 (2013): 24–39, https://www.tandfonline.com/doi/abs/10.2753/PPC1075-8216600203.

40. "Putin: Glavnoe, shtoby my byli vmeste," *Vzglyad*, February 23, 2012, https://vz.ru/news/2012/2/23/563536.html.

41. In a study from Azerbaijan, Fredrik Sjoberg found that video cameras displaced fraud to settings outside the voting booth. Fredrik M. Sjoberg, "Autocratic Adaptation: The Strategic Use of Transparency and the Persistence of Electoral Fraud," *Electoral Studies* 33 (2014): 233–45.

42. Nikolai Petrov and Darrell Slider, "United Russia's 'Primaries': A Preview of the Duma Elections?," *Russian Analytical Digest*, no. 186, July, 15, 2016; "Administratsiya prezidenta zaprosila

pomoshchi uchenykh," *Vedomosti*, July 15, 2014; "V Kremle izuchayut amerikanskie tekhnologii v kontektse vyborov v Dumu v 2016 godu," *Vedomosti*, March 11, 2015.

43. Leonid Bershidsky, "Russia Has the Most Boring Election in the World," *Bloomberg*, July 8, 2016, https://www.bloomberg.com/opinion/articles/2016-07-08/russia-has-the-most -boring-election-of-2016.

44. "Regiony vstupili v borbu za yavku: informirovat' o prezidentskikh vyborov budut na zavodakh i doma," *Kommersant'*, January 25, 2018.

45. Vladimir Kara-Murza, "Protests Return to Moscow as Opposition Candidates Are Banned," *Washington Post*, July 22, 2019, https://www.washingtonpost.com/opinions/2019/07 /22/protests-return-moscow-opposition-candidates-are-banned-crucial-election/.

46. Timothy Colton, "Regimeness, Hybridity, and Russian System Building as an Educative Project," *Comparative Politics* (April 2018): 455–70.

Chapter 6. Neither as Strong nor as Weak as It Looks: Russia's Economy

1. It is possible that a large devaluation may increase Russia's GDP at purchasing power parity to place it within the top five economies in the coming years, but such a change would further reduce Russian's ability to import goods and services.

2. She is also the spouse of Vyacheslav Kuzminov, the head of the Higher School of Economics.

3. "Russian Central Bank Governor Voted Best in Europe in 2017," *Euractiv*, January 10, 2017, https://www.euractiv.com/section/euro-finance/news/russian-central-bank-governor-voted -best-in-europe-for-2017/. See, in general, Juliet Johnson, *Priests of Prosperity: How Central Bankers Transformed the Postcommunist World* (Ithaca, NY: Cornell University Press, 2016).

4. "Central Bank Identified in the Bank 'Ugra' Signs of Withdrawal of Assets and Manipulation of the Deposits," *TASS*, July 11, 2017, http://freenews-en.tk/2017/07/11/the-central-bank -identified-in-the-bank-ugra-signs-of-withdrawal-of-assets-and-manipulation-of-the-deposits/.

5. Henry Foy, "Russian Central Bank Withdraws the License of Bank Yugra," *Financial Times*, July 28, 2017, https://www.ft.com/content/b209b5be-fca2-3010-b85c-6e57d51bc197.

6. Daron Acemoglu, Suresh Naidu, Pascual Restrepo, and James Robinson, "Does Democracy Cause Growth?," *Journal of Political Economy* 127, no. 1 (2019): 47–100, https://doi.org/10 .1086/700936.

7. Kunal Sen, Lant Pritchett, Sabyasachi Kar, and Selim Raihan, "Democracy versus Dictatorship? The Political Determinants of Growth Episodes," March 2017, ESID Working Paper No. 70, http://dx.doi.org/10.2139/ssrn.2893112; Ruchir Sharma, *The Rise and Fall of Nations: Ten Rules of Change in the Post-Crisis World* (New York: W. W. Norton and Company, 2016).

8. Luis R. Martinez, "How Much Should We Trust the Dictator's GDP Estimates," (unpublished manuscript, University of Chicago, April 2018), 1–59.

9. Barbara Geddes, Joseph Wright, and Erica Frantz, *How Dictatorships Work* (New York: Cambridge University Press, 2018). See also Eric Chang and Miriam Golden, "Sources of Corruption in Authoritarian Regimes," *Social Science Quarterly* 91, no. 1 (2010): 1–20.

10. Rory Carroll, "Hugo Chávez Revolution Mired by Claims of Corruption," *Guardian*, April 18, 2010, https://www.theguardian.com/world/2010/apr/18/hugo-chavez-revolution -corruption-claims.

11. Balint Magyar, *Post-Communist Mafia State: The Case of Hungary* (Budapest: Central European University Press, 2015), chapter 5; Javier Corrales and Michael Penfold, *Dragon in the Tropics: Hugo Chavez and the Political Economy of Revolution in Venezuela* (Washington, DC: Brookings Institution Press), 60–62.

12. For an explicit comparison of cronyism in Hungary and Russia, see Maria Snegovaya, "Russia: The Mafia State," *Meduza*, December 17, 2015, https://meduza.io/en/feature/2015/12/17/opinion-russia-the-mafia-state.

13. Anders Aslund, *Russia's Crony Capitalism: The Path from Market Economy to Kleptocracy* (New Haven, CT: Yale University Press, 2019), 175.

14. "Foreign Direct Investment into Russia Is Falling," *Moscow Times*, May 22, 2019, https://www.themoscowtimes.com/2019/05/22/foreign-direct-investment-into-russia-is-falling-a65690.

15. Ben Aris, "Russia's National Projects: Economic Reboot or Mucky Bog?," *Russia Matters*, May 30, 2019, https://www.russiamatters.org/analysis/russias-national-projects-economic-reboot-or-mucky-bog.

16. Bank of Finland Report, March 19, 2020.

17. Bert Ely, "Russia Is an Economic Pipsqueak," *Hill*, July 13, 2018, https://thehill.com/opinion/international/396877-russia-is-an-economic-pipsqueak-trumps-infatuation-is-baffling. See also Matthew Lynn, "Opinion: Putin's Russia Is Too Weak to Threaten Anyone," *MarketWatch*, April 12, 2017, https://www.marketwatch.com/story/putins-russia-is-too-weak-to-threaten-anyone-2017-04-11.

18. Data from the World Economic Outlook, https://knoema.com/nwnfkne/world-gdp-ranking-2019-gdp-by-country-data-and-charts.

19. "GDP—Per Capita (PPP) 2018 Country Ranks, by Rank," CIA World Fact Book, Countries of the World, 2018, https://photius.com/rankings/2018/economy/gdp_per_capita_2018_0.html.

20. "Russia GDP Growth Rate," *Trading Economics*, 2018, https://tradingeconomics.com/russia/gdp-growth.

21. Novatek recently surpassed Gazprom in liquefied natural gas (LNG) production. After Gazprom stumbled with LNG projects, the government opened the door to Novatek, which finished the Yamal project ahead of schedule. Two observers note that "Yamal LNG has arguably been the most successful LNG project in the world during the last decade." James Henderson and Vitaly Yermakov, "Russian LNG Becomes Global Force," Oxford Institute for Energy Studies, November 2019, 14, https://www.oxfordenergy.org/wpcms/wp-content/uploads/2019/11/Russian-LNG-Becoming-a-Global-Force-NG-154.pdf.

22. James Henderson and Arild Moe, "Gazprom's LNG Offensive: A Demonstration of Monopoly Strength or Impetus for Russian Gas Sector Reform?," *Post-Communist Economies* 28, no. 3 (2016): 281–99, https://www.tandfonline.com/doi/pdf/10.1080/14631377.2016.1203206.

23. Julia S. P. Loe, "'But It Is Our Duty!': Exploring Gazprom's Reluctance to Russian Gas Sector Reform," *Post-Soviet Affairs* 35, no. 1 (2019): 63–76.

24. "Number of Russians in Poverty Hits Decade High," *Radio Free Europe / Radio Liberty*, April 6, 2017, https://www.rferl.org/a/recession-sanctions-left-20-million-russians-living-poverty-2016-up-300000-2015/28413387.html.

25. *Private Health Care Market in Russia, 2017–19*, KPMG, 2017, https://assets.kpmg.com/content/dam/kpmg/ru/pdf/2017/03/ru-en-research-on-development-of-the-private-medical-services-market.pdf.

26. Noah Buckley, "Calculating Corruption," (PhD diss., Columbia University, 2017).

27. Henry Foy, "Russia's Middle Class Opens Door to Private Health Providers," *Financial Times*, February 21, 2018, https://www.ft.com/content/672684ea-1649-11e8-9376 -4a6390addb44.

28. "Six Months into the Coronavirus Outbreak Russia's Statistics Still Provide More Questions Than Answers," *Moscow Times*, August 11, 2020, https://www.themoscowtimes.com/2020 /08/11/six-months-into-the-coronavirus-outbreak-russias-statistics-still-provide-more -questions-than-answers-a71069.

29. Talia Khan Burki, "The Russian Vaccine for Covid-19," *Lancet: Respiratory Medicine*, September 4, 2020, https://www.thelancet.com/journals/lanres/article/PIIS2213-2600(20)30402-1 /fulltext.

30. "Novost' o sozdanii vaktsiny ot koronavirusa u 46 rossiyan vyzvala negativnye emotsii," Levada Center, August 28, 2020, https://www.levada.ru/2020/08/28/novost-o-sozdanii -vaktsiny-ot-koronavirusa-u-46-rossiyan-vyzvala-negativnye-emotsii/.

31. *Wellcome Global Monitor*, June 19, 2019, chapter 5, https://wellcome.org/reports /wellcome-global-monitor/2018.

32. *Education at a Glance 2016*, OECD, 2016, 282, 54, https://read.oecd-ilibrary.org/education /education-at-a-glance-2016/russian-federation_eag-2016-76-en#page3.

33. Tatyana Lomskaya and Maksim Taikalo, "Rossiya bolee korumpirovanna chem mozhno ozhidat'," *Vedomosti*, January 8, 2019, https://www.vedomosti.ru/economics/characters/2019 /01/08/790919-glavnii-ekonomist-ebrr.

34. "Top Russian Universities in World University Rankings," Study in Russia, https:// studyinrussia.ru/en/why-russia/world-university-rankings/qs/.

35. Filip Novokmet, Thomas Piketty, and Gabriel Zucman, "From Soviets to Oligarchs: Inequality and Property in Russia, 1905–2016," VOX EU, November 9, 2017, https://voxeu.org /article/inequality-and-property-russia-1905-2016. See also the working paper version at https://www.nber.org/papers/w23712.

36. Credit Suisse, Global Wealth Databook, 100, 108, https://publications.credit-suisse.com /tasks/render/file/index.cfm?fileid=17711FFC-0524-76AB-CEB0FE206E46C125.

37. Novokmet, Piketty, and Zucman, "From Soviets to Oligarchs: Inequality and Property in Russia."

38. Daniel Treisman, "Russia's Billionaires," *American Economic Review Papers and Proceedings* 106, no. 5 (2016): 236–41.

39. "Gini Index (World Bank Estimate)," World Bank Data, https://data.worldbank.org /indicator/SI.POV.GINI.

40. Giles Whittell, "This Is Russia's Real Revolution," *Times*, July 14, 2018, https://www .thetimes.co.uk/article/towering-skyscrapers-smooth-new-roads-uber-airbnb-porsche-and -jaguar-dealers-this-is-russia-s-real-revolution-tfffz5f8g.

41. Natalia Zubarevich, "Four Russias: Rethinking the Post-Soviet Map," *Open Democracy*, March 29, 2012, https://www.opendemocracy.net/en/odr/four-russias-rethinking-post-soviet -map/.

42. "Russia GDP," Trading Economics, https://tradingeconomics.com/russia/gdp.

43. See Karen Dawisha, *Putin's Kleptocracy: Who Owns Russia?* (New York: Simon and Schuster, 2014); Aslund, *Russia's Crony Capitalism*.

44. Natalia Lamberova and Konstantin Sonin, "The Role of Business Elites in Shaping Economic Policy," in *The New Autocracy: Information, Politics, and Policy in Putin's Russia*, ed. Daniel Treisman (Washington, DC: Brookings Institution Press, 2018), 137–58.

45. David Szakonyi, "Businesspeople in Elected Office: Identifying Private Benefits from Firm-Level Returns," *American Political Science Review* 112, no. 2 (2018): 322–38.

46. "Hello, my name is Alexander Shabolov. I am a representative of a Russian [Chinese, US, German ...] information technology [retail, agriculture, transport, tourism ...] sector company. I would like to get some information about investment possibilities in your region. Specifically, I'm interested in programs supporting small [medium-size] businesses. Sincerely, Alexander Shabolov, Council for Entrepreneurial Development of United Russia [KPRF, LDPR, Yabloko ...]."

47. Michael Rochlitz, Evhenia Mitrokhina, and Irina Nizvola, "Bureaucratic Discrimination in Electoral Authoritarian Regimes: Experimental Evidence from Russia," Bremen Papers on Economics and Innovation, 2020, 1–35. This paper has not yet undergone peer review.

48. Magyar, *Post-Communist Mafia State*, 73–208; Corrales and Penfold, *Dragon in the Tropics*, 60–62.

49. Stanislav Markus, *Property, Protection, and Predation: Piranha Capitalism in Russia and Ukraine* (New York: Cambridge University Press, 2015); Jordan Gans-Morse, *Property Rights in Post-Soviet Russia: Violence, Corruption, and Demand for the Rule of Law* (New York: Cambridge University Press, 2017).

50. As a former minister of justice commented, "It is well known that over the past years, the threat of a prison sentence in particular has become a widespread source of corruption. Cases for those types of crimes hardly ever go to court, but are actively used as a means to pressure businessmen." Oleg Shvartsman, "For Us, the Party Is Represented by the Power Bloc Headed by Igor' Ivanovich Sechin," *Kommersant'*, December 3, 2007.

51. Joera Mulders, "Legal Reforms: Medvedev's Achievements," *Russia Watchers*, April 25, 2011.

52. "An Amnesty for Russian Business," *Russian Survey*, September 2013, http://www.russian-survey.com/main/200-an-amnesty-for-russian-business.

53. "Kolichestvo ugolovnikh del protiv biznesa rezko vozroslo," *Vedomosti*, February 19, 2020.

54. Timothy Frye and Andrei Yakovlev, "Elections and Property Rights: A Natural Experiment from Russia," *Comparative Political Studies* 49, no. 4 (2016): 499–528, https://doi.org/10.1177/0010414015621074; Timothy Frye, *Property Rights and Property Wrongs: How Power, Institutions, and Norms Shape Economic Conflict in Russia* (New York: Cambridge University Press, 2017).

55. Rostislav Kapeliushnikov, Andrei Kuznetsov, Natalia Demina, and Olga Kuznetsova, "Threats to Security of Property Rights in a Transition Economy," *Journal of Comparative Economics* 41, no. 1 (2013): 245–64.

56. "Russia Loses $30Bln a Year in Post-Crimea Investment Climate," *Moscow Times*, May 13, 2019, https://www.themoscowtimes.com/2019/05/13/russia-loses-30bln-a-year-in-post-crimea-investment-climate-economist-a65555.

57. "Russia's Capital Outflow More than Doubled," *Moscow Times*, January 18, 2019, https://www.themoscowtimes.com/2019/01/18/russias-capital-outflow-more-than-doubled-2018-68-billion-reports-a64193.

58. Polina Devitt, "Declare Offshore Wealth? Russian Tycoons Would Rather Ship Themselves Offshore," *Reuters*, June 6, 2017, https://www.reuters.com/article/us-russia-economy-tax-insight/declare-offshore-wealth-russia-tycoons-would-rather-ship-themselves-off-shore-idUSKBN18X0XJ..

59. Alexander Sazonov, "Cash (in US Dollars) Is King for Russia's Millionaires," *Bloomberg*, April 15, 2019, https://www.bloomberg.com/news/articles/2019-04-05/russia-s-millionaires-hoard-cash-as-banks-pitch-alternatives.

60. "Putin Gets Tough on Extortion Masquerading as State Service," *Moscow Times*, March 5, 2013.

61. Vladimir Novikov, "A Business Amnesty: Mission Impossible," RAPSI, Russian Legal Information Agency, May 31, 2013, http://www.rapsinews.com/legislation_publication/20130531/267663712.5.html.

62. Joshua Yaffa, "Putin's Shadow Cabinet and the Bridge to Crimea," *New Yorker*, May 29, 2017, https://www.newyorker.com/magazine/2017/05/29/putins-shadow-cabinet-and-the-bridge-to-crimea.

63. "Road Rage," *Russia Today*, December 12, 2012, https://www.rt.com/news/ekaterinburg-road-city-manager-855/.

64. Andrew Osborne, "Russian Corruption Means Foie Gras Roads Would Have Been Cheaper," *Telegraph*, July 22, 2010, https://www.telegraph.co.uk/news/worldnews/europe/russia/7902905/Russian-corruption-means-foie-gras-roads-would-be-cheaper.html.

65. "The Winter Olympics in Sochi Cost 51 Billion Dollars," *Bloomberg*, February 1, 2014, https://www.bloomberg.com/news/articles/2014-01-02/the-2014-winter-olympics-in-sochi-cost-51-billion.

66. Andrew E. Kramer, "In Moscow a Financial District That Is Anything But," *New York Times*, November 26, 2014, https://www.nytimes.com/2014/11/26/realestate/commercial/in-moscow-a-financial-district-that-is-anything-but.html.

67. Haakon Gjerløw and Carl Henrik Knutsen, "Autocrats and Skyscrapers: Modern White Elephants in Dictatorships," *Political Research Quarterly* 72, no. 2 (2019): 504–20.

68. Buckley, "Calculating Corruption."

69. Davydov Index, LiveJournal.com, June 7, 2016, https://davydov-index.livejournal.com/2635820.html.

70. "Deputatam i chinovnikam razreshyat utaivat' dokhodi byvshikh zhen," *Lenta.ru*, January 17, 2017, https://lenta.ru/news/2017/01/17/money_control/.

71. Darina Gribova, "Study Finds One in Nine Russian Duma Deputies Are Academic Phonies," *World*, January 20, 2016, https://www.pri.org/stories/2016-01-20/study-finds-one-nine-russian-duma-deputies-are-academic-phonies.

72. Valerie Strauss, "Russia's Plagiarism Problem: Even Putin Has Done It!," *Washington Post*, March 18, 2014, https://www.washingtonpost.com/news/answer-sheet/wp/2014/03/18/russias-plagiarism-problem-even-putin-has-done-it/?utm_term=.f796cecdcac2. Putin's degree is a *kandidatskaya*, which requires more work than a master's degree, but less than a PhD.

73. Fiona Hill, Clifford Gaddy, and Igor Danchenko, "The Mystery of Vladimir Putin's Dissertation," Brookings Institution, March 30, 2006, https://www.brookings.edu/events/the-mystery-of-vladimir-putins-dissertation/.

74. Prior to the economic shock of COVID-19, most observers saw Russia locked into growth rates of 1 to 2 percent. "Russia Economic Report," World Bank, December 4, 2018, http://www.worldbank.org/en/country/russia/publication/rer.

Chapter 7. Hitting Them with Carrots: The Role of Repression

1. Valerie Sperling, *Sex, Politics, and Putin: Political Legitimacy in Russia* (New York: Cambridge University Press, 2015).

2. Christian Davenport, "Multi-Dimensional Threat Perception and State Repression: An Inquiry into Why States Apply Negative Sanctions," *American Journal of Political Science* 39, no. 3 (1995): 683–713, www.jstor.org/stable/2111650. See also Sergei Guriev and Oleg Tsivinskii, "Ot repressii k repressiyam," *Vedomosti*, July 31, 2012, https://www.vedomosti.ru/opinion/articles /2012/07/31/ot_repressij_k_repressiyam.

3. For a good discussion on elite politics, see Andrew Monaghan, "Beyond Putin: Deciphering Power in Russia," Manchester Open Hive, August 17, 2016.

4. Mark Kramer, "The Soviet Legacy in Russian Foreign Policy," *Political Science Quarterly* 134, no. 4 (2019–20): 585–610.

5. Kirill Shamiev and Luke Mchelidze, "Is Russia a Militocracy?," *Riddle*, September 20, 2018. Precise measurement of siloviki penetration of state organizations is difficult because the degree of involvement with the security services varies a great deal. Some siloviki are career professionals in the security services, but others worked in related organizations, have past work experience in the services, or studied at service academies and have more tenuous links to these organizations. These distinctions are often lost in popular discussions.

6. Andrei Soldatov and Irina Borogan, "Russia's New Nobility," *Foreign Affairs*, September 1, 2010, https://www.foreignaffairs.com/articles/russia-fsu/2010-09-01/russias-new-nobility.

7. Andrei Soldatov and Irina Borogan, "The Country's New Nobility," *Moscow Times*, September 9, 2010, 3, https://www.themoscowtimes.com/2010/09/16/the-countrys-new -nobility-a1496.

8. "Rossiyane schitayut armiyu i gozbezopastnost' samymi avtoritetnimi institutami," *Vedomosti*, February 5, 2020.

9. Robert Mueller, "Report on the Investigation into Russian Electoral Interference in 2016," 2019, https://www.justice.gov/storage/report.pdf.

10. "Russian National Guard Reaches 340,000," *Moscow Times*, November 25, 2016, https:// www.themoscowtimes.com/2016/11/25/russian-national-guard-reaches-340000-personnel -a56308.

11. Margarete Klein, "Putin's New National Guard: Bulwark against Mass Protests and Illoyal Elites," SWP Comments, September 1–4, 2016, https://www.swp-berlin.org/fileadmin/contents /products/comments/2016C41_kle.pdf.

12. Stephen Sestanovich, "The Day after Putin," *Foreign Affairs*, March 4, 2020, https:// thecsspoint.com/the-day-after-putin-by-stephen-sestanovich/.

13. Leonid Kosals and Anastassiya Dubova, "Commercialization of Police and the Informal Economy: The Russian Case," *Economic Sociology: European Electronic Newsletter* 13, no. 2 (2012): 21–28, https://ecsoclab.hse.ru/data/2012/07/27/1258192823/ econ_soc_13–2_cut.pdf.

14. Ekaterina Karacheva, "Sledstvennomy Komitetu rashirit polnomochiya po vozbuzh-deniyu del protiv VIP-person," Iz.ru, September 10, 2012, https://iz.ru/news/534747.

15. Lucian Kim, "In Putin's Russia, an 'Adhocracy' Marked by Ambiguity and Plausible Deni-ability," NPR, July 21, 2017, https://www.npr.org/sections/parallels/2017/07/21/538535186/in-putins-russia-an-adhocracy-marked-by-ambiguity-and-plausible-deniability.

16. Lisa Blaydes, State of Repression: Iraq under Saddam Hussein (Princeton, NJ: Princeton University Press, 2018).

17. Michael Ellman, "Soviet Repression Statistics: Some Comments," Europe-Asia Studies 54, no. 7 (2002): 1151–72. He notes that "the best estimate that can currently be made of the number of repression deaths in 1937–38 is in the range 950,000–1.2 million, i.e., about a million. This is the estimate which should be used by historians, teachers and journalists concerned with twentieth century Russian—and world—history."

18. Yuri Zhukov and Roya Talibova, "Stalin's Terror and the Long-Term Political Effects of Mass Terror," Journal of Peace Research 55, no. 2 (2018): 267–83, http://journals.sagepub.com/doi/abs/10.1177/0022343317751261?journalCode=jpra.

19. Noah Buckley, Timothy Frye, Scott Gehlbach, and Lauren A. McCarthy, "Cooperating with the State: Evidence from a Survey Experiment on Policing," Journal of Experimental Political Science 3, no. 2 (2016): 124–39.

20. Noah Buckley, Ora John Reuter, Michael Rochlitz, and Anton Aisin, "Staying Out of Trouble: Criminal Cases against Russian Mayors," Bremen Papers on Economics and Innovation, no. 2013, July 9, 2020, 1–26. This paper has not yet undergone peer review.

21. Ella Panayakh, "Faking Enforcement Together: Systems of Performance Evaluation in Russian Enforcement Agencies and Production of Bias and Privilege," Post-Soviet Affairs 30, no. 2–3 (2014): 115–36.

22. Javier Corrales, "The Authoritarian Resurgence: Autocratic Legalism in Venezuela," Journal of Democracy 26, no. 2 (2015): 37–51; Kim Lane Scheppele, "Autocratic Legalism," University of Chicago Law Review 85 (2018): 545–83.

23. Daniela Ikawa, "Hungary's Anti-NGO Tax Law Violates Free Speech," Open Society Justice Initiative, December 18, 2018, https://www.justiceinitiative.org/voices/hungary-s-anti-ngo-tax-law-violates-free-speech-and-freedom-association.

24. In Venezuela, state agencies are prohibited from advertising in private media. Corrales, "The Authoritarian Resurgence."

25. Similarly, within forty-eight hours after being elected party head for the opposition in Turkey, Canan Kaftancioglu faced charges of terrorism by the Erdoğan government. Nick Ash-down, "A Motorcycle Riding Leftist Feminist Is Coming for Erdogan," Foreign Policy, May 1, 2020, https://foreignpolicy.com/2020/05/01/canan-kaftancioglu-turkey-erdogan-chp-profile/.

26. Chávez and Erdoğan went after the high courts in their countries shortly after taking power. This is also a key issue in Poland.

27. "Chechnya No Longer Helps Foreign Journalists," Guardian, October 10, 2016, https://www.theguardian.com/world/2016/oct/10/chechnya-no-longer-help-foreign-journalists-ramzan-kadyrov.

28. Egor Lazarev, "Laws in Conflict: Legacies of War, Gender, and Legal Pluralism in Chech-nya," World Politics, 71, no. 4 (2019): 667–709.

29. Joshua Yaffa, *Between Two Fires: Truth, Ambition, and Compromise in Putin's Russia* (New York: Tim Duggan Books, 2020), 93.

30. Lazarev, 2019.

31. These types of studies are controversial because they involve some deception of respondents as the scholars were acting on behalf of a fictitious NGO. The concern is that this approach may undermine the activities of legitimate NGOs. At the same time, none of the advertisements were placed on the web as the scholars were only interested in studying how the firms responded to their requests so the broader effects in Russia were likely limited.

32. Charles Crabtree, Christopher J. Fariss, and Holger L. Kern, "Truth Replaced by Silence: A Field Experiment on Private Censorship in Russia," December 25, 2015, https://ssrn.com/abstract=2708274. This paper has not undergone peer review.

33. In this way, repression is a substitute for other ways that the Kremlin tries to make its rule legitimate.

34. Human Rights Watch, World Report, Russia, 2018, https://www.hrw.org/world-report/2018/country-chapters/russia.

35. Alexis M. Lerner, "The Co-optation of Dissent in Hybrid States: Post-Soviet Graffiti in Moscow," *Comparative Political Studies* (October 31, 2019). https://journals.sagepub.com/doi/full/10.1177/0010414019879949.

36. Eduard Limonov's National Bolshevik Party, a small yet dedicated radical nationalist movement, received longer prison sentences for protesting.

37. "Lukin: There Were No Riots on Bolotnaya Square," HRO.org, July 2, 2012, http://hro.rightsinrussia.info/archive/right-of-assembly-1/may-2012/lukin/no-riots.

38. Early in his career, Navalny associated with some ugly nationalist groups in Russia, but he has kept his distance from them in recent years.

39. Zolotov raged, "You're rotten and moldering inside, you have neither spirituality nor morality, nothing whatsoever, you're just tumbleweed, you have neither country nor Fatherland. . . . You are just an oppositionist little mite of a dog who has convinced himself he's an elephant. . . . I am simply challenging you to a one-on-one fight—in a boxing a ring, on a tatami, wherever—where I promise to turn you into a nice, juicy schnitzel within minutes." *BBC Monitoring*, January 1, 2019.

40. Ruben Enikolopov, Maria Petrova, and Konstantin Sonin, "Social Media and Corruption," *American Economic Review* 10, no. 1 (2018): 152.

41. This sentence was overturned by the Russian Supreme Court after the European Court of Human Rights found that Navalny had not received a fair trial.

42. Some also believe that the mayor of Moscow thought having a competitor would increase his standing—perhaps as a successor to Putin.

43. Julia Ioffe, "What Russia's Latest Protests Mean for Putin," *Atlantic*, March 27, 2017, https://www.theatlantic.com/international/archive/2017/03/navalny-protests-russia-putin/520878/.

44. "FBK inostrannim agentom," *Vedomosti*, October 10, 2019, https://www.vedomosti.ru/politics/articles/2019/10/10/813309-fbk-inostrannim-agentom.

45. "As US and Allies Demand Answers, Russia Dismisses Poisoning Accusations," *CBS News*, September 9, 2020, https://www.cbsnews.com/news/alexei-navalny-poisoning-g7-push-for-sanctions-russia-says-united-states-germany-demand-answers/.

46. "OPCW Issues Technical Report on Request for Assistance from Germany," October 6, 2020, https://www.justice.gov/storage/report.pdf.

47. Andrew E. Kramer, "Russia Spins Alternative Theories in Poisoning of Navalny," *New York Times*, September 3, 2020; "As US and Allies Demand Answers, Russia Dismisses Poisoning Accusations," *CBS News*, September 9, 2020, https://www.cbsnews.com/news/alexei-navalny -poisoning-g7-push-for-sanctions-russia-says-united-states-germany-demand-answers/.

48. "Russia: Germany Has Provided No Proof of Poisoning," *Associated Press*, September 4, 2020, https://www.hotsr.com/news/2020/sep/04/russia-germany-has-provided-no-proof-of -poisoning/.

49. "Putin's Attempt to Explain the Poisoning of Alexei Navalny to France Failed," *Fr24news*, September 23, 2020, https://www.fr24news.com/a/2020/09/putins-attempt-to-explain-the -poisoning-of-alexei-navalny-to-france-failed-and-helped-unite-europe-against-him -intelligence-sources-say.html.

50. "Russian Oligarch and Opposition Nemesis Buys Civil Suit Debt Owed by Navalny," *Meduza*, August 26, 2020, https://meduza.io/en/news/2020/08/26/russian-oligarch-and -opposition-nemesis-buys-civil-suit-debt-owed-by-navalny-and-company-says-he-ll-ruin-him -if-he-survives-poisoning.

51. Tatiana Stanovaya, "Navalny's Poisoning Is the Act of a Sickly Regime," Carnegie Moscow Center, September 8, 2020, https://carnegie.ru/commentary/82574.

52. "Ot 'Salar'eva' do 'Kommunarki': zapushen novii uchastok Sokolnicheskoi linii metro," Mos.ru, June 20, 2019, https://www.mos.ru/mayor/themes/4299/5736050.

53. Tomila Lankina and Rodion Skovoroda, "Regional Protest and Electoral Fraud: Evidence from Analysis of New Data on Russian Protest," *East Eastern Politics* 33, no. 2 (2017): 25–74, https://www.tandfonline.com/doi/full/10.1080/21599165.2016.1261018; Tomila Lankina, "Young Russians Are Protesting Again," *Washington Post*, March 31, 2017, https://www.washingtonpost .com/news/monkey-cage/wp/2017/03/31/russians-are-protesting-part-8-young-russians-arent -a-brainwashed-lost-generation-after-all/.

54. Tomila Lankina, "Release of Lankina Russian Protest Event Dataset," October 12, 2018, https://popularmobilization.net/2018/10/12/release-of-lankina-russian-protest-event-dataset/.

55. Katerina Tertychnaya, *Deterred: Dissent in Electoral Autocracies* (unpublished book manuscript, London, January 2020).

56. Regina Smyth, Anton Sobolev, and Irina Soboleva, "A Well-Organized Play," *Problems of Post-Communism* 60, no. 2 (2013): 24–39, https://www.tandfonline.com/doi/abs/10.2753 /PPC1075-8216600203.

57. Timothy Frye and Ekaterina Borisova, "Elections, Protest, and Trust: A Natural Experiment from Russia," *Journal of Politics* 81, no. 3 (2019): 820–32, https://www.journals.uchicago .edu/doi/abs/10.1086/702944?mobileUi=0.

58. "20k People Donate to Russian Liberal Outlet to Pay Government Fine," *Moscow Times*, November 13, 2018, https://themoscowtimes.com/news/20k-people-donate-russian-liberal -outlet-pay-government-fine-63483.

59. "The Advocacy Group PEN Has Declared Serebrennikov an 'Artist at Risk," Pen America, https://pen.org/advocacy-case/kirill-serebrennikov/.

60. "Kak Kirill Serebrennikov vodit ekskursii po Prechistenke," *Vedomosti*, November 13, 2018.

61. Anna Nemtsova, "A Russian Journalist's Arrest Counters the Image of Putin the Puppet Master," *Atlantic*, June 11, 2019, https://www.theatlantic.com/international/archive/2019/06/ivan-golunov-putin-puppet-master-myth/591469/.

62. "5 Moscow Police Officials Fired over Investigative Journalist's Arrest," *Moscow Times*, July 10, 2019, https://www.themoscowtimes.com/2019/07/10/5-moscow-police-officials-fired-over-investigative-journalists-arrest-a66355.

63. Andrei Yakovlev and Anton Kazun, "Doverie professionalam i potentsial obshestvennoi mobilizatsii," (unpublished manuscript, Moscow, May 2020).

64. The arrest and continued detention of Michael Calvey, a US businessman detained since February 2019 following a business dispute with partners, is a good example.

65. "VShE ne stala prodlevat' kontrakt eshche c 4 oppozitsionnimi prepodavatelyami," https://www.rbc.ru/politics/11/08/2020/5f326a669a79472db1f306b9. Sergei Medvedev, a well-known professor who left the HSE in October 2020, explained his reasoning on Facebook. See https://www.facebook.com/sergei.medvedev3/posts/10224043950394870.

66. For a good discussion of this balancing act, see this statement by the HSE rector, Yaroslav Kuzminov, from January 24, 2020, https://www.hse.ru/our/news/335436253.html.

67. Vladimir Gel'man, "The Politics of Fear," *Russian Politics* 1, no. 1 (2016): 27–45, https://brill.com/view/journals/rupo/1/1/article-p27_2.xml?language=en.

68. Bryn Rosenfeld, "Putin's Support Is Weakening: Will That Show Up in Russia's Regional Elections?," *Washington Post*, September 10, 2020, https://www.washingtonpost.com/politics/2020/09/10/putins-support-is-weakening-will-that-show-up-russias-regional-elections-this-weekend/?utm_campaign=wp_monkeycage&utm_source=twitter&utm_medium=social.

69. Christian Davenport, "Multi-Dimensional Threat Perception and State Repression: An Inquiry into Why States Apply Negative Sanctions," *American Journal of Political Science* 39, no. 2 (1995): 683–713, www.jstor.org/stable/2111650. See also Sergei Guriev and Oleg Tsivinskii, "Ot represii k repressiyam," *Vedomosti*, July 31, 2012,
https://www.vedomosti.ru/opinion/articles/2012/07/31/ot_repressij_k_repressiyam.

70. Anastasiya Kornya, "Rossiya bolshe vsekh ve Evrope tratit na tyurmi, no menshe vsekh na zaklyuchennykh," *Vedomosti*, April 3, 2019.

Chapter 8. Mysterious Ways: Media Manipulation at Home

1. "Festive Flight to Moscow Resumes US-Soviet Air Service," *New York Times*, April 30, 1986, https://www.nytimes.com/1986/04/30/world/festive-flight-to-moscow-resumes-us-soviet-air-service.html. Pan Am ended these flights in 1979 following the Soviet invasion of Afghanistan.

2. Pomerantsev continues, "We saw one example when Russian media spread a multitude of conspiracy theories about the downing of Malaysia Airlines Flight 17 over eastern Ukraine in July, from claiming that radar data showed Ukrainian jets had flown near the plane to suggesting that the plane was shot down by Ukrainians aiming at Mr. Putin's presidential jet. The aim was to distract people from the evidence, which pointed to the separatists, and to muddy the water to a point where the audience simply gave up on the search for truth." Peter Pomerantsev, "Russia's Ideology: There Is No Truth," *New York Times*, December 12, 2014, https://www.nytimes.com/2014/12/12/opinion/russias-ideology-there-is-no-truth.html.

3. Daniel Treisman, "Introduction: Rethinking Russia's Political Order," in *The New Autocracy: Information, Politics, and Policy in Putin's Russia*, ed. Daniel Treisman (Washington, DC: Brookings Institution Press, 2017), 13–14. See also Sergei Guriev and Daniel Treisman, "Informational Autocrats," *Journal of Economic Perspectives* 33, no. 4 (2019): 100–127.

4. Elisabeth Zerofsky, "Viktor Orbán's Far-Right Vision for Europe," *New Yorker*, January 7, 2019, https://www.newyorker.com/magazine/2019/01/14/viktor-orbans-far-right-vision-for-europe.

5. For a detailed description of these techniques, see Marius Dragomir, "The State of Hungary Media: Endgame," LSE, August 29, 2017, https://blogs.lse.ac.uk/medialse/2017/08/29/the-state-of-hungarian-media-endgame/.

6. Zia Weise, "How Did Things Get So Bad for Turkey's Journalists?," *Atlantic*, August 23, 2018.

7. Hamdi Firat Buyuk, "Under Erdogan, Independent Turkish Media Find Revenues Squeezed," *Balkan Insight*, March 3, 2020, https://balkaninsight.com/2020/03/03/under-erdogan-independent-turkish-media-find-revenues-squeezed/.

8. Katelyn Fossett, "How the Venezuelan Government Made the Media Its Most Powerful Ally," *Foreign Policy*, March 11, 2014, https://foreignpolicy.com/2014/03/11/how-the-venezuelan-government-made-the-media-into-its-most-powerful-ally/.

9. Jan Allsop, "Venezuela's War on the Press," *Columbia Journalism Review*, January 25, 2019.

10. Vera Tolz and Yuri Tepper, "Broadcasting Agitainment: A New Media Strategy of Putin's Third Presidency," *Post-Soviet Affairs* 34, no. 4 (2018): 213–27.

11. Lidia Kelley, "Russia Can Turn US into Radioactive Ash: Kremlin-Backed Journalist," *Reuters*, March 16, 2014, https://www.reuters.com/article/ukraine-crisis-russia-kiselyov/russia-can-turn-us-to-radioactive-ash-kremlin-backed-journalist-idINL6N0MD0P920140316.

12. For an insightful and humorous take on Russian state television, see Gary Shteyngart, "Out of My Mouth Comes Unimpeachable Manly Truth," *New York Times*, February 8, 2015, https://www.nytimes.com/2015/02/22/magazine/out-of-my-mouth-comes-unimpeachable-manly-truth.html.

13. How Russia's Independent Media Was Dismantled Piece by Piece," *Guardian*, May 25, 2016, https://www.theguardian.com/world/2016/may/25/how-russia-independent-media-was-dismantled-piece-by-piece.

14. Rolf Fredheim, "The Loyal Editor Effect: Russian Online Journalism after Independence," *Post-Soviet Affairs* 33, no. 1 (2016): 34–48, https://www.tandfonline.com/doi/abs/10.1080/1060586X.2016.1200797.

15. Carolina Vendil Pallin, "Internet Control through Ownership: The Case of Russia," *Post-Soviet Affairs* 33, no. 1 (2017): 16–33.

16. On April 13, 2020, *Vedomosti* pulled an op-ed two hours after its publication as the piece argued that Rosneft' head Sechin might be blamed for the 2020 economic crisis. For details, see "On Leadership and Hard Times," *Meduza*, April 14, 2020, https://meduza.io/en/feature/2020/04/13/on-leadership-and-hard-times?utm_source=email&utm_medium=briefly&utm_campaign=2020-04-14. Coverage following the change in ownership has become much less critical of the government.

17. Data from the Committee to Protect Journalists, https://cpj.org/europe/russia/. During the same period, Brazil and Mexico had, respectively, thirty-nine and forty-four journalists murdered.

18. Robert Coalson, "Twelve Who Left: A New Wave of Russian Emigration," *Radio Free Europe / Radio Liberty*, May 21, 2020, http://www.rferl.org/a/russia-emigration-emigrants /26970465.html.

19. Bruce Etling, Karina Alexanyan, John Kelly, Rob Faris, John Palfrey, and Urs Gasser, "Public Discourse in the Russian Blogosphere: Mapping RuNet Politics and Mobilization," https://dash.harvard.edu/handle/1/8789613.

20. Christopher Brennan, "Putin Says CIA Created the Internet," *Moscow Times*, April 24, 2014, https://www.themoscowtimes.com/2014/04/24/putin-says-cia-created-the-internet -cites-foreign-influence-at-yandex-a34639.

21. Shan Wang, "Paywalls and Politics," Neiman Lab, July 2016, http://www.niemanlab.org /2016/07/paywalls-and-politics-independent-russian-television-station-tv-rain-turns-to -subscriptions-as-its-future/.

22. "Internet Censorship Skyrockets in Russia in 2017, Study Says," *Moscow Times*, February 5, 2018. See also "Russian Troll Describes Work in Infamous Troll Factory," *NBC News*, November 16, 2017, https://www.nbcnews.com/news/all/russian-troll-describes-work -infamous-misinformation-factory-n821486.

23. Neil MacFarquhar, "Inside the Russian Troll Factory: Zombies and a Breakneck Pace," *New York Times*, February 18, 2018, https://www.nytimes.com/2018/02/18/world/europe /russia-troll-factory.html.

24. Seva Gunitsky, "Corrupting the Cyber-Commons: Social Media as a Tool of Autocratic Stability," *Perspectives on Politics* 13, no. 1 (2015): 42–54.

25. Sergei Sanovich, Denis Stukal, and Joshua A. Tucker, "Turning the Virtual Tables: Government Strategies for Addressing Online Opposition with an Application to Russia," *Comparative Politics* 50, no. 3 (2018): 435–82.

26. Beth Knobel, "*The Great Game* and the Evolving Nature of Political Talk Shows on Russian Television," *Post-Soviet Affairs* 36, no. 4 (2020): 346–64.

27. "Za schet chego Vladimir Putin ustanovil vybornii record, *Vedomosti*, March 19, 2018, https://www.vedomosti.ru/politics/articles/2018/03/19/754245-putin-rekord.

28. Abbas Gallyamov cited in Elena Mukhametshina and Svetlana Bocharova, "Politilogi: Zaderzhanie miliardera Magomodeva stavit v dvusmyslennoe polozhenie Medvedeva," *Vedomosti*, March 31, 2018, https://www.vedomosti.ru/business/articles/2018/03/31/755493 -dvusmislennoe-polozhenie-medvedeva.

29. Nikolai Mironin, cited in Margarita Alekhina, Vasilii Marinin, Irina Parfemyeva, and Vladimir Dergachev, "Delo Brat'ev Magomedovykh," *RBC*, April 1, 2018, https://www.rbc.ru /society/01/04/2018/5abfdc6b9a7947dbabdb519e.

30. Mikhail Vinogradov, cited in Galina Starinskaya, Irina Sinitsina, Elena Mukhametshina, and Svetlana Bochareva, "Kak Brat'ya Magomedovykh skladivali 'summu,'" *Vedomosti*, April 3, 2018, https://www.vedomosti.ru/business/articles/2018/04/03/755752-magomedovi -summu.

31. "Delo Brat'ev Magomedovykh," *RBC*, April 1, 2018, https://www.rbc.ru/society/01/04/2018/5abfdc6b9a7947dbabdb519e.

32. Pavel Aptekar' and Maria Zheleznova, "O chem govorit' kogda vse skazano?," *Vedomosti*, December 21, 2018.

33. "Ne protiv khrama, a za golosa srednova klassa," *Nezavisimaya Gazeta*, May 25, 2019.

34. "Srednii po Putinu," *Moskovsky Komsommelets*, May 25, 2020.

35. Yuri Dud', https://www.youtube.com/channel/UCMCgOm8GZkHp8zJ6l7_hIuA.

36. Yuri Dud', *Kolyma: Birthplace of Our Fear*, 2019, https://www.reddit.com/r/Documentaries/comments/bqu53z/kolyma_birthplace_of_our_fear_2019_english/.

37. Yuri Dud', *HIV in Russia*, February 11, 2020, https://www.youtube.com/watch?v=GTRAEpllGZo.

38. Judith Twygg and Michael Rendelman, "A Turning Point for Russia on HIV," Center for Strategic and International Studies, March 11, 2020, https://www.csis.org/analysis/turning-point-russia-and-hiv.

39. Alexei Navalny's Twitter account, October 7, 2020, https://twitter.com/navalny/status/1313928014728757248.

40. Sanovich, Stukal, and Tucker, "Turning the Virtual Tables."

41. Henry Farrell, "If You Are Worried That Russian Bots Are Brainwashing the World, Take a Deep Breath," *Washington Post*, February 24, 2020, https://www.washingtonpost.com/politics/2020/02/24/if-youre-worried-that-russian-bots-are-brainwashing-world-take-deep-breath. For more information, see Hugo Mercier, *Not Born Yesterday: The Science of Who We Trust and What We Believe* (Princeton, NJ: Princeton University Press, 2020).

42. This approach gets around the problem, highlighted above, that viewers select their sources of information.

43. Ruben Enikolopov, Michael Rochlitz, Koen Schoors, and Nikita Zakharov, "Independent Media and Elections," (unpublished manuscript, December 2018), 1–47. This paper has not yet undergone peer review.

44. Maria Lipman, Anna Kachkaeva, and Michael Poyker, "Media in Russia: Between Modernization and Monopoly," in *The New Autocracy: Information, Politics, and Policy in Putin's Russia*, ed. Daniel Treisman (Washington, DC: Brookings Institution Press, 2018), 160.

45. The following data all come from the Levada Center, http://www.levada.ru/28-07-2015/sobytiya-na-vostoke-ukrainy-vnimanie-i-uchastie-rossii.

46. Support for giving aid to refugees from the conflict fell from 81 percent in July 2014 to 67 percent in August 2015.

47. "Menee polovini Rossiyan vystupili za podderzhku Rossiei DNR i LNR," Levada Center, October 31, 2017, https://www.levada.ru/2017/10/30/menee-poloviny-rossiyan-vystupili-za-podderzhku-rossiej-dnr-i-lnr/.

48. "Russian Reporters Attacked at Secret Burial," *BBC*, August 27, 2014, https://www.bbc.com/news/world-europe-28949582.

49. "MH-17 Plane Crash Trial Opens in the Netherlands," *Guardian*, March 9, 2020, https://www.theguardian.com/world/2020/mar/09/mh17-plane-crash-trial-opens-in-the-hague-malaysia-airlines-flight.

50. "Who Downed the Malaysian Boeing in Eastern Ukraine?," Levada Center, October 3, 2014, https://www.levada.ru/en/2014/10/03/who-downed-the-malaysian-boeing-in-eastern-ukraine/.

51. Russian state television showed doctored footage to support the Kremlin's claim that the Ukrainian government shot down the plane, but this was quickly debunked. Konstantin Ernst, the director of state television, later admitted that the video was manipulated. Joshua Yaffa, "The Kremlin's Creative Director," *New Yorker*, December 16, 2019, https://www.newyorker.com/magazine/2019/12/16/the-kremlins-creative-director.

52. Arturas Rozenas and Denis Stukal, "How Autocrats Manipulate Economic News: Evidence from Russia's State Controlled Television," *Journal of Politics* 81, no. 3 (2019): 989.

53. Rozenas and Stukal, 2019, 989.

54. Rozenas and Stukal, 2019, 989.

55. Rozenas and Stukal, 2019, 989.

56. For example, more than a hundred children died in a schoolhouse fire in 1961 that was not made public until the early 1990s. See "Fifty-Seven Years Ago, 106 Children Died in a Fire at a Village School. The Soviet Public Didn't Know about It until the 1990s," *Meduza*, March 28, 2018, https://meduza.io/en/feature/2018/03/28/fifty-years-ago-106-children-died-in-a-fire-at-a-village-school-the-soviet-public-didn-t-know-about-it-until-the-1990s.

57. Bryn Rosenfeld, "Reevaluating the Middle-Class Protest Paradigm: A Case-Control Study of Democratic Protest Coalitions in Russia," *American Political Science Review* 111, no. 4 (2017): 638.

58. Frye, "Economic Sanctions and Public Opinion."

59. Anton Sobolev, "How Pro-Government Trolls Influence Online Conversations in Russia," (working paper, Los Angeles, 2018), https://asobolev.com/publications/#published-works.

60. Ellen Mickiewicz, cited in Scott Gehlbach and Konstantin Sonin, "Government Control of the Media," *Journal of Public Economics* 118 (October 2014): 164.

61. Denis Volkov and Stepan Goncharov, "Russian Media Landscape: Television, the Internet, and Social Media," Levada Center, May 2020, https://www.levada.ru/cp/wp-content/uploads/2020/05/Medialandshaft-2020-fin.pdf.

62. For instance, "early in the crisis Putin held regular press conferences and state media reported diligently on the virus, but the public was skeptical. In March 2020, 59 percent of Russians surveyed reported that they did not believe the state's figures on the number of coronavirus deaths. "A Majority of Russians Doubt Official Coronavirus Data," *Moscow Times*, March 27, 2020, https://www.themoscowtimes.com/2020/03/27/majority-of-russians-doubt-official-coronavirus-data-poll-a69768. One researcher noted a surprisingly large number of death reports that ended in the figures ninety-nine or ninety-eight, suggesting that local officials were faking the results. "Permission to Die Rejected," *Meduza*, May 14, 2020, https://meduza.io/en/feature/2020/05/14/permission-to-die-rejected.

63. Stepan Goncharov, "The Whys and Wherefores of Russians' Trust in the Media," *Riddle*, June 27, 2019, https://www.ridl.io/en/the-whys-and-wherefores-of-russians-trust-in-their-media/.

64. "Istochniki informatsii," Levada Center, September 28, 2020, https://www.levada.ru/2020/09/28/ggh/.

Chapter 9. Great Power Posing: Russian Foreign Policy

1. Thomas Graham, "A Russia Problem, Not a Putin Problem," *Perspectives on Russia*, Carnegie Corporation of New York, https://perspectives.carnegie.org/us-russia/a-russia-problem-not-a-putin-problem/.

2. The continuity thesis tends to take Russia's power as a given. This line of argument treats Russia as a "damaged, but formidable" power that regularly experiences periods of retrenchment and expansion, yet offers less guidance as to the sources of its strengths and weaknesses.

3. Reihan Salaam, "Vladimir Putin's Strategy: Russia's President Has Played a Weak Hand Well," *National Review*, February 9, 2018, https://www.nationalreview.com/corner/vladimir-putin-strategy-russias-president-played-weak-hand-well/. See also Brian D. Taylor, *The Code of Putinism* (New York: Oxford University Press, 2018).

4. Timothy Frye, "Putin Touts Russia as a Great Power: He Has Made It a Weak One," *Washington Post*, June 6, 2019, https://www.washingtonpost.com/opinions/2019/06/06/putin-touts-russia-great-power-hes-made-it-weak-one/.

5. Studying Russian foreign policy raises special challenges. Fewer scholars write on Russian foreign policy than on domestic politics. Academics are drawn to current events, and for much of the 1990s and early 2000s, younger researchers devoted more attention to domestic politics than to foreign policy. This imbalance is being corrected, although slowly. A second challenge is inherent to the topic. Foreign policy making is opaque, and we have limited access to relevant data. We are often forced to make due with public pronouncements by leaders, and it is hard to separate self-serving rationalizations and political spin from rare moments of candor. Studying Russian domestic politics is hard, and studying Russian foreign policy is harder. Given these evidentiary challenges, it is not surprising that foreign policy is among the most contentious and politicized topics for Russia watchers and the general public. Finally, because no single chapter can capture the full range of topics in Russian foreign policy, I limit the analysis to a few key themes. For more complete treatments, see Andrei Tsygankov, *Routledge Handbook of Russian Foreign Policy* (Abingdon, UK: Routledge Press, 2018); Angela Stent, *The Limits of Partnership: US-Russian Relations in the 21st Century* (Princeton, NJ: Princeton University Press, 2014).

6. NATO's intervention in Kosovo is sometimes seen as a second case, but the differences are stark. NATO did not incorporate Kosovo as a territory, there was no threat of ethnic cleansing in Crimea, and the United Nations condemned Russia's annexation of Crimea, but oversaw Kosovo in the immediate aftermath of the intervention via the UN Interim Administration Mission in Kosovo.

7. Samuel Charap and Timothy Colton, *Everyone Loses: The Ukraine Crisis and the Ruinous Contest for Post-Soviet Eurasia* (London: International Institute for Strategic Studies, 2017).

8. *The Eurasian Economic Union: Power, Politics, and Trade, International Crisis Group*, July 20, 2016, https://css.ethz.ch/content/dam/ethz/special-interest/gess/cis/center-for-securities-studies/resources/docs/Crisis%20Group%20the-eurasian-economic-union-power-politics-and-trade.pdf.

9. Nikolay Kozhanov, "Russia Policy across the Middle East: Motivations and Methods," Chatham House, London, February 21, 2018; Dmitri Trenin, *What Is Russia Up to in the Middle East?* (Medford, MA: Polity Press, 2018).

10. Stacey Closson, "Russian Foreign Policy in the Arctic: Balancing Cooperation and Competition," *Wilson Center*, 2018, https://www.wilsoncenter.org/publication/kennan-cable-n024-russian-foreign-policy-the-arctic-balancing-cooperation; Kimberly Marten, "Russia Is Back in Africa: Is the Cold War Returning?," *Washington Quarterly* 42, no. 4 (2019): 1455–70, https://www.tandfonline.com/doi/full/10.1080/0163660X.2019.1693105.

11. Alexander Lukin, *China and Russia: The New Rapprochement* (Medford, MA: Polity Press. 2018).

12. Yinan Wang, "In Battle for Putin's Affections, Cupid Favors Xi over Trump," *AP News*, July 28, 2018, https://www.apnews.com/ad5da44ccaba4ea885b69d450b590637.

13. In a May 2019 phone call with Trump, Putin offered to withdraw military support from Venezuela if the United States would do the same in Ukraine. "Putin Is Ready to Give Up Venezuela for the Right Price," *Moscow Times*, May 5, 2019, https://www.themoscowtimes.com/2019/05/05/putin-is-ready-to-give-up-venezuela-for-the-right-price-a65487.

14. "Presidential Address to the Federal Assembly," President of Russia, March 1, 2018, http://en.kremlin.ru/events/president/news/56957.

15. "Nuclear Weapons: Who Has What at a Glance," Arms Control Association, August 2020, https://www.armscontrol.org/factsheets/Nuclearweaponswhohaswhat.

16. "Trends in World Military Expenditure, 2017," SIPRI Fact Sheet, May 2018, https://www.sipri.org/sites/default/files/2018-05/sipri_fs_1805_milex_2017.pdf.

17. "The Strengths and Weaknesses of Russia's Military," *Deutsche Welle*, July 4, 2018, https://www.dw.com/en/the-strengths-and-weaknesses-of-russias-military/a-43293017.

18. Holly Ellyatt, "Russia Drops Out of the Top 5 Military Spenders while the US and China Up the Ante," *MSNBC*, April 29, 2019, https://www.cnbc.com/2019/04/29/russia-drops-out-of-top-5-global-military-spenders.html.

19. "Putin Speaks for Investment in Defense," *Sputnik News*, February 20, 2012, https://sputniknews.com/military/20120220171406103/.

20. Peter Rutland, "The 2020 Oil Crash: Is Russia Still an Energy Superpower?," PONARS Memo, 642, March 2020.

21. Venezuela too has tried to use the energy tool to leverage its power abroad to curb criticism.

22. Clark Letterman, "Image of Putin, Russia Suffers, Internationally," Pew Research Center, December 6, 2018, https://www.pewresearch.org/global/2018/12/06/image-of-putin-russia-suffers-internationally.

23. Jerry Hendrix, "When Putin Invades the Baltics," *National Review Plus*, February 5, 2018, https://www.nationalreview.com/magazine/2018/02/05/vladimir-putin-invade-baltics/.

24. Taylor, *The Code of Putinism*.

25. Robert Legvold, *Return to Cold War* (Medford, MA, Polity Press, 2016).

26. Danielle Lussier, "Ideology among Russian Elites: Attitudes toward the United States as a Belief System," *Post-Soviet Affairs* 35, no. 5–6 (2019): 433–49, https://www.tandfonline.com/doi/full/10.1080/1060586X.2019.1662201.

27. Sharon Rivera and James D. Bryan, "Understanding the Sources of Anti-Americanism in the Russian Elite," *Post-Soviet Affairs* 35, no. 5–6 (2019): 376–92, https://www.tandfonline.com/doi/full/10.1080/1060586X.2019.1662194.

28. Sharon Werning Rivera, "Survey of Russian Elites," July 28, 2020, Hamilton College, 1–52.

29. "Andrei Gromyko," *Time Note*, https://timenote.info/en/Andrei-Gromyko.

30. Seva Gunitsky, "One Word to Fix US-Russia Policy," *New Republic*, April 27, 2018, https://newrepublic.com/article/148140/one-word-fix-us-russia-policy.

31. Thomas Graham and Rajan Menon, "The Putin Problem," *Boston Review*, September 12, 2017, http://bostonreview.net/politics/thomas-graham-rajan-menon-putin-problem.

32. Keir Giles, *Moscow Rules: What Drives Russia to Confront the West* (London: Chatham House, 2019), 15.

33. Sergei Lavrov, "Russia in the 21st-Century World of Power," *Russia in Global Affairs*, December 27, 2012, https://eng.globalaffairs.ru/number/Russia-in-the-21st-Century-World-of -Power-15809.

34. Martin Malia, *Russia Under Western Eyes: From the Bronze Horseman to the Lenin Mausoleum* (Cambridge, MA: Harvard University Press, 2000).

35. For one expert's view of how this might work, see Charles A. Kupchan, "NATO's Final Frontier: Why Russia Should Join the Atlantic Alliance," *Foreign Affairs*, May–June 2010, https://www.foreignaffairs.com/articles/russian-federation/2010-05-01/natos-final-frontier.

36. James M. Goldgeier, *Not Whether But When: The US Decision to Enlarge NATO* (Washington, DC: Brookings Institution Press, 1999).

37. Stent, *The Limits of Partnership*, 163–68.

38. Andrei Tsygankov, "Vladimir Putin's Last Stand: The Sources of Ukraine Policy," *Post-Soviet Affairs* 31, no. 4 (2015): 279–303; John J. Mearsheimer, "Why the Ukraine Crisis Is the West's Fault: The Liberal Delusions That Provoked Putin," *Foreign Affairs*, September–October 2014, https://www.foreignaffairs.com/articles/russia-fsu/2014-08-18/why-ukraine -crisis-west-s-fault.

39. "Speech and the Following Discussion at the Munich Security Conference," February 10, 2007, http://en.kremlin.ru/events/president/transcripts/24034.

40. Cited in Tsygankov, "Vladimir Putin's Last Stand," 279.

41. Steven Sestanovich, "Could It Have Been Otherwise?," *American Interest*, May–June 2015, https://www.the-american-interest.com/2015/04/14/could-it-have-been-otherwise.

42. Michael McFaul, *From Cold War to Hot Peace: An American Ambassador in Putin's Russia* (New York: Houghton Mifflin Harcourt, 2018), 190.

43. Stephen Kotkin, "Russia's Perpetual Geopolitics: Putin Returns to the Historical Pattern," *Foreign Affairs* 95, no. 1 (2016): 6.

44. Dimitar Bechev, *Rival Power: Russia in Southeast Europe* (New Haven, CT: Yale University Press, 2019), 29.

45. Bechev, *Rival Power*, 23. See also Martin Jirusek, Thomas Vilcek, and James Henderson, "Russia's Energy Relations in Southeastern Europe: An Analysis of Motives in Bulgaria and Greece," *Post-Soviet Affairs* 33, no. 5 (2017): 335–55.

46. Seva Gunitsky and Andrei Tsygankov, "The Wilsonian Bias in the Study of Russian Foreign Policy," *Problems of Post-Communism* 65, no. 6 (2018): 385–93, https://www.tandfonline .com/doi/full/10.1080/10758216.2018.1468270.

47. Christopher Smart, "Economic Constraints on Russian Foreign Policy," Carnegie Endowment for International Peace, November 17, 2017, https://carnegieendowment.org/2017/11 /17/economic-constraints-on-russian-foreign-policy-pub-74805.

48. "China Is on Track to Replace Russia as Ukraine's Biggest Trade Partner," *Kyiv Post*, November 7, 2018, https://www.unian.info/economics/10328907-china-on-track-to-replace -russia-as-ukraine-s-biggest-trading-partner-kyiv-post.html.

49. Janusz Bugajski, "Trump's Criticisms Have Reinvigorated NATO," *Hill*, February 7, 2019, https://thehill.com/opinion/national-security/428920-trumps-criticisms-have -reinvigorated-nato.

50. US Department of State, https://www.state.gov/e/eb/tfs/spi/ukrainerussia/.

51. Robin Emmott, "Sanctions Impact on Russia to Be Longer Term, U.S. Says," *Reuters*, January 12, 2016, https://www.reuters.com/article/us-ukraine-crisis-sanctions/sanctions -impact-on-russia-to-be-longer-term-u-s-says-idUSKCN0UQ1ML20160112.

52. "How Far Do EU-US Sanctions Go?," *BBC*, September 15, 2014, http://www.bbc.com /news/world-europe-28400218.

53. "Deripaska Sues US Treasury to Block Sanctions Against Him," *Bloomberg*, March 15, 2019, https://www.bloomberg.com/news/articles/2019-03-15/deripaska-sues-u-s-treasury-to-block -sanctions-against-him. These particular sanctions were poorly designed and caused global prices on aluminum to spike, leading the US government to reverse course.

54. Henry Foy, "Russian Billionaire Pushes Back Against Sanctions," *Financial Times*, May 31, 2019, https://www.ft.com/content/1133c42e-82c9-11e9-b592-5fe435b57a3b?shareType=nongift.

55. Dmitry Medvedev, "Novaya real'nost': Rossiya i global'nye vyzovy," *Voprosy Ekonomiki* 86, no. 10 (2015) : 5–29, http://www.vopreco.ru/rus/redaction.files/10-15.pdf, cited in Richard Connolly and Philip Hanson, "Import Substitution and Economic Sovereignty in Russia," research paper, Chatham House, June 2016, 12.

56. OECD Stat, https://stats.oecd.org/Index.aspx?DataSetCode=LEVEL.

57. "Russia Economic Report," World Bank, December 2019, http://www.worldbank.org/en /country/russia/publication/rer.

58. "Kudrin predlozhil otsenivat' effektivnost' vneshnei politiki RF po rezhimu sanktsii," *Interfax*, October 10, 2018, https://www.interfax.ru/russia/632682.

59. Thomas Sherlock, "Russian Society and Foreign Policy: Mass and Elite Orientations after Crimea," *Problems of Post-Communism* 67, no. 1 (2020): 1–23, https://www.tandfonline.com /doi/abs/10.1080/10758216.2018.1561190.

60. Levada Center, "Russia as a Great Power," January 1, 2017, http://www.levada.ru/en/2017 /01/09/russia-as-a-great-power/. Sergei Belanovsky and Mikhail Dmitriev, two of Russia's most respected social scientists, reached similar conclusions in a series of focus groups in 2018.

61. Russian Academy of Sciences, "Rossiya v XXI veke: Globalnye vyzovy i perspektivi razvitiya," Third International Forum, October 21–22, 2014, Moscow. See also Viktor Khamrayev, "Blagopoluchie dorozhe velichiya," *Kommersant'*, November 6, 2018, https://www.kommersant .ru/doc/3792003.

62. "Rossiya na mezhdunarodnoi arena: otsenka vneshnei politiki," FOM, April 18, 2019, http://bd.fom.ru/report/map/dominant/dom_1519/d151906.

63. "Rossiyan vse menshe interesuet voennaya moshch strany," Znak.com, November 6, 2018, https://www.znak.com/2018-11-06/sociologiya_rossiyan_vse_menshe_interesuet_voennaya _moch_strany.

64. Bjorn Alexander Duben, "There Is No Ukraine. Fact Checking the Kremlin's Version of Ukrainian History," https://blogs.lse.ac.uk/lseih/2020/07/01/there-is-no-ukraine-fact

-checking-the-kremlins-version-of-ukrainian-history; Russian Presidential Address to Parliament, March 18, 2014, http://en.kremlin.ru/events/president/news/20603.

65. "Russian Ukraine Relations," Levada Center, poll, January 28, 2020, https://www.levada.ru/en/2020/02/28/russia-ukraine-relations-6/.

66. "Pochti chetvert' grazhdan podderzhivayut ideyu ob'edineniya s Belorussiei," Levada Center, poll, September 17, 2020, https://www.levada.ru/2020/09/17/pochti-chetvert-grazhdan-podderzhivayut-ideyu-obedineniya-s-belorussiej/.

67. "Russia-Ukraine Relations," Levada Center, poll, February 28, 2020, https://www.levada.ru/en/2020/02/28/russia-ukraine-relations-6/.

68. "Soyuzniki i vragi sredi stran," Levada Center, poll, June 14, 2019, https://www.levada.ru/2019/06/14/soyuzniki-i-vragi-sredi-stran/.

69. Similarly, a September 2020 poll found that 42 percent of Russians had a positive view of the United States, even as 60 percent named it as an unfriendly/hostile country toward Russia. Levada Center, poll, September 9, 2020, https://www.levada.ru/2020/09/16/23555/.

70. "Zapad Stanovitsya Blizhe," Levada Center, poll, February 18, 2020, https://www.levada.ru/2020/02/18/zapad-stanovitsya-blizhe/print/.

71. Russia is an autocracy, and popular support does not necessarily translate into actual policies. Even in democracies, powerful minorities can keep policies in place. It is important to consider how those closest to Putin—not surprisingly from the security services—view great-power status.

72. Javier Corrales, "The Authoritarian Resurgence: Autocratic Legalism in Venezuela," *Journal of Democracy* 26, no. 2 (2015): 46–50.

73. Keith Johnson and Robbie Gramer, "Who Lost Turkey?," *Foreign Policy*, July 19, 2019, https://foreignpolicy.com/2019/07/19/who-lost-turkey-middle-east-s-400-missile-deal-russia-syria-iraq-kurdish-united-states-nato-alliance-partners-allies-adversaries/.

74. Elisabeth Zerofsky, "Viktor Orbán's Far-Right Vision for Europe," *New Yorker*, January 7, 2019, https://www.newyorker.com/magazine/2019/01/14/viktor-orbans-far-right-vision-for-europe.

75. Cited in "Hungary Is Winning Again," *Hungary Today*, June 6, 2020, https://hungarytoday.hu/orban-at-trianon-100-event-hungary-is-winning-again/.

76. Michael Kofman "Raiding and International Brigandry: Russia's Strategy for Great Power Competition," *War on the Rocks*, 2018, https://warontherocks.com/2018/06/raiding-and-international-brigandry-russias-strategy-for-great-power-competition.

77. The disorder in the West has done a great favor to Putin by making democracy less attractive to ordinary Russians and reducing demands for greater political rights in Russia, thereby giving the Kremlin more space for foreign policy adventurism.

78. Steven Cook, "Russia Is in the Middle East to Stay," *Foreign Policy*, March 16, 2018, https://foreignpolicy.com/2018/03/16/the-middle-east-needs-a-steady-boyfriend/.

79. Nikolay Kozhanov, "Russia Policy across the Middle East: Motivations and Methods," Chatham House, London, February 21, 2018, https://www.chathamhouse.org/sites/default/files/publications/research/2018-02-21-russian-policy-middle-east-kozhanov.pdf.

80. Dmitri V. Trenin, *Getting Russia Right* (New York: Carnegie Endowment for International Peace, 2007), 76.

81. Robert Legvold, "Into the Unknown," *Russia in Global Affairs*, no. 2, June 6, 2017, https://eng.globalaffairs.ru/articles/into-the-unknown/.

82. Andrew Kuchins, "Northern Distribution Network and Afghanistan," Center for Strategic and International Studies, January 2010, https://www.csis.org/analysis/northern-distribution-network-and-afghanistan.

83. Global Security.org Northern Distribution Network, https://www.globalsecurity.org/military/facility/ndn.htm.

84. Cited in Michael Bohm, "Why Putin Wants US Bases in Afghanistan," *Moscow Times*, May 16, 2013, https://themoscowtimes.com/articles/why-putin-wants-us-bases-in-afghanistan-24084.

85. "New START at a Glance," Arms Control Association, January 2020, https://www.armscontrol.org/factsheets/NewSTART. New START is set to expire in February 2021 and prospects for renewal look uncertain.

86. Cooperation has also not been held back by popular attitudes in Russia or the United States. For much of the post–Cold War era, Gallup polls showed that a majority of Americans had a favorable view of Russia, while the Pew Research Center found similar a view in Russia about the United States. These positive views plummeted on both sides following the annexation of Crimea.

87. "What Is the Status of the Iranian Nuclear Agreement," Council on Foreign Relations, January 7, 2020, https://www.cfr.org/backgrounder/impact-iran-nuclear-agreement.

88. McFaul, *From Cold War to Hot Peace*, 158–75.

89. Cited in Eliza Collins, "Obama Offers Some Praise of Putin," *Politico*, July 14, 2015, https://www.politico.com/story/2015/07/obama-offers-praise-of-putin-120127. On Putin's refusal to discuss foreign policy issues as prime minister, See McFaul, *From Cold War to Hot Peace*.

90. Compare to Mark Peceny, Caroline Beer, and Shannon Sanchez Terry, "Dictatorial Peace?," *American Political Science Review* 96, no. 1 (2002): 15–27; Alexandre Debs and Hein E. Goemans, "Regime Type, the Fate of Leaders, and War," *Journal of Peace Research* 104, no. 3 (2010): 430–45; Jessica L. Weeks, "Strawmen and Strongmen: Authoritarian Regimes and the Initiation of International Conflict," *International Organization* 106, no. 2 (May 2012): 326–45.

Chapter 10. Why Russia Hacks:
Digital Persuasion and Coercion Abroad

1. Emily Tankin, "10 Years after the Landmark Attack on Estonia, Is the World Better Prepared for Cyber Threats?," *Foreign Policy*, April 27, 2017, https://foreignpolicy.com/2017/04/27/10-years-after-the-landmark-attack-on-estonia-is-the-world-better-prepared-for-cyber-threats/.

2. David Sanger, *The Perfect Weapon: War, Sabotage, and Fear in the Cyber Age* (New York: Crown, 2018), 47.

3. These two types of activity are not exclusive as information stolen from private firms or political parties can then be released to the public to shape public attitudes, as happened during the US and French presidential elections in 2016 and 2017, respectively, but digital persuasion and coercion also have different mechanisms and targets.

4. "Foreign versus Domestic: An Examination of Amplification of Discarded Ballots," Election Integrity Project, October 7, 2020, https://www.eipartnership.net/rapid-response/vast

-majority-of-discarded-ballot-amplification-isnt-from-foreign-sources; "Mail in Voter Fraud: Anatomy of a Disinformation Campaign," Berkman Klein Center Harvard, October 1, 2020, https://cyber.harvard.edu/publication/2020/Mail-in-Voter-Fraud-Disinformation-2020.

5. Robert Orttung and Elizabeth Nelson, "State International Broadcasting Strategy and Effectiveness: RT's Impact on YouTube," *Post-Soviet Affairs* 35, no. 2 (2019): 77–92, https://www.tandfonline.com/doi/full/10.1080/1060586X.2018.1531650?scroll=top&needAccess=true.

6. Cited in Orttung and Nelson, "State International Broadcasting Strategy and Effectiveness." 80.

7. Interview with Vitaly Bespalov, a former worker at the Internet Research Agency, in Ben Popkin and Kelly Cobiela, *NBC News*, November 16, 2017, https://www.nbcnews.com/news/all/russian-troll-describes-work-infamous-misinformation-factory-n821486.

8. Sanger, *The Perfect Weapon*, 124–70.

9. Jen Kirby, "Yes Russia Is Interfering in the Election Again," *Vox*, September 21, 2020, https://www.vox.com/2020/9/21/21401149/russia-2020-election-meddling-trump-biden.

10. Jen Kirby, "Yes Russia Is Interfering in the Election Again."

11. Mark Clayton, "Ukraine Election Narrowly Avoided Wanton Destruction from Hackers," *CSM*, June 17, 2014, https://www.csmonitor.com/World/Passcode/2014/0617/Ukraine-election-narrowly-avoided-wanton-destruction-from-hackers.

12. Adam Nossiter, David E. Sanger, and Nicole Perlroth, "Hackers Came But French Were Prepared," *New York Times*, May 9, 2017, https://www.nytimes.com/2017/05/09/world/europe/hackers-came-but-the-french-were-prepared.html.

13. Jake Tapper interview with Rand Paul on CNN, July 15, 2018. https://www.youtube.com/watch?v=hOBTv5SBIkM.

14. Dov Levin, "When the Great Power Gets a Vote: The Effects of Great Power Electoral Interventions on Election Results," *International Studies Quarterly* 60, no. 2 (2016): 189–202.

15. Thomas Carothers, "Is the US Hypocritical to Criticize Russian Election Meddling?," *Foreign Affairs*, March 12, 2018, https://www.foreignaffairs.com/articles/united-states/2018-03-12/us-hypocritical-criticize-russian-election-meddling.

16. Oliver Roeder, "Why We're Sharing 3 Million Russian Troll Tweets," *FiveThirtyEight*, July 31, 2018, https://fivethirtyeight.com/features/why-were-sharing-3-million-russian-troll-tweets/.

17. Elizabeth Dwoskin and Tony Romm, "Facebook Says It Has Uncovered Coordinated Disinformation Campaign," *Washington Post*, July 31, 2018, https://www.washingtonpost.com/technology/2018/07/31/facebook-says-it-has-uncovered-coordinated-disinformation-operation-ahead-midterm-elections/?utm_term=.d6cbd473f320.

18. Christine Huang and Jeremiah Cha, "Russia and Putin Receive Low Ratings Globally," Pew Research Center, February 7, 2020, https://www.pewresearch.org/fact-tank/2020/02/07/russia-and-putin-receive-low-ratings-globally/.

19. Chloe Arnold, "Is Russian Dying Out in the Former Soviet Republics?," Radio Free Europe / Radio Liberty, August 26, 2007, https://www.rferl.org/a/1078355.html.

20. Arturas Rozenas and Leonid Pesiakhin, "Electoral Effects of Biased Media: Russian Television in Ukraine," *American Journal of Political Science* 62, no. 3 (2018): 535–50, https://onlinelibrary.wiley.com/doi/abs/10.1111/ajps.12355.

21. Lucan Way and Adam Casey, "Russian Foreign Elections Interventions since 1991," PONARS, research memo, March 2018, http://www.ponarseurasia.org/memo/russian-foreign -election-interventions-since-1991.

22. Sean Illing, "Former Top Spy James Clapper Explains How Russia Swung the Election to Trump," *Vox*, May 31, 2018, https://www.vox.com/2018/5/31/17384444/james-clapper-trump -russia-mueller-2016-election.

23. Cited in Max Boot, "Without the Russians, Trump Wouldn't Have Won," *Washington Post*, July 24, 2018, https://www.washingtonpost.com/opinions/without-the-russians-trump -wouldnt-have-won/2018/07/24/f4c87894-8f6b-11e8-bcd5-9d911c784c38_story.html?utm _term=.18010ad317db.

24. Kathleen Hall Jamieson, *Cyberwar: How Russian Trolls and Hackers Helped Elect a President: What We Don't, Can't, and Do Know* (New York: Oxford University Press, 2018), 275.

25. Yochai Benkler, Robert Raris, and Hal Roberts, "Network Propaganda: Manipulation, Disinformation, and Radicalization in American Politics," *Washington Post*, October 25, 2018.

26. Yochai Benkler, "The Russians Didn't Swing the 2016 Election to Trump but Fox News Might Have," *Bangor Daily News*, October 26, 2018, https://bangordailynews.com/2018/10/26 /opinion/contributors/the-russians-didnt-swing-the-2016-election-to-trump-but-fox-news -might-have/.

27. Nate Silver, "How Much Did Russian Interference Affect the 2016 Election?," *FiveThirtyEight*, February 16, 2018, https://fivethirtyeight.com/features/how-much-did-russian -interference-affect-the-2016-election/.

28. Andrew M. Guess, Brendan Nyhan, and Jason Reifler, "Exposure to Untrustworthy Websites in the 2016 US Presidential Election, *Nature: Human Behaviour*, no. 4 (2019) 472–480. 2019, https://www.nature.com/articles/s41562-020-0833-x.epdf?author_access_token=nZl PzDV78YgOACoB8eDfCtRgNojAjWel9jnR3ZoTvoMSqVwVNQWYD-7ScS8YYGbMCO4 NJbd3OYEqA1DhbR8gVHnEwrFfNN5vvElr6V4Y7QCZp5QMl4WveRWdZxrNcgakM8jj _ziw-fjDkK5Fe5e_2w%3D%3D.

29. Guess, Nyhan, and Reifler, "Exposure to Untrustworthy Websites in the 2016 US Presidential Election."

30. Alexander Coppock, Seth J. Hill, and Lynn Vavreck, "The Small Effects of Political Advertising Are Small Regardless of Context, Sender, or Message: Evidence from 59 Randomized Experiments," *Science Advances*, September 2, 2020, https://advances.sciencemag.org/content /6/36/eabc4046.

31. Hunt Allcott and Allen Gentzkow, "Social Media and Fake News in the 2016 Presidential Election," *Journal of Economic Perspectives* 31, no. 2 (2017): 211–236, https://pubs.aeaweb.org/doi /pdfplus/10.1257/jep.31.2.211. See also Jacob L. Nelson and Harsh Tenaja, "The Small, Disloyal Fake News Audience: The Role of Audience Availability in Fake News Consumption," *New Media and Society* 20, no. 10 (2018): 3720–37.

32. Mike Glenn, "A Houston Protest Organized by Russian Trolls," *Houston Chronicle*, February 20, 2018, https://www.houstonchronicle.com/local/gray-matters/article/A-Houston -protest-organized-by-Russian-trolls-12625481.php.

33. Leon Yin, Franziska Roscher, Richard Bonneau, Johnathan Nagler, and Joshua A. Tucker, "Your Friendly Neighborhood Troll: Internet Research Agency's Use of Local News in the 2016

US Presidential Election," https://s18798.pcdn.co/smapp/wp-content/uploads/sites/1693/2018/11/SMaPP_Data_Report_2018_01_IRA_Links_1.pdf.

34. Casey Michel, "Russia's Long and Mostly Unsuccessful History of Election Interference," *Politico*, October 26, 2019, https://www.politico.com/magazine/story/2019/10/26/russias-long-and-mostly-unsuccessful-history-of-election-interference-229884.

35. Ashley Parker and David E. Sanger, "Donald Trump Calls on Russia to Find Hillary Clinton's Missing Emails," *New York Times*, July 27, 2016, https://www.nytimes.com/2016/07/28/us/politics/donald-trump-russia-clinton-emails.html; "Donald Trump Calls on Ukraine and China to Interfere in US elections," *MSNBC*, October 3, 2019, https://www.msnbc.com/mtp-daily/watch/trump-calls-on-ukraine-china-to-interfere-in-2020-election-70569541695.

36. US Senate Select Committee on Intelligence, *Report on Russian Active Measures Campaigns and Interference in the 2016 Election*, https://www.intelligence.senate.gov/sites/default/files/documents/Report_Volume2.pdf.

37. The literature on the Trump-Russia connection is voluminous.

38. See "Ukraine Crisis: Transcript of Leaked Nuland-Pyatt Call," *BBC News*, February 7, 2014, https://www.bbc.com/news/world-europe-26079957.

39. Sanger, *The Perfect Weapon*.

40. Sanger, *The Perfect Weapon*, 84.

41. Adam Segal, *Hacked World Order: How Nations Fight, Trade, and Manipulate in the Digital Age* (New York: Public Affairs, 2016), 82.

42. Evgeny Morozov, "An Army of Ones and Zeroes: How I Became a Soldier in the Georgia-Russia Cyberwar," *Slate*, August 14, 2008, https://slate.com/technology/2008/08/how-i-became-a-soldier-in-the-georgia-russia-cyberwar.html.

43. "Russia Hacked Danish Defense Ministry for Two Years," *Reuters*, April 23, 2017, https://www.reuters.com/article/us-denmark-security-russia-idUSKBN17P0NR; Hans van der Bouchard, "Merkel Blames Russia for 'Outrageous' Cyberattack on German Parliament," *Politico*, May 13, 2020, https://www.politico.eu/article/merkel-blames-russia-for-outrageous-cyber-attack-on-german-parliament/; Jack Cloherty and Pierre Thomas, "'Trojan Horse' Bug Lurking in Vital US Computers since 2011," *ABC News*, November 6, 2014, https://abcnews.go.com/US/trojan-horse-bug-lurking-vital-us-computers-2011/story?id=26737476; "Data Breach at the Storting," October 13, 2020, https://www.regjeringen.no/en/aktuelt/datainnbruddet-i-stortinget/id2770135/.

44. Andrei Soldatov and Irina Borogan, *Red Web: The Struggle between Russia's Digital Dictators and the New Online Revolutionaries* (New York: Public Affairs, 2018).

45. "It Is Our Time to Serve the Motherland," *Meduza*, August 7, 2018, https://meduza.io/en/feature/2018/08/07/it-s-our-time-to-serve-the-motherland?utm_source=email&utm_medium=briefly&utm_campaign=2018-08-08.

46. "Cyber Operations Tracker," Council on Foreign Relations, https://www.cfr.org/cyber-operations/.

47. Brandon Valeriano, Benjamin Jensen, and Ryan C. Maness, *Cyber Strategy: The Evolving Character of Power and Coercion* (Oxford: Oxford University Press, 2017).

48. Brandon Valeriano and Benjamin Jensen, "No Matter What Trump Says, Russia Is Unique in Trying to Hack Other Countries' Democracies," *Washington Post*, July 17, 2018, https://www.washingtonpost.com/news/monkey-cage/wp/2018/07/17/no-matter-what

-trump-says-russia-is-the-only-nation-that-tries-to-hack-other-countries-democracies/?utm
_term=.9fe4338c4c42.

49. Brandon Valeriano, Ryan C. Maness, and Benjamin Jensen, "Cyberwarfare Has Taken a New Turn. Yes, It's Time to Worry," *Washington Post,* July 13, 2017, https://www.washingtonpost .com/news/monkey-cage/wp/2017/07/13/cyber-warfare-has-taken-a-new-turn-yes-its-time -to-worry/?utm_term=.93a0881461ff.

50. Valeriano, Jensen, and Maness, *Cyber Strategy,* 110–21.

51. Valeriano, Jensen, and Maness, "Cyberwarfare Has Taken a New Turn."

52. Segal, *Hacked World Order,* 100.

53. Cynthia McFadden, William M. Arkin, and Kevin Monahan, "Russia Penetrated US Voter Systems," *NBC News,* February 7, 2018, https://www.nbcnews.com/politics/elections /russians-penetrated-u-s-voter-systems-says-top-u-s-n845721.

54. David Shimer, *Rigged: America, Russia, and One Hundred Years of Covert Influence* (New York: Penguin, 2020). See also Timothy Frye, "Inside Job: The Challenge of Foreign Online Electoral Interference," *War on the Rocks,* October 6, 2020, https://warontherocks.com/2020 /10/inside-job-the-challenge-of-foreign-online-influence-in-u-s-elections.

55. Adam Segal, *Hacked World Order,* 82–84.

56. McFadden, Arkin, and Monahan, "Russians Penetrated U.S. Voter Systems."

57. Nicole Perlroth and David E. Sanger, "Ransomware Attacks Take on New Urgency Ahead of Vote," *New York Times,* September 27, 2020, https://www.nytimes.com/2020/09/27 /technology/2020-election-security-threats.html.

58. Sanger, *The Perfect Weapon.*

59. David E. Sanger and Nicole Perlroth, "U.S. Escalates Online Attacks on Russia's Power Grid," *New York Times,* June 15, 2019, www.nytimes.com/2019/06/15/us/politics/trump-cyber -russia-grid.html?action=click&module=Top%20Stories&pgtype=Homepage.

60. Valeriano, Jensen, and Maness, *Cyber Strategy.*

61. Segal, *Hacked World Order,* 82–84.

Chapter 11. Conclusion: The Death of Expertise?

1. Anne Applebaum, "The False Romance of Russia," *Atlantic,* December 12, 2019.

2. Rachel Maddow, *Blowout: Corrupted Democracy, Rogue State Russia, and the Most Destructive Industry on Earth* (New York: Crown, 2019).

3. "Doverie Politikam VTsIOM," https://wciom.ru/news/ratings/doverie_politikam.

4. "Basmannii sud arestoval byvshego gubernatora Ivanovskoi Oblasti," *Vesti,* June 3, 2019, http://www.vesti.ru/doc.html?id=3154220&3154220.

5. Yevgeny Razumnii, "Schem svyazano delo protiv Sergeya Petrova," *Vedomosti,* June 27, 2019, https://www.vedomosti.ru/politics/articles/2019/06/27/805280-sergeya-petrova?utm _campaign=editorchoice29062019&utm_content=805280-sergeya-petrova&utm_medium =email&utm_source=newsletter#%2Fpolitics%2Farticles%2F2019%2F06%2F27%2F805280 -sergeya-petrova%23!%23%2Fboxes%2F140737494499096.

6. "Kontrakt po Druzhbe," *RBC,* December 10, 2018, https://www.rbc.ru/society/10/12/2018 /5c05308e9a7947cc01d961af. See also "Dobycha poleznikh okhranyaemykh," *Kommersant',*

January 18, 2019,; "Vperviie soobshchila o zaderzhanii svoego vysokopostavlennogo ofitsera," *Vedomosti*, April 26, 2019, https://www.vedomosti.ru/politics/articles/2019/04/25/800273-fsb -zaderzhanii-ofitsera?utm_campaign=newspaper_26_4_2019&utm_medium=email&utm _source=vedomosti.

7. Henry Hale, *Patronal Politics: Eurasian Regime Dynamics in Comparative Perspective* (New York: Cambridge University Press, 2014).

8. Of course, the record of academics on predicting events, particularly about Russia, is nothing to boast about. Philip Tetlock, *Expert Political Judgment: How Good Is it? How Can We Know?* (Princeton, NJ: Princeton University Press, 2005).

9. H. E. Goemans, "Putin's Peers," in *The Policy World Meets Academia: Designing US Policy toward Russia*, ed. Timothy Colton, Timothy Frye, and Robert Legvold (Cambridge, MA: American Academy of Arts and Sciences, 2010), 79–92, https://www.amacad.org/sites/default /files/publication/downloads/policyTowardRussia.pdf.

10. Vladimir Gel'man, "Bringing Actors Back In: Political Choices and Sources of Post-Soviet Regime Dynamics," *Post-Soviet Affairs* 34, no. 5 (2018): 282–96.

11. Denis Volkov, Stepan Goncharov, and Maria Snegovaya, "Russian Youth and Civic Engagement," Levada Center and CEPA, September 29, 2020, https://cepa.org/russian-youth-and -civic-engagement/?fbclid=IwAR2-dsu4SXOsKnX-sgmEYuJGr4U4vkAZNcJHn1u1lr4vsX1E Yq7TPMleBBI.

12. Oliver Bullough, *Moneyland: Why Thieves and Crooks Now Rule the World and How to Take It Back* (London: Profile, 2019), https://www.nytimes.com/2017/09/19/opinion/brexit -britain-corruption.html.

13. Konstantin Sonin, "Why the Rich Favor Weak Property Rights," *Journal of Comparative Economics* 31 (2003): 715–31.

14. Timothy Colton, *Russia: What Everyone Needs to Know* (Oxford: Oxford University Press, 2016). Some recent surveys appear to show a decline in support for democratic values in Russia. See Richard Wike and Shannon Schumacher, "Democratic Rights Popular Globally but Commitment to Them Not Always Strong," Pew Research Center, February 27, 2020, https:// www.pewresearch.org/global/2020/02/27/democratic-rights-popular-globally-but -commitment-to-them-not-always-strong/; "A Rift in Democratic Attitudes is Opening Around the World," August 22, 2020, *Economist*, https://www.economist.com/graphic-detail/2020/08 /22/a-rift-in-democratic-attitudes-is-opening-up-around-the-world.

15. Scholars long debated the pluses and minuses of tight links between policy makers and academics during the Cold War, with many arguing that it had a pernicious effect on Soviet studies.

16. Tom Nichols, *The Death of Expertise: The Campaign against Established Knowledge and Why It Matters* (New York: Oxford University Press, 2017).

17. The Upshot in the *New York Times*, Monkey Cage in the *Washington Post*, and websites like www.Vox.com and Nate Silver's www.538.com have become important platforms for translating social science research for nonacademic audiences, but academia still does far too little to recognize the efforts of those who publish in these outlets.

18. Albert O. Hirschman, *A Bias for Hope: Essays on Development and Latin America* (New Haven, CT: Yale University Press, 1974).

INDEX

abortion, 7

Abyzov, Mikhail, 198

Access Hollywood, 185

adat law, 116

adhocracy, 24

advertisements, 4, 71, 117–18, 233n31

Afghanistan, 3, 21, 132, 172–73, 211n1, 235n1, 245n1

African Americans, 181

Agora, 139–40

agriculture, 89, 95–96, 167–68, 202, 229n46

Albats, Evgeniya, 126

Alfa-Bank, 85

Alliance of Tolerance, 170

Amnesty International, 120

Amuragrocenter, 66

Anderson, Perry, 53

Angola, 160

Anticorruption Foundation, 123–24

Applebaum, Anne, 7, 212n11, 249n1

approval ratings, 47, 52–54, 57–59, 61–65, 92, 129

Arashukov, Rauf, 198

Argentina, 33, 75, 91

Armenia, 129, 154, 157, 171

Aslund, Anders, 227n13

Assad, Bashar al-, 18

Associated Press, 57

Australia, 166, 172

Austria, 159

authoritarianism, 14; elections and, 67, 69; exceptional Russia and, 9–10; media and, 144; Putinology and, 32, 35; reassessment and, 200, 205; repression and, 112, 130; scholarly study of, 6; U.S. public opinion on, 8

autocracy: Chávez and, 11, 23, 39, 52, 70, 72, 87, 170; China and, 6; coercion and, 40, 47–48; constraints and, 200; corruption and, 45; coups and, 12–13, 38–39, 43–49, 219n16, 220n24; courts and, 39–40, 42; democracy and, 6, 12, 39, 54, 69, 72, 201, 203, 223n3; dictatorships and, 39, 42–44; dilemmas of, 37–49; dual threats to, 44–47; economic issues and, xx, 86–93, 96–97, 99, 103, 105; elections and, 38–39, 42, 44, 48, 67–72, 76–77, 84; elites and, 40–41, 44–48, 219n9; Erdoğan and, 11, 21, 23, 39, 52, 70, 72, 117, 135, 171, 232nn25–26; foreign policy and, 14, 40, 152–53, 156–57, 165–74; human rights and, 12–13; Hungary and, 38–39; information, 134–40; Iran and, 6, 38; legalism and, 112–18; limits of, 37, 41, 47–49; media and, 134–35; military and, 11, 38–43, 46–47, 49; nuclear weapons and, 37, 152; oligarchs and, 41; personalist, 11–14, 23, 37–52, 84, 87–91, 97, 99, 135, 153, 170–71, 174, 200–1; police and, 48; political economy of, 96–99; polls and, 54–58; powerful minorities and, 244n71; protests and, 38, 42–48, 220n24, 220n27; public opinion and, 6, 49, 51, 54, 64, 134, 222n34, 244n71; Putinology and, 16, 19, 22–23, 25, 28, 35–36; Putin's popularity and, 51–54, 64–65; reassessment and, 200–5; repression and, 12–14, 38, 40,

A NOTE ON THE TYPE

This book has been composed in Arno, an Old-style serif typeface in the classic Venetian tradition, designed by Robert Slimbach at Adobe.

CPSIA information can be obtained
at www.ICGtesting.com
Printed in the USA
JSHW050931110822
29112JS00004B/4